United States Foreign Policy and the
Prospects for Peace Education

United States Foreign Policy and the Prospects for Peace Education

CARL MIRRA

with forewords by
Johan Galtung *and* Staughton Lynd

McFarland & Company, Inc., Publishers
Jefferson, North Carolina, and London

LIBRARY OF CONGRESS CATALOGUING-IN-PUBLICATION DATA

Mirra, Carl.
    United States foreign policy and the prospects for peace education
/ Carl Mirra ; with forewords by Johan Galtung and Staughton Lynd.
        p.   cm.
    Includes bibliographical references and index.

    ISBN: 978-0-7864-3321-6
    softcover : 50# alkaline paper ∞

    1. Peace — Study and teaching — United States.   2. United
States — Foreign relations — Study and teaching.   3. United
States — Foreign relations — 1945–1989.   4. United States — Foreign
relations — 1989–   I. Title.
JZ5534.M57   2008
303.6'6 — dc22   2008006228

British Library cataloguing data are available

Cover photograph ©2008 Shutterstock

Manufactured in the United States of America

McFarland & Company, Inc., Publishers
  Box 611, Jefferson, North Carolina 28640
  www.mcfarlandpub.com

To Sabrina Grace

Acknowledgments

I owe a special debt to past teachers and my doctoral adviser Douglas Sloan stands out in particular. He provided a potent example of how a teacher should develop his/her students and has been a tireless supporter of my work. He is a true peace educator who has taught me a great deal. My undergraduate English professor, Laura Otis, was important in encouraging me to pursue my ideas and encouraged me to enter graduate school. Civil rights lawyer Ron Kuby demonstrated first-hand for me that intellectual pursuits can have practical and worthwhile consequences and this pugnacious attorney very much led to my decision to return to college and follow my intellectual dreams. New York City public school teacher, Warren Donin, taught me the power of pivotal questions in the classroom and how to facilitate an open, yet critical, environment that allows students to express their views. In many ways, I still model my own teaching on his approach. Donin's influence is one key reason why I became a teacher. Conversations with the historian Staughton Lynd altered the direction of the final chapter and helped to sharpen my thinking on the importance of ethical norms. Staughton has been something of an intellectual and existential mentor to me; exchanging ideas with him has thoroughly expanded and sharpened my thinking. I am indebted to Johan Galtung for reading the manuscript and offering positive feedback and agreeing to draft a foreword. His work remains a genuine inspiration to so many of us concerned about peace.

In addition to those named above, several people read parts of the manuscript and offered penetrating comments, critiques and suggestions. Remarks from Betty Reardon improved the manuscript, although some of her probing questions probably remain unanswered. I should also say that I was fortunate to have been a student of Dr. Reardon's and fondly remember her course at Teachers College, "The Fundamental Concepts of Peace Education." Professor Marvin J. Berlowitz, director of the Urban Center for Peace

Education at the University of Cincinnati, offered comments that were stimulating, uplifting and helpful. His recent work on African-Americans and peace education warrants attention. Monisha Bajaj, a professor at Teachers College/Columbia University who specializes in peace education, kindly read chapter one and provided some useful sources. Professor Bajaj's work is part of the gradual trend in peace education toward examining U.S. foreign policy issues. She helped to direct a summer institute in 2005 through "Global Kids" for high school students, which explores U.S. foreign policy as well as labor and human rights.

I should also express my gratitude to the International Association of University Presidents/United Nations Commission on Disarmament Education, Conflict Resolution and Peace, where I had the opportunity to present part of the research on this book. Supportive remarks from Dr. Eudora Pettigrew, Sister Francesca Onley, Moya Kaporch and Steve Zeisler were greatly appreciated. Karl Grossman was especially important in my joining the Commission and I owe him many thanks. I remain solely responsible for the opinions expressed throughout this text.

Let me also make clear my appreciation for all those who identify themselves as peace educators. Many scholars and workers in this field are carrying out crucial work across the globe and in the United States. My call to have peace educators study U.S. foreign policy is not to dismiss or diminish the various efforts that have been undertaken that do not deal with this topic. Of course, peace education needs multiple entry points for facilitating a more humane world, and all of the various approaches to the field are necessary. I am merely opening a dialogue on how U.S. foreign policy can be taken seriously as one of the entry points of peace education. Most of the people whom I have encountered who call themselves "peace educators" are worthy of my admiration.

As always, the support of my family is crucial both to my professional and personal growth. Of special importance is my wife, Eneida, whom I cherish for many reasons. My daughter, Sabrina, expanded my appreciation for the beauty of all life.

Contents

Foreword: What Would the World Like the United States of America to Know about Peace? On Peace Education for Those Most in Need

by Johan Galtung

Most non–Americans, according to the polls, have an attitude very similar to my own: I love the U.S. Republic, and I hate the U.S. Empire. Hence, what is badly needed in the United States of America from a world public opinion point of view would be some knowledge of how the U.S. Empire works and then the much more constructive knowledge of what it would take to undo it peacefully from the inside and turn the United States into a peace actor, or just into a more normal country.

There might be some advantages to doing this before the outside does the job in ways that may not necessarily be peaceful, like the way Anglo-America and the Soviet Union did it to Germany and Japan not too long ago, Stalingrad being the turning point, or the national liberation movements did it to the colonial empires, with the noble exception of Gandhi. And that example brings out the by and large nonviolent way in which the Soviet Empire was dismantled, also to a large extent from the inside. Often as pure self-defense like the way many today are fighting United States/United Kingdom aggression in Iraq (the Stalingrad of the U.S. Empire?), and not for, say, pedagogical reasons to raise the United States from predator to world citizenship.

This baffles some: "Love and hate of things U.S., often at the same time, and often within the same person"— is not that either schizophrenic or simply, good old formula, "anti–American"? No.

The United States itself has brilliant and dark spots, like all societies. But the U.S. Empire is overwhelmingly dark and dirty, addicted to violence like the alcoholic to liquor. There are brilliant spots to build on in getting sober. But some knowledge is useful. And true friends of the United States do not give the drunkard more liquor, but say, with some determination, I am not with you on that; rather, let us mediate the conflict between Anglo-America/Christian and Arabia/Islamic fundamentalism.

What does so much of the world have against the U.S. Empire? Mainly that it kills, exploits, manipulates and dictates:

- The U.S. Empire has killed 12–16 million in 70 interventions after the Second World War alone to obtain the following three below.

- The U.S. Empire, through its hyper-capitalism, brings wealth to some but condemns very many to misery, and kills them through malnutrition and lack of affordable prevention/therapy.

- The U.S. Empire manipulates all over, including the United Nations politically, like in John Perkins's *Confessions of an Economic Hit Man*.

- The U.S. Empire thinks it has a God-given monopoly on truth, imposes its own approach, and is today unfit for dialogue.

A system like that is condemned to decline and fall by the resistance it generates, and that will also eventually happen to the U.S. Empire. And what would so much of the world like to see from this great country? It derives easily from the list above; namely, that the United States of America stops killing globally; stops spreading misery along with wealth; stops manipulating, arm-twisting, spying, coercing and enters into dialogue as an equal party, especially in the United Nations.

In short, that the United States of America joins the world. Step down from that platform above Planet Earth "under God" as Chosen People with a Promised Land and Manifest Destiny to cut the world to your desire. This mentality came with the Pilgrims; the only new point with George W. Bush is that he is more explicit, more open, and honest. This short list above defines the major tasks for peace education in the United States schools — and colleges and universities, we might add. It is not that revolutionary, mainly common sense, but the United States of America has drilled itself into some holes where common sense has become uncommon.

Most violence springs out of untransformed conflicts that have been left to fester until violence by one party or the other seems to be the only recourse. There is also some evil in the world, but more important are the intractable, protracted conflicts. Hence, the "ABC" of peace studies: learn to distinguish between the A for attitudes like hatred (like in the ubiquitous "why do they hate us;" well, look at the four points above); B for behavior, like in violence, with the United States far ahead of all others in number of wars per year of existence as a state actor (see George Kohn's "War Participation Index" in *Dictionary of Wars* and the U.S. Congressional Research Service, *Instances of Use of United States Armed Forces Abroad*); and C for contradiction, meaning the root of conflicts, incompatible goals.

A culture of peaceful conflict transformation, mainly through mediation, and not only of the conflicts of others but of conflicts where the United States of America is involved, has to blossom (and of course not only in the United States!). But attention to the economics of peace is also essential. Somehow U.S. economists have to discover that "equity" refers to something more important than collateral for loans and "exploitation" is a major root of conflicts, including when it refers to mining.

And the world is today increasingly a community of societies with globalization all over, not only of stock exchanges to dump excess U.S. economic surplus at the top of society for speculation. Communities have citizens with rights and duties, and so does the world community. The United States of America has to learn and internalize the norms, ratify all human rights conventions, living by international law. And all of that presupposes listening and questioning: dialogue.

The country that would benefit most from the decline and fall of the United States Empire and from joining the world as a good world citizen would be the United States of America itself, getting rid of that killing, strangling, manipulating, autistic albatross around its neck. People from the outside join you in that struggle as nothing much can be expected from paranoid politicians seeing any dissent as a security threat, unable to see the underlying conflicts and simply go about solving them. One step might be to stop talking about "anti–American," presumably being a misnomer for "anti–USA." We on the outside know perfectly well how to differentiate between Germany and Nazism, Russia and Stalinism, England and colonialism and so on, even if they were all deeply rooted. Most of us love the former and hate the latter. The United States of America is not (yet?) fascist; but geo-fascist, killing directly and structurally all over the world. Solid peace education may make people wake up and see the realities, not only the myths, and roads to a much better future. Carl Mirra's outstanding study helps us to see the realities of U.S. foreign policy and it is a valuable contribution to peace education in the United States.

Johan Galtung, a professor of peace studies, is the founder and co-director of TRANSCEND

Foreword

by Staughton Lynd

I

The anthropologist Gregory Bateson used to say that the history of the United States was revealed on the faces of the old American nickel. On one side of the coin was the profile of a Native American and the word, "Liberty." On the other side was the image of a buffalo and the words, "E pluribus unum," or in Bateson's translation, "There used to be a lot of us and now there's only one."

When it comes to African-American slavery the layers of shame, guilt and hypocrisy go deeper. The history profession in this country is still in the process of facing the fact that the United States, with the consent of all those gathered at the constitutional convention in 1787, was created as an economy, society, and government based on chattel slavery. In the words of Gordon Wood:

> Not only does the overwhelming presence of slavery in early America cast a dark shadow [sic] over the sunny aspects of the founding, but it is also driving a huge rethinking of our history. Previous historians of early America, of course, never entirely ignored slavery (how could they?), but they did not bring its harsh brutality and its influence front and center....[1]

George Washington was the only Founding Father who provided in his will that his slaves should be freed. But at roughly the same time that he was drafting his will, Washington persistently sought to recover, by illegal, duplicitous, and forceful means, a favorite slave of his wife's who had run away. The slave's name was Ona Judge. Ms. Judge had escaped because, so she explained, she "wanted to be free ... wanted to learn to read and write." President Washington instructed a federal customs official to have Ms. Judge seized and returned to the possession of the Washingtons by force. Instead, the official warned Ms. Judge, who fled into the interior of New England and apparently remained free.[2]

As historian Edmund Morgan concedes: "Whatever guilt we may feel for slavery stops short of repudiating our national heroes because of their role in oppressing the whole race."[3]

II

At the same time, if we are ever to get to the bottom of the forces driving our tormented national self-identity, we must recognize that it has afflicted good persons as well as bad.

The most revolutionary change in our nation's history was the abolition of slavery during the Civil War. This monumental conflict evoked rhetoric of the very kind Carl Mirra deplores on behalf of emancipating, without compensation, the 2 million human beings held as slaves.

Carl Mirra rightly remarks that the "Battle Hymn of the Republic" took its rhetoric from the Book of Revelations. Edmund Wilson describes the circumstances in which Julia Ward Howe composed the song. As Union troops were mobilizing in Washington, D.C., Ms. Howe was making her way across the city in a carriage. The carriage was brought to a standstill by a mass of marching conscripts singing the song, "John Brown's Body." Immobilized, obliged to listen, Ms. Howe wrote new words for the tune.

Consider the words that she wrote. Just in the first verse, the Lord is trampling out the "grapes of wrath," and hath "loosed the fateful lightning of his terrible swift sword." The words derive from that part of the Bible which imagines that when the grapes are trodden in the great winepress of the wrath, "blood [will come] out of the winepress even unto the horse['s] bridles," Revelations 14:18–20. The song is a procession of apocalyptic, violent images.

This was also the ideological world of the antislavery martyr, John Brown. A wife recalled:

My husband always believed that he was to be an instrument in the hands of Providence, and I believed it too...; Many a night he had lain awake and prayed concerning it....

But this was not Laura Bush commenting on her husband George; it was Mary Brown remembering her husband John.[4] John Brown himself confirmed what she remembered as he lay covered in blood on the floor after his capture, and the governor of Virginia questioned him.

Q. Do you consider this a religious movement?

A. It is in my opinion the greatest service man can render to God.

Q. Do you consider yourself an instrument in the hands of Providence?

A. I do.[5]

The most exasperating trait exhibited by George W. Bush and his associates is an air of complete certainty, an inability to admit mistakes, a refusal to change course in the face of overwhelming evidence of failure. Even those who most loved and respected him were frustrated by the identical quality in John Brown.[6] These failings foreshadowed both John Brown's insistent advocacy of the Harpers Ferry strategy in the face of objections by Frederick Douglass and others, and the tactical failure to retreat into the Allegheny Mountains during the morning of the Harpers Ferry assault, even without the additional arms and ammunition for which Brown waited too long.

III

If historians have been in denial regarding the centrality of slavery in the national experience, it is at least equally so with respect to the persistent appetite of United States governments for imperialist war. Daniel Ellsberg in his *Secrets: A Memoir of Vietnam and the Pentagon Papers* has observed that the Pentagon Papers were controversial because they demonstrated that all presidents of the United States since the Second World War — Truman, Eisenhower, Kennedy, Johnson, and by implication, Nixon — lied to the electorate about the true intentions of the United States in Southeast Asia.

U.S. history is replete with controversy over reasons initially offered for going to war. Congressman Abraham Lincoln challenged President Polk as to the "spot" where the armies of Mexico and the United States first fired on each other in the 1840s. Today many of us would be ready to join Henry Thoreau in his Concord jail to protest the war against Mexico. The circumstances causing the battleship *Maine* and steamship *Lusitania* to be sunk are still debated. Within living memory, it now seems, the Johnson administration deliberately falsified the alleged events that occasioned the so-called Tonkin Gulf Resolution in August 1964. The blundering or hypocrisy or chicanery which brought on the Vietnam War seems to us today unacceptable. In short, if we could only approximate this understanding, we might be helped in our grasp of the practical alternatives that are presently before us. Mirra's critique of U.S. policy aims to open our understanding to these alternatives.

And it is not only official explanations of the reasons for going to war that require examination and correction. The underlying assumptions of policymakers are often enough, from an historian's vantage point, simply false. After a trip to Hanoi in the mid 1960s, I had the opportunity to meet Robert Kennedy. If memory serves, Kennedy said that "everybody knows" that Communists can't win democratic elections. But in fact, former President Eisenhower's memoirs prove that ten years earlier the United States had sabotaged the Geneva agreements, which ended the French war in Indochina, because American policymakers knew that if nationwide democratic elections were held in Vietnam, Ho Chi Minh would win. The same fallacy — that the "bad guys" are bound to lose in a fair election — now plagues United States foreign policy in Iran, Palestine, Venezuela, Haiti, and elsewhere.

The syndrome of underlying American assumptions and attitudes — a syndrome which Walter Lippman has called "Wilsonian" and E. H. Carr "Utopian" — throws up significant obstacles to the making of peace. George Kennan has shown how the tendency of American international behavior to oscillate between extremes of idealism and realism is magnified by the country's habitual self-righteousness. "Whoever says there is a law," Kennan observes, "must of course be indignant against the lawbreaker and feel a moral superiority to him. And when such indignation spills over to military contest, it knows no bounds short of reduction of the lawbreaker to the point of complete submissiveness."[7]

A debate that has no obvious "politically correct" answer but that desperately requires to be joined concerns the question: How new is the Bush administration policy of "preventive" or "preemptive" war? Writing in the *New York Review of Books*, Professor Arthur Schlesinger opines that preemption represents a "fatal change in the foreign policy of the United States." During the long years of the Cold War, Schlesinger assures the reader, "preventative war was unmentionable. Its advocates were regarded as loonies."[8] Yet some of Schlesinger's colleagues in the administration of John F. Kennedy explicitly advocated attacking communism in Vietnam while it was still relatively weak: McGeorge Bundy "concluded that a preemptive strike was desirable."[9]

On the one hand, commentators point to the brazen way in which policymakers in the Bush administration destroy multinational agreements painstakingly drafted over many decades, and blithely leap from rationale to rationale in seeking to justify United States aggression. This, it is suggested, is something new under the sun. On the other hand, anyone viewing the history of treaties with Native Americans might conclude that both in style and substance, neoconservatism began with the extermination of the Pequot Indians.

Most fundamentally and grievously of all: Radical historians, anxious to prove the meticulous character of their scholarship, have too often confined the scope of their research to small, "manageable" topics. Mirra suggests that there might be a similar tendency in the field of peace education. Creation of the master narrative devolves to professors who view the world broadly, but from the parochial perspective of Ivy League departments whose tenured members — think of the Bundys, the Rostows, Professor Wolfowitz — in even years make the policy that in odd years their scholarship grandly justifies.

For example, Tony Judt finds such parochialism and "triumphalism" in the sweeping Cold War history of Yale professor John Lewis Gaddis.[10] Among the topics he finds lacking substantial treatment in Gaddis's work are: the sources and psychology of Soviet strategy; the degree to which United States diplomats like Harriman, Acheson, Kennan and Bohlen brought to the table a "worldly, cosmopolitan" outlook just as cold and hard as that of their Marxist counterparts; the Third World, including the overthrow of elected governments in Iran, Guatemala and Chile; Polish Solidarity and Hungary in 1956; Soviet intelligence; the fact that McCarthyism did not occur in Western Europe despite spying in those countries at least as serious as that charged to the Rosenbergs and Alger Hiss; Charles de Gaulle; Eurocommunism; the international New Left; the prehistory of the Cold War from 1917 to 1945; and its posthistory, including the invasion of Iraq. One might pardonably conclude that this master narrative is not just Hamlet without the Prince of Denmark, but Hamlet without the entire court at Elsinore.

To revise is more than to criticize. Radical historians must take risks that will expose them, in turn, to criticism. Historians and scholars have a responsibility to reconstruct the master narrative as well as to polish particular tiles in the mosaic. Since William Appleman Williams, few if any historians on the Left have had the chutzpah to try to tell the whole story of U.S. foreign policy, or even the whole story of U.S. foreign policy since the Second World War. That should be next on our agenda.

IV

How, then, may we extricate ourselves from what Carl Mirra terms "the sense that it was the United States' destiny to spread freedom and prosperity" without reproducing a Left version of the same mind-set with a new cast of villains? Carl Mirra is abundantly persuasive when he asks that those who project political direction for the United States cultivate, before all else, the quality of humility.

A good beginning might be to reexamine the same figure invoked by John Winthrop, Thomas Jefferson, John Brown, Martin Luther King, Jr., and George W. Bush, namely, Jesus of Nazareth. There are two obvious ways to do this.

A first approach is by way of recent scholarship of the so-called Jesus Seminar. The work of John Dominic Crossan is perhaps the most relevant. Crossan presents Jesus as a "Mediterranean Jewish peasant," who resisted the globalization sponsored by the Roman Empire.[11] In the Nazareth of Jesus' lifetime, according to Crossan, Rome built cities and promoted the spread of a commercial economy. As a result, artisans and small farmers fell into debt and lost their livelihoods and lands. Those who attempted to resist the Roman authorities were, like rebellious slaves before them, crucified. Crossan's Jesus is not an agent of empire but an anti-imperialist revolutionary.[12]

Another approach to the historical Jesus, even for those who must read the texts in English rather than Hebrew, Greek or Aramaic, is to look again at the Bible itself. Luke 4:16–24 portrays what is often described as Jesus' first sermon. In fact, Jesus stood up in the congregation, read from the prophet Isaiah, handed the scroll back to "the minister," and sat down. What Jesus read was Isaiah 61:1:

> The spirit of the Lord God is upon me; because the Lord hath anointed me to preach good tidings unto the meek; he hath sent me to bind up the broken hearted, to proclaim liberty to the captives, and opening of the prison to them that are bound.

In addition to advocating the release of all prisoners, Jesus opposed the death penalty and insisted that his followers visit those presently incarcerated so that it might be said of them at the last judgment, "I was in prison, and ye came unto me."[13] This is not a Jesus who would condone the indefinite imprisonment without charge of "enemy combatants" or the dropping of cluster bombs on civilians whose deaths are dismissed as "collateral damage."

This Jesus also instructed his followers to turn the other cheek and to return good for evil; he told Peter to put up his sword. This Jesus would have condemned John Brown, four of his sons, and his son-in-law Henry Thompson, who, in May 1856, after they "sharpened and honed their short-bladed, heavy swords to razor fineness,"[14] took five unarmed pro-slavery men from their homes in Pottawatomie, Kansas, and slaughtered them.

Abraham Lincoln's Second Inaugural Address struggled to reconcile the vengeful God of Revelations with the teaching of Jesus. Astonishingly for a U.S. president in the midst of the bloodiest war in our history, he recognized the irony that each side in the conflict prayed to the same God. He advocated charity for all. But in the Old Testament cadence of Julia Ward Howe and John Brown, Lincoln also stated that if the war must continue until every drop of blood drawn by the lash had been paid for by a drop of blood drawn by the sword, still must it be said as it was said of old, the judgments of the Lord are true and righteous altogether.

As Howard Zinn and I have recalled, and Carl Mirra emphasizes, Thomas Paine, and after him other ordinary workingmen, William Lloyd Garrison and Albert Parsons, transcended any form of nationalism with the words, "My country is the world."[15] This was and is an astonishingly radical idea. It is the thesis that dissenters in the United States cannot be content with *any* interpretation of the U.S. experience confined within national boundaries. So long as we limit ourselves to that which has occurred within the framework of a single nation, we will always arrive at a place that is parochial and chauvinistic. A merely "American" set of values will always be Athenian in the sense that whatever equality it extends to those who are considered "citizens," and even if that designation is extended to, say, Native Americans, women, people of color, and legalized Hispanic immigrants, there will always be those whom the Greeks called "barbarians" who are not included. A society which affirms anything less than the belief that every human being on the face of the earth is equally entitled to the good things that the earth provides will, in the end, find some group of enemy combatants to hate.[16]

The Supreme Court of the United States has recently offered impressive support for the concept that there are universal rights, the existence of which arises not from the laws of any nation but from human nature itself. In the majority decision about the rights of prisoners at the Guantánamo detention facility, the justices turned historian and cited the eighteenth-century case in which Lord Mansfield set free an African slave purchased in Virginia, bound for Jamaica, but temporarily detained on a ship docked in England.[17] In another decision about the kidnapping of a Mexican doctor by drug enforcement agents, the Court continued to probe the "ambient law" of the Revolutionary era, concluding that courts of that period were opened to claims based on "the law of nations" and that a court today should likewise entertain a claim that rests "on a norm of international character accepted by the civilized world."[18] And in *Hamden v. Rumsfeld*, in 2006, the Supreme Court held that the United States government was bound by Common Article 3 of the Geneva Conventions concerning the treatment of prisoners even in a conflict not between sovereign states.[19]

These decisions are consistent with the tradition that "my country is the world." The most riveting expressions of that tradition, however, come from Henry David Thoreau. In Thoreau's essay on "Civil Disobedience," he says that it is more important for the "American" people to abolish slavery and to end war on Mexico than that the United States should survive as a nation.

> If I have unjustly wrested a plank from a drowning man, I must restore it him though I drown myself. This, according to Paley [a writer on moral questions], would be inconvenient. But he that would save his life, in such a case, shall loose it. This people must cease to hold slaves, and to make war with Mexico, though it cost them their existence as a people.[20]

In "Slavery in Massachusetts," written after the abduction of a fugitive slave from Boston, Thoreau called on his countrymen to be "men first, and Americans only at a late and convenient hour."[21]

Here is an American Revolutionary tradition on which scholars, activists, and even courts of law can take a stand together.

Staughton Lynd, former history professor at Spelman College and Yale University, was coordinator of the 1964 Mississippi Freedom Schools and made a widely publicized trip to Hanoi in 1965-66.

Preface

Under the presidency of George W. Bush, a public debate over the role of the United States in world affairs has swept across the nation. This lively conversation has occurred in the halls of Congress, in movie theaters after Michael Moore's *Fahrenheit 9/11*, on street corners, and of course, in classrooms. Scholars have undertaken studies that tackle the once taboo subject of empire. A proliferation of titles dealing with the U.S. Empire from across the political spectrum fill libraries and book stores as "the war on terrorism" unfolds.

Consider the appearance of texts such as Andrew Bacevich's edited volume, *The Imperial Tense: Prospects and Problems of the American Empire* (2003) and Noam Chomsky's *Hegemony or Survival: America's Quest for Global Dominance* (2004). Chomsky's study captured the attention of Venezuela's president, Hugo Chavez, who brandished a copy of the book at a speech before the United Nations in 2005, having demanded that U.S. citizens should read it to better understand that the threat resides in "their house." That a Latin American president was urging Americans to read about U.S. interventionism illustrates how far and wide the debate over U.S. power reaches. The outspoken Venezuelan leader is part of a broader dialogue concerning the U.S. role in world affairs.

Other scholarly forays into empire include Chalmers Johnson's *The Sorrows of Empire: Militarism, Secrecy, and the End of the Republic* (2004); Stephen Walt's *Taming American Power: The Global Response to U.S. Primacy* (2005); Niall Ferguson's *Colossus: The Rise and Fall of the American Empire* (2005); Greg Gradin's *Empire's Workshop: Latin America, the United States, and the Rise of the New Imperialism* (2006); and John Bellamy Foster's more explicit work, *Naked Imperialism: The U.S. Pursuit of Global Dominance* (2006). Even theologians have entered the discussion regarding empire. Cornel West, professor of religion at Princeton University, published *Democracy Matters: Winning the Fight against Imperialism* in 2004. Biblical scholar John Dominic Crossan's *God and Empire: Jesus against Rome, Then and Now* (2007) joins the public conversation over the meaning of empire.

The present study suggests that American peace educators have an especially valuable role to play in assessing the American Empire. Peace education is an expansive field, one which performs a crucial role in fostering conflict resolution skills and developing a broader culture of peace. All of the various endeavors in the field are necessary and foreign policy should not dominate every aspect of peace education. However, this book suggests that U.S. interventionism contributes to global violence and that a viable peace education must address its various dimensions. The United States as the remaining superpower wields an unprecedented degree of power and force throughout the globe. Given this reality, it might be well for peace education to develop a sustained analysis of U.S. military might. Developing curriculum, opening channels of communication for controversial forays into foreign policy and specific case studies can strengthen the field of peace education.

Regardless of one's views about the necessity of U.S. interventions, the repeated use of the armed forces by the United States merits special attention. The field of peace education, particularly in the United States, has not paid sufficient attention to addressing U.S. diplomacy. This field is uniquely prepared to offer well-established alternatives to force can contribute strongly to altering U.S. foreign policy behavior.

Hence, this book differs from competing works insofar as it offers concrete proposals for addressing contentious foreign policy issues in the classroom. Recent, related works such as Johan Galtung's *Searching for Peace*, Ian Harris's *Peace Education* (McFarland, 2003) or Alicia Cabezudo and Betty Reardon's *Learning to Abolish War: Teaching toward a Culture of Peace* offer a range of important views on peace education, but treat U.S. foreign policy in a secondary manner. Given that the Bush policy of unilateralism has unleashed a national and international debate on the use of force — a debate that frequently casts critical educators as threats to national security — it is surprising that no full length study attempts to analyze the pitfalls of U.S. policy, while offering approaches to educators (and all concerned citizens) for building peace. This book attempts to fill this gap by providing a framework for analyzing U.S. policy with suggestions for opening constructive dialogue.

It is of pivotal importance that educators begin to develop the skills to critique U.S. adventurism without succumbing to pessimism or indoctrination. This text aims to fills a significant void in both international relations and educational theory by combining a critical appraisal of U.S. policy with constructive ideas for bringing such analysis into the public schools, colleges and the broader public sphere.

Historically, the field of peace education has not paid particular attention to U.S. foreign policy. Recent events such as the September 11 tragedy and the U.S. invasion of Iraq have made it nearly impossible for peace educators to ignore America's global role. Indeed, many peace educators are increasingly evaluating U.S. foreign policy. Conferences and scholarly articles in the field have looked at American adventurism, yet there is a need to develop a focused narrative within the field on foreign policy issues. The architects of American diplomacy embrace a narrative of spreading democracy abroad, which has justified U.S. interventionism for at least the past century. The present study argues that peace educators can more readily build a culture of peace if they develop a narrative that questions easy answers and simple formulas for exercising military might in distant lands. In short, this book offers a critical appraisal of U.S. foreign policy alongside a constructive attempt to build a more peaceful world.

Introduction

The purpose of this book is to examine the prospects for peace education in light of U.S. foreign policy since 1945. It will first document the disparity between U.S. pronouncements about protecting human rights and its systematic erosion of those rights in the international arena. Second, it shall evaluate the challenges that the war on terrorism poses for peace education by way of exploring the importance of international treaties in upholding security. Investigating these nonviolent alternatives to the U.S. penchant for military force further illustrates how the contradiction between U.S. rhetoric and reality constrains peace education efforts. A final section will explore new ways of thinking and relating that are ultimately necessary for the realization of these nonviolent options.

It is understood here that U.S. foreign policy presents a significant obstacle to the project of peace education. The Congressional Research Service lists 168 U.S. military interventions from 1798 to 1945, while the former State Department official, William Blum, identifies fifty-five military actions since the Second World War. Despite the end of the Cold War in 1991, U.S. military strikes are increasing.[1] Supporters of these intrusions argue that they are necessary to protect freedom and American interests abroad, while critics charge they reveal the cold, calculated expansion of empire.[2] Whether or not one defends or criticizes U.S. policy, the sheer volume of interventions warrants an investigation into alternatives. These options, from conflict resolution strategies to international treaties and tribunals, constitute the foundation of peace education. The United States' propensity for military force rather than negotiation, poses a challenge to this enterprise. In short, this study will illustrate how past and present U.S. policy abroad hinders peace education at home, the attempt to teach and learn about nonviolent alternatives to military campaigns.

The challenge is to introduce U.S. foreign policy behavior into existing peace education approaches in a manner that is not excessively threatening to national privileges, thereby provoking further conflict and debate. One way to begin this undertaking is to explore the creation of a new U.S. national metaphor to aid in the pressing task of including U.S. international affairs in peace education. However, we shall first outline U.S. policy in chapter 2, "The Contours of U.S. Foreign Policy: A Critical Peace Education Perspective," aiming to situate these amply documented, but often overlooked, facets of U.S. power within the conceptual framework of peace education.

One fundamental reason why some peace educators might avoid direct criticisms of U.S. policy stems from the shame and guilt that it evokes. Critiques regarding the extermination of the Amerindians, 244 years of slavery, and warfare aimed at Vietnamese citizens provoke a profound sense of dishonor and disgrace. Many thoughtful peace educators avoid "taking sides" against U.S. policy as it risks instigating conflict, the very thing they seek to reduce. Yet, it is exactly this general evasion of shame and guilt that perpetuates the cycle of violence that plagues the modern world. Chapter 3 takes on the topic of repressed guilt and its role in exacerbating militarism and violence.

Psychologist Ervin Staub characterizes the avoidance of subjects that evoke feelings of guilt as cognitive screening.[3] Uncomfortable facts that challenge national consciousness or collective self-images are filtered from the memory, as Staub explains. Scholars sometimes label it historical amnesia, the tendency to forget unpleasant events. As the screening and accompanying distortions of reality are shared collectively, they are hard to discover or "remember." Drawing attention to these buried realities elicits contempt. Yet, Staub writes that the most effective way to overcome the dangers of cognitive screening is to identify, discuss and analyze its presence. Successful peace education efforts must locate how cognitive screening, or the refusal to acknowledge guilt concerning past atrocities, propels violence.

Bertrand Russell, Thomas Scheff, Roy Baumeister and Johan Galtung find that unacknowledged guilt leads to violence. Anger and hatred of others serves as a means to escape shame, the painful experience of disgrace. Individuals or nation-states that cause others to suffer must somehow release themselves from the distress of shame and the torment of guilt, the realization that one is responsible for one's wrongdoing. The easiest way to circumvent guilt is to cast one's enemies as inhumane, and wholly deserving of violent treatment. Alongside this strategy is the tendency to depict oneself as morally superior and ethically virtuous, which further conceals one's guilt. Psychologists and historians have documented how vicious regimes, from ancient societies to Nazi Germany, shroud their pernicious crimes behind a veil of moral superiority. The underlying problem is that violence proceeds from these two competing images of oneself. Aggression arises from the strained denial of shame embedded within this contradiction. While Franklin Ford locates this dynamic in ancient civilization and Bertrand Russell and Thomas Scheff masterfully identify it in the outbreak of the First World War, few scholars apply this trend to U.S. society. Studies by the Norwegian scholar, Johan Galtung, are alone in suggesting that the U.S. penchant for violence is, in part, driven by its refusal to acknowledge guilt.[4] To avoid misunderstanding, the present study does not suggest that unacknowledged guilt is the sole contributing factor behind violent military campaigns. The role of suppressed guilt in stimulating violence is well documented in psychological studies, yet further research is needed on its role in collective violence.

Hence, the analysis of the gap between U.S. principles and practice offered here seeks to uncover the contradiction that lies at the heart of violence, thereby expanding Galtung's critique. This book's critical assessment of U.S. foreign policy does not aim to take sides against America, but instead seeks to uncover the collective shame and guilt that fuels the U.S. tendency to flex its military muscles during crises. When guilt remains unacknowledged, it is easier to blame and hurt others. When guilt is acknowledged it becomes more difficult to strike out against others, which paves the way for the consideration of alternatives to violent action. That a U.S. State Department report boasts, "human rights pervades every aspect of U.S. foreign policy" and George H. Bush's memorable comment that "I will never apologize for the United States" reveal what philosopher Cornel West calls an insecure culture trapped in the tension between its pristine self-image and its vile conduct.[5] Chapters 2, 4 and 5 chronicle the audacious policy statements regarding U.S. superiority that point to a nation plagued by unacknowledged shame and guilt and relate these remarks to specific interventions. Chapter 3, "Unacknowledged Guilt and U.S. Militarism," illustrates the long history of U.S. metaphors of superiority, saturated in quasi-religious discourse, that point to a hidden sense of shame and guilt.

The pressure to ignore U.S. wrongdoing was greatly amplified immediately following the horrific attacks of September 11. While nothing excuses those barbaric acts, a detailed examination into why terrorists target the United States reveals that the projection of U.S. military power across the globe is not without consequences, what the CIA calls "blowback." U.S. policymakers frequently follow violent policies and form improper alliances that regularly ignite anti–U.S. sentiment expressed in heretofore unimaginable ways on September 11. When placed in the proper historical perspective, it is clear that the war on terrorism and Operation Iraqi Freedom entail the same reckless and dangerous policies that place U.S. citizens at risk and undermine our security. Some simple and effective policy changes may reduce the likelihood of future attacks and save innocent lives. These strategies can be implemented only if peace educators and the American people examine exactly how the United States continues to erode basic human rights and risks sparking another incident of "blowback" in the war on terrorism. Therefore, chapter 4, "George W. Bush and the Resurrection of the Chosenness Syndrome after September 11: A Unique Challenge for Peace Education" and chapter 5, "The War on 'Terrorism,' Iraq and the Challenges for Peace Education," explore the U.S. war that began on October 7, 2001, uncovering how U.S. defense planning continues to erode safety and security while undermining peacemaking alternatives.

Chapter 6, "The International Criminal Court as a Peace Educator," examines the U.S. rejection of a key antiterrorist device and peacemaking tool, the International Criminal Court. It seeks to bring to justice the world's worst human rights violators, individuals who commit war crimes, genocide and crimes against humanity. The entire European Union backs the court, yet the United States opposes it. U.S. leaders fear that they might be targeted by the ICC. The United States' suspicion regarding the court is unfortunate insofar as many significant theoretical approaches to peace education are based on such institutions. Ian Harris reminds us that international education, as a species of peace education, explores the international system and the importance of how the United Nations "can adjudicate conflicts between nations, so that they don't go to war." Human Rights education is inseparable from movements to create institutions such as the International Criminal Court. Focusing on the dignity of all people, human rights education "attempt[s] to replace enemy images with understanding," Harris writes, "to break through a process of numbing and denial about atrocities committed in intractable conflicts."[6] Clearly, the International Criminal Court is a vital tool in overcoming the tendency among violent perpetrators to conceal their crimes. Yet, the United States rejects this potent tool for maintaining peace and justice. Chapter 6 examines the U.S. opposition to the court insofar as it illuminates the fact that U.S. leaders are more concerned with shielding themselves from guilt than they are with upholding an essential instrument for peace educators and those concerned with reducing terrorism.

Chapter 7, "Toward a Critical Peace Pedagogy of Nonviolent Tension," discusses the importance of recognizing unacknowledged guilt for the project of peace education. To accept responsibility for past and present misdeeds forces one to wrestle with guilt, and begins a process of healing by refraining from revenge or "justified" violence. Indeed, as the cognitive scientist Noam Chomsky observes, "confessions of overwhelming guilt can be good therapy."[7] This difficult engagement not only inspires new ways of formulating U.S. foreign policy, it also encourages new ways of thinking and relating to one another.

Effective peace education encourages new ways of thinking that transcend the realism that underlies U.S. foreign policy. Realpolitik, or power politics, animates U.S. diplomacy. A 1954 executive branch panel, for example, felt that, "acceptable norms of human conduct do not apply"[8] in the fight against communism, which forces us to adopt a "fundamentally repugnant" foreign policy. It is worth noting that this realism behind U.S. foreign policy really amounts to an idealistic mythology. The notion that U.S. liberal democracy (the good) must contain, at all costs, the spread of communism (evil) is little more than a celebratory theodicy of good defeating evil.

"Repugnant" realism, canonized in Western philosophy by Hobbes and Machiavelli, is related to the dominant, modern ways of thinking. Modern consciousness began roughly in the seventeenth century with Descartes's famous mind-body or subject-object dualism, which institutionalized Francis Bacon's earlier rhetoric that man must master nature, "put her on a rack and torture secrets from her." In effect, a master-slave narrative informs modern thought. The conquest of nature lends itself to the conquest of whole cultures, the mastery of the civilized nations (the subject) uplifting and modernizing the uncivilized (the object). This patriarchal presupposition that man resides outside of nature is funneled through our modern social structures and political ideologies thereby fueling more complicated divisions of race, gender, class and nation. This onlooker, dualistic thinking, can be found in the "deep culture" of U.S. foreign relations, especially the largely unexamined assumption that the United States sides with the good against a distant, incomprehensible evil.

Peace education must facilitate a concept of foreign policy that moves beyond the realist, dualist paradigm. As peace educator Riitta Wahlström writes, dualistic thinking lends itself to the "formation of enemy images" and proliferates militaristic attitudes.[9] Instead peace educators should promote images that are flexible enough to recognize our interrelatedness by way of facilitating a holistic awareness. At the same time these alternative images and strategies must remain practical enough to provide lasting security. To avoid misunderstanding, a holistic paradigm does not reject modern scientific thought and practical political strategies. The aim is to promote the clear thinking and individuality that modernity provides, while highlighting its almost excessive drive to carve up and conquer the entire spectrum of reality, from atoms to nations. Reexamining U.S. policy entails reassessing our dominant assumptions. Such an exploration simply recognizes that a transformation of our thinking is needed to maintain an enduring peace, a condition based on a holistic consciousness, which is inextricably linked with cooperative exchanges and respect for human dignity. Such an endeavor requires more than factual analysis, and imagines novel ways of thinking and behaving.

This seemingly naïve enterprise is anything but childish. Instead of clinging to rigid distinctions of good versus evil, a holistic consciousness demands that we travel into the dark side of human existence, recognizing its presence in ourselves as well as our enemies. We must come to terms with, rather than distancing ourselves from, evil. This process begins with understanding the seductive appeal of violence and war for both our adversaries and ourselves. Violence seduces us with the idea that we can overcome our alienation and isolation through war. In the quest to defeat an evil enemy, war yields a sense of unified action, while simultaneously erasing our past failures and misdeeds. Recall, for instance, the expression of relief in some quarters at the outbreak of World War I, the "war to end all wars." Or, consider the ascendancy of U.S. power and self-confidence after incinerating over 100,000 Japanese in August 1945. The widespread feeling that war is redemptive strongly suggests that it serves an emotional outlet for frustrated emotions such as unacknowledged guilt.

As the aforementioned studies illustrate, repressed guilt is often released by way of war. Consider the tendency to insist that "September 11 changes everything," that this "new" war demands that we stand behind the president and avoid the temptation "to blame America first." The root conflict, the contradiction between the United States' lofty principles and ignoble practices, is conveniently discarded. Focusing on the enemy dissolves the responsibility of grappling with guilt, the recognition of one's capacity for evil. To evade this painful process is to avoid the root causes of violence and war.

This book shall conclude with an exploration into new ways of thinking, ones that begin by coming to terms with the United States' guilt. This process starts with a critique of U.S. misdeeds, not to inflict shame and ridicule, but to pave the way for the consideration of nonviolent alternatives to U.S. policy. These alternatives, such as the International Criminal Court and police force, promote ways of thinking that will gradually transform our consciousness. But, they will be implemented only when the United States recognizes that its current preference for military action erodes safety and security, a realization that starts by deconstructing U.S. policy. In short, this study will outline American transgressions in the international arena, offer solutions to this military option and explore ways of thinking that move beyond our modern balkanization and fragmentation.

1

The Tasks of Peace Education

The development of learning that will enable humankind to renounce the institution of war and replace it with institutions more consistent with the visions and values being articulated in the body of international standards [such as] the norms of a peaceful society [articulated in] the Universal Declaration of Human Rights remains a core of the peace education task.

— Betty Reardon[1]

Education shall be directed to the full development of the human personality and to the strengthening of respect for human rights and fundamental freedoms. It shall promote understanding, tolerance and friendship among all nations, racial or religious groups, and shall further the activities of the United Nations for the maintenance of peace.

— United Nations Declaration of Human Rights, Article 26

Citizens and intellectuals in the United States have a particular responsibility for what goes on between the United States and the rest of the world, a responsibility that is in no way discharged or fulfilled by saying that the Soviet Union, Britain, France or China were, or are, worse. The fact is that we are indeed responsible for, and therefore more capable of, influencing *this* country in ways that we were not for the pre–Gorbachev Soviet Union, or other countries ... it behooves us as intellectuals and humanists and secular critics to understand the United States in the world of nations and power from *within* the actuality.

— Edward Said[2]

While in this book peace education is defined broadly as pedagogy about peace, it is important to define the field for clarification. Reardon notes that definitions of peace education are not always uniform owing principally to the field's multidisciplinary nature and its application in different arenas. The "whole field of peace education," Birgit Brock-Utne similarly notes, "is extremely difficult to treat in a scholarly manner" as it is subject to a variety of interpretations. In an attempt to define this broad field, Reardon writes that peace education is the "transmission of knowledge about requirements of, the obstacles to and possibilities for achieving and maintaining peace, training in skills for interpreting the knowledge, and the development of reflective and participatory capacities for applying the knowledge to overcoming problems and achieving possibilities."[3] In secondary schools, peace education encompasses conflict resolution programs, violence prevention curricula, multicultural education and human rights education. Theoretical approaches, such as world order studies, are located in colleges and universities, and found within departments of anthropology, sociology, teacher education and peace studies. Civic groups and nongovernmental organizations add important contributions to the field outside the university setting.[4] A common focus on the prevention and elimination of violence binds these disparate groups together. This study is not an investigation into the myriad approaches to the field; instead, it is an examination into the root causes of violence in the modern world coupled with practical peacemaking strategies, using U.S. foreign policy as a case example. As such, it represents critical peace research that expands the general practice of peace education.

That the notion of peace itself is also contested further complicates this investigation. Johan Galtung, widely regarded as the father of peace studies, clarifies matters with his distinction between negative and positive peace. Negative peace signifies the absence of war, a desirable condition although it is frequently accompanied with a stalemate, where warring parties are at "peace" but hostilities and threats remain. Positive peace indicates the presence of justice and peace values, such as nonviolent conflict resolution skills and a genuine respect for human dignity. A social order characterized by economic, gender and racial equality exists alongside nonviolent dispute resolution strategies under conditions of positive peace. The distinction between negative and positive peace does not suggest a conflict among them; rather, they comprise a larger whole that constitutes peace, the absence of war and the realization of justice. Effective peace education connects the two understandings of peace by raising awareness about the causes of war and the barriers to nonviolence while building the skills needed to create a world defined by economic, gender and racial equality. American policy often masks these nonviolent alternatives, while perpetuating structural violence that frequently sparks conflict and war.

A reliable yardstick for assessing these transgressions is the Universal Declaration of Human Rights. Adopted by the United Nations in 1948, the declaration promotes the conditions of positive peace in its preamble by insisting that the "inherent dignity and the equal and inalienable rights of all members of the human family is the foundation of freedom, justice and peace in the world." Some critics charge that the declaration contains a Western prejudice. Other commentators believe that the United States manipulates the concept of human rights to justify intervention against weaker states. My aim is not to enter this debate, but to record the incongruity between U.S. proclamations about upholding human rights and its violation of those rights. Such an analysis is important to peace education for several reasons. For one thing, many peace researchers note that human rights are the "most promising conceptual area" for linking negative and positive peace.[5] Recording precisely how the U.S. military erodes basic human rights is a significant step toward the abolition of war, whereas upholding the dignity and equality of all people as a fundamental right contributes to ways of thinking and behaving that are essential to positive peace.

The notion of human rights also helps peace educators to reliably assess the shortcomings of U.S. foreign policy, an exercise that is often neglected. U.S. foreign policy, Betty Reardon observes, "has yet to receive significant place in American peace education."[6] While peace educators have done a great deal of work in the area of human rights since Reardon made this remark, the link between human rights education and U.S. foreign policy has yet to *fully* materialize. In the late 1990s, human rights education approaches seemed to proliferate (along with other approaches such as conflict resolution). As Reardon observes, the incorporation of human rights into peace education is rapidly expanding. Both the Global Campaign for Peace Education and UNESCO's Integrated Framework of Action on Education for Peace, Human Rights and Democracy give centrality to the issue of human rights. This expansion provides a "dimension of concrete possibilities for alternatives to current world conditions," Reardon writes, while presenting a "constructive action dimension to complement and apply to all the diverse forms of peace education." Peace educators such as Aline Stomfay-Stitz and Edyth Wheeler have argued that human rights and peace education become part of mainstream school curricula.[7] Indeed, the field has increasingly concentrated on human rights education and a greater application of this approach in the area of U.S. international relations might benefit peace education in the United States. Just as human rights education has grown over the past several decades, the field of peace education seems to be moving in the direction of addressing "current world conditions," such as the United States' role in the international arena. U.S. foreign policy has captured the attention of peace educators but greater specificity on actual international policy within in the field is needed. The debates in the field center more on the causes of war and violence than on the purposes or concepts of peace education.[8] This book suggests that both the purpose of peace education and studies into the causes of war should creatively incorporate U.S. foreign policy into existing work.

Peace scholars abroad, Johan Galtung and Magnus Haavelsrud among them, pay attention to U.S. foreign policy, yet peace educators in the United States have only recently started to wrestle seriously with American diplomacy.

Nguyen My Chau, a peace researcher from Vietnam who completed a thesis at Gifu University in Japan, sees a "crucial failing" in American peace education. Having worked with Vietnamese victims of U.S. napalm sprayings, Nguyen observes that American peace educators do not encourage teachers "to tell the truth" regarding the U.S. invasion of foreign nations. A greater discussion of U.S. "wrongdoing" would facilitate a better understanding with the outside world, the Vietnamese peace researcher adds.[9] That peace education is an expansive field, with a variety of objectives, makes it nearly impossible to chart the various trends that have shaped, and continue to shape, the field. It is clear, however, that U.S. foreign policy plays a tangential, although expanding, role in most of these trends.

Robin J. Burns and Robert Aspeslagh's widely cited anthology, *Three Decades of Peace Education around the World*, includes a single chapter on foreign policy issues. In an essay titled, "Adult Education for Peacebuilding," Chadwick Alger argues that peace education needs to examine foreign policy matters. A professor emeritus of political science at Ohio State University, Alger correctly critiques the "ideology of the state system." This ideology holds that ordinary people are incapable of grasping the complexity of international relations.[10] Peace researchers and peace education curricula can help to debunk this myth. To properly accomplish this task, discussions of foreign policy must be particularized. When peace education addresses foreign policy, it often remains abstract or part of more technical discussions on where it might fit within the field. Incorporating specific case studies into peace education aids ordinary people in realizing that foreign policy is not the purview of a few elites.

Some scholars maintain that an analysis of U.S. policy and empire is invisible not only in peace education but also in the entire scope of education studies. According to radical educator Peter McLaren, "there is little discussion of empire and imperialism in education journals." There has been a rise in "generalized critique[s]" of the Bush administration in recent years; however, there is a lack of "substantial treatments of U.S. militarism and empire by educationalists."[11] The pendulum appears to be swinging in the direction of greater analysis of American international behavior, although more work is needed. One step in this direction is McLaren's own research. His coauthored book with Ramin Farahmandpour, *Teaching against Global Capitalism and the New Imperialism: A Critical Pedagogy* (2004) and McLaren's *Capitalists and Conquerors: A Critical Pedagogy against Empire* (2005), both published by Rowman and Littlefield, represent critical pedagogy's attempt to tackle U.S. foreign policy. Peace education is not alone in failing to concentrate on the overall narrative of U.S. foreign policy. Staughton Lynd's foreword reminds us that even among radical historians the "whole story" of American interventionism has been largely left to more conservative interpretations. Few left historians have had the nerve, Lynd insists, to present an alternative narrative of U.S. foreign relations. This task should indeed be next on our agenda, not only for historians, but peace educators as well.

Aline Stomfay-Stitz's excellent overview, *Peace Education in America, 1828–1990*, covers various templates in the field over the past two centuries, yet there are few cases of peace educators offering critiques or a detailed analysis of U.S. foreign policy. In the early decades of the twentieth century, an aim of peace education was to stop the United States' participation in World War I. Limited reviews of foreign policy, such as John Dewey's Outlawry of War campaign, received some attention at this time. After World War II, peace education became increasingly concerned with the threat of nuclear war. From the 1960s until today four major streams of peace education dominate the field: nonviolence, global education, world order studies and conflict resolution. Each category receives different emphasis depending on the historical moment. By the 1980s the field became preoccupied with global and disarmament education, tilting heavily toward the "technicalities of the arms race," with little research on alternative conflict resolution strategies, as Elise Boulding and Birgit Brock-Utne noted.[12] Even during this intense period of chronicling the proliferation of nuclear weapons, few educators documented the role of U.S. interventions in accelerating the problem. As for the 1990s, Marcia Johnson's brief article, "Trends in Peace Education," highlights the proliferation of teaching for respect and tolerance during the decade, but does not mention the presence of foreign policy issues.[13] Whereas the pendulum swung in the direction of technical aspects of militarization during the eighties, at the turn of the twenty-first century the field is largely dominated by conflict resolution methodology.[14] This emphasis is both necessary and valuable in fostering peacemaking skills, especially in the international arena. The focus on conflict resolution has generally overshadowed any systematic evaluation of U.S. foreign affairs.

In January 2007, the United States Institute for Peace released a report titled "Building Global Peace, Conflict, and Security Curricula at Undergraduate Institutions: A Curriculum Development Guide for Colleges and Universities." It provides a coherent and solid set of sample curricula for core programs related to peace and security studies. The sample for a Bachelor of Arts degree in Peace Studies lists some twenty-seven courses. Four are devoted to international relations, three in general and one focused specifically on Europe, "War and Peace in 20th Century Europe." The only sample curriculum that includes courses specific to U.S. foreign policy is in the area of security studies, which has a heavy emphasis on international relations.[15] Returning to peace studies, one might argue that some of the general introductory courses subsume American foreign policy topics. Perhaps this is true; however, the absence of any specific reference or coursework in the area suggests that U.S.

foreign policy behavior is not part of the conceptual framework in the field. Including a course on European foreign policy yet omitting any direct reference to U.S. policy in the course listings might signal to cautious educators to minimize U.S. foreign relations.

The Five College Consortium in Peace and World Security Studies based at Hampshire College produces an exemplary international conflict resolution curriculum. As a variant of peace education, it draws upon world order studies to analyze the global effects of militarism, while promoting conflict resolution strategies. Writing in the consortium's curriculum guide, George Lopez rightly notes that militarization has "at times been invisible" in peace research, but it should be given "prominence." An area that Lopez, director of the Institute for International Peace Studies at the University of Notre Dame, identifies as requiring further study concerns the economics of arms sales. His important recommendation does not, however, specifically chart the U.S. role in global arms sales and its impact on human rights. The consortium has not systematically documented the U.S. role in undermining international cooperation and human rights, with the exception of Michael Klare's *Supplying Repression: U.S. Support for Authoritarian Regimes Abroad,* which links U.S. military aid to human rights abuses. Moreover, both the consortium and Klare's investigation into U.S. misdeeds are principally concerned with security studies and not peace education per se.[16]

While the United States is hardly alone in undermining human rights, the fact that it has intervened over fifty times in the past half-century, and accounts for roughly 50 percent of global arms sales, warrants close attention by anyone concerned about peace. Peace research and peace education have contributed significantly to our knowledge about militarism, particularly regarding how the arms race has proliferated militaristic attitudes and anxiety. The "dramatic expenditure" on weapons systems, Magnus Haavelsrud observes, leads to militaristic attitudes and an "increasing reliance on military means of coercion." Studies into militarism can be extended into research on U.S. policy. A United Nations publication confirms that the United States produces nearly 50 percent of the world's arms. Defense contractor Lockheed Martin's arms sales exceed the defense spending of "all but ten countries in the world," the UN report continues.[17] "The US defence budget," notes a leading industry consultant, "has increased over 60% in constant US$ over the past ten years, reaching $442 billion in 2003." It is clear that "US [defense] spending will continue to outstrip the rest of the world by a huge margin well into the future ... the USA will continue to dominate," concludes the market services firm.[18] The United States leads the world in arms sales, exporting war products across the globe. The United States also leads the world in military interventions. A viable peace education must address the United States' "dominance" over the military industry and warfare. Surely, a field that seeks to eliminate war must include a close examination of the nation most active in warfare on its agenda.[19]

A sustained and focused inquiry into U.S. interventionism remains on the periphery of peace education. Part of the reason why U.S. policy does not receive greater attention from peace educators may stem from its controversial nature. Ian Harris reports that proponents of conflict resolution education view it as "more acceptable than teaching strategies for peace that might threaten national policies."[20] Educators across disciplines are mindful of the danger of scrutinizing foreign policy. For instance, Hunt and Metcalf in their landmark book on social studies curriculum, *Teaching High School Social Studies*, label foreign policy a "closed area of society." They suggest that social studies educators tend to avoid controversies in international affairs as it is laden with inconsistencies and conflict. Hunt and Metcalf nonetheless recommend that teachers adopt a "closed areas approach" to teach students the skills to resolve such conflict constructively.[21] No field is better equipped to handle this approach than peace education. Indeed, conflict resolution education is an essential and established approach for developing a peace consciousness. One central goal of this study is to develop a conception of peace education that links this accepted strategy to the more precarious international arena in such a way that we can begin to evaluate and change U.S. foreign policy behavior.

Along these lines, Carolyn Stephenson notes that more recent trends in peace studies have broadened the concept of security in dealing with international affairs. There is an attempt to not only examine national security and the causes of war, but also collective security and the steps toward positive peace.[22] Peace researchers Galtung, Jacobson and Brand-Jacobson have developed a "Transcend" approach to conflict mediation that enables peace educators to conceptually link U.S. policy to this broader concern for conflict resolution. They contend that a genuine conflict transformation can occur only by way of engaging the entire civil society in dialogue. Most conflict mediation strategies, the authors argue, focus too heavily on "reaching an agreement" at the expense of grasping the deep structures that underlie a given conflict.[23] This book similarly seeks to examine the deep structures that underlie U.S. militarism, while fostering a civic dialogue that works toward positive peace.

Schools, of course, are an essential part of this civic dialogue. Within the field of social studies, the increasingly influential National Council for the Social Studies rightly insists that the field must include civic competence. Surely, civic competence entails the ability to honestly examine one's cultural and political assumptions, including the U.S. role in world affairs. Such an approach requires effective conflict resolution curricula to empower students to uncover the contradictions of U.S. power, yet without becoming vindictive or cynical. Educators who encourage a critical analysis of U.S. policy must place a priority on *resolution*, taking as its example the civil rights movement and its powerful images of reconciliation and redemptive love. As peace researcher Michael Henderson notes, conflict resolution "must help individuals and nations break free of their past," and becomes "most effective when initiated by those whose people perpetuated wrongs rather than when demanded by those who see themselves as victims." Henderson cites the work of former U.S. State Department officer Joseph Montville, who argues that aggressors must acknowledge the harm caused by their actions. "When the acknowledgement is sincere," Montville writes, "the victim group can begin to trust" the aggressor group and build a future relationship.[24] For example, the U.S. government formally apologized to the Japanese Americans victimized by internment during the Second World War. What remains is the acknowledgment of the deeper structures that lead to destruction and preventable wars such as Vietnam and the March 2003 invasion of Iraq. In short, conflict resolution curricula can contribute to a civic conversation that prompts both U.S. citizens and officials to acknowledge the global scale of U.S. military violence.

Whereas Harris reminds us that some peace educators prefer approaches that do not threaten national policies, Martin Luther King, Jr. followed a different trajectory for eradicating violence. "There is a type of constructive, nonviolent tension that is necessary for growth," King explains, "it [is] necessary to create a tension in the mind so that individuals could rise from the bondage of myths and half-truths."[25] An authentic conflict resolution curriculum entails uncovering myths and distortions. The twenty-first century is marked by warfare, with the United States as the central actor. Building a genuine peace demands a "constructive, nonviolent tension," which this book takes as its principal aim.

Since the September 11 tragedy and the seemingly endless war on terrorism, the field of peace education has turned its gaze toward foreign policy issues. In October 2002, the Peace and Justice Association held a conference in Washington, D.C., titled, "Confronting Injustice, Ending War: The Role of Peace Educators and Activists after 9/11." In October 2004, the Peace Education Center at Teachers College, Columbia University, sponsored a day long event, "The Law of Force or the Force of Law?" which included U.S. diplomacy on its agenda. The founding director emeritus, Betty Reardon, spoke passionately about the pitfalls of Bush's preemptive war doctrine, while encouraging educators to support the World Tribunal on Iraq. The tribunal is an international, nongovernmental body that aims to document U.S. misdeeds during the Iraq war that began in March 2003. John Synott's editorial in the *Journal of Peace Education*, "Peace Education as an Educational Paradigm: Review of a Changing Field Using Old Measures," notices that the field has expanded rapidly over the past decade. One area of growth is in peace education's global orientation, which is "especially relevant" to a more interdependent, globalized world, Synott correctly argues. Many new trends are emerging as "the futility of violent solutions to international conflicts (as in Iraq)" has "encouraged ... the introduction of peace education into schools." Synott's article focuses on peace education as a legitimate educational paradigm and his mention of U.S. policy is significant. However, Synott stops short of arguing for any specific treatment of American foreign policy behavior. And, Ian Harris and Mary Lee Morrison in their influential text, *Peace Education*, warn that, "Following the World Trade Center attacks in 2001, President George Bush was able to dramatically increase the defense budget of the U.S." Therefore, "a primary goal for peace educators must be to challenge students to think through what is a reasonable defense."[26]

Part of this process entails an open, critical and informative appraisal of U.S. diplomacy. Awareness of information alone can change attitudes toward war. Harris and Morrison point to a study on nuclear weapons conducted by the Physicians for Social Responsibility in San Francisco. The physicians group distributed a questionnaire before presenting information on the effects of nuclear weapons, whereby 10 percent of the some 1,300 respondents felt that the use of nuclear weapons was sometimes worth it. After the presentation of information on the dangers of nuclear war, half of those in favor of their use changed their position, saying that using nuclear weapons was not justified.[27] The present study holds that a fair-minded and careful presentation of information can change perceptions. An honest and informative analysis of U.S. foreign policy will likely contribute to altering support for aggressive policies. While many peace educators are increasingly addressing foreign policy issues, there still is no single full-length manuscript in the field devoted to systematically analyzing U.S. foreign policy alongside a constructive proposal for peace educators to address such policies. A full-length inquiry into U.S. foreign policy seems long overdue. This book does not pretend to be a comprehensive appraisal, but merely an invitation to a deeper, thought-provoking evaluation of U.S. diplomacy within the field of peace education.

To be sure, peace educators should not indoctrinate students or inundate them with a completely biased portrait of U.S. foreign policy. There is much concern, some of it bordering on the hysterical, about maintaining "balance" in the classroom. Peace educators can present information and pose questions without insisting on the "correct" point of view. Students must be comfortable to evaluate these facts without coercion or concern about the teacher's biases. It must be made clear to students that they are never graded based on their political predilections, but instead on their grasp of the curriculum. Open-ended questions that invite criticism of peace education and critical approaches to foreign policy must also be part of any sound and healthy curriculum. It is worth recalling radical, nonviolent activist Dave Dellinger's observation that, "If freedom is one of our goals, we must include in our conception of [nonviolent] revolution the freedom of everyone else to choose or reject any aspect of what seems [progressive] to us."[28]

Consider also that many high schools and college campuses welcome Reserve Officers' Training Corps (ROTC) programs, which are basically prowar without any corresponding nonviolent, antiwar alternative. Henry Giroux reminds us that the public schools are not only subject to military recruiters. They also have "military personnel teaching in the classroom" under junior ROTC programs that are "becoming a conventional part of the school day." Moreover, it is estimated that at least 10 million people (probably youngsters) have downloaded *American Army*, a video game that the military uses in recruiting.[29] Peace educators should not settle for isolated pockets of sympathetic faculty to introduce alternatives to war in the curriculum, but should seek to serve as a viable alternative to ROTC programs, CIA recruiting on campuses and international affairs programs specifically designed to prepare students for U.S. foreign service. Since these programs have every right to operate, so too does peace education have the right to call for a direct, systematic alternative to these "militarized pedagogies" without the reactionary charge that we are "biased" or "anti–American."[30] If schools welcome military recruiters and military training, it is only fair that they welcome peace education as well. A peace education that systematically analyzes U.S. foreign policy is a step in this direction of offering an alternative to war.

In a certain sense, this book appears to fit with the Hague Appeal for Peace, Global Campaign for Peace Education as outlined in Alicia Cabezudo and Betty Reardon's valuable manual *Learning to Abolish War: Teaching toward a Culture of Peace*. The Hague Appeal offers a fifty-step plan for building a peace culture, which entails the investigation of the roots causes of war, international institutions in upholding peace and the transformation of violent conflict. Taken together, these strategies aid in the study of the root causes of U.S. interventionism, while highlighting the role of international institutions in facilitating a positive peace. The Hague Appeal offers a significant contribution toward a peace education that explores the root causes of war. Eradicating war entails an "understanding of culture as the values and worldviews that determine significant aspects of human identity." Similarly, the Hague Appeal rightly maintains that peace education should be "culturally contextualized" to address those needs most relevant in a particular setting.[31]

The U.S. setting is characterized by the enduring myth of American progress and growth, which is inseparable from expansion and empire. The sense that the United States is destined for limitless abundance and prosperity, expressed in the nineteenth century as its manifest destiny, contributes to a U.S. national identity that facilitates war. This identity was described by William Appleman Williams as "empire as a way of life," the feeling that U.S.

expansionism spreads freedom and goodwill. Conservative analyst Andrew Bacevich also urges citizens to recognize the perils of a U.S. culture that promotes the "sense that the nation's role in the world could not be understood except as benign." Notions of the United States as a beacon of freedom or the best hope for the world are variations of this theme. Within the United States, it is essential that this expansionist ethos, which is inseparable from U.S. foreign policy and global violence, is explored so as to fully accomplish the Hague Appeal's call to develop the "critical capacities ... to challenging the structures of the war system."[32] It seems that a culturally specific peace education in the United States must come to terms with the U.S. role in accelerating violent conflict. While many peace educators call for such an analysis, the field would benefit from greater specificity. That is, a focused and sustained discussion of the U.S. role in the world, from massive arms sales to its ranking the highest on war participation indexes, is a project that still needs to be completed.

The model of "chosenness" is employed here to probe unacknowledged guilt for several reasons. The theme of chosenness, or the belief that the United States is God's favored nation, saturates the speeches of every post–World War II American president. The notion that the United States is God's chosen land is presented as a truism in presidential speeches, government reports and sometimes popular culture in the postwar period. Unless we accept this highly speculative discourse as a truism, we must uncover the reasons for the articulation of such dramatic expressions. Sociology, psychology and history teach us that these chosenness sensibilities are frequently related to deeper feelings of unacknowledged guilt. Given the pervasiveness of chosenness themes in U.S. foreign policy rhetoric, it serves as an excellent model for examining the deeper sources of guilt. Respected studies by Eric Hoffer, Ervin Staub, Thomas Scheff and Johan Galtung are cited in support of the model of chosenness and its relationship to unacknowledged guilt.

This model is directed principally toward peace educators, but should be relevant to students of U.S. foreign policy and concerned citizens. Peace educators, however, are uniquely trained to address such controversial issues and can properly introduce U.S. foreign policy into existing conflict resolution materials. The metaphor of chosenness can be refashioned to transcend narrow, nationalist interests toward a more global, inclusive vision, much like the planetary stewardship that Reardon promotes. Although most U.S. presidents manipulate the sense of chosenness to justify war, Abraham Lincoln serves as one exemplar for reinventing the U.S. national narrative. During the Civil War, Lincoln articulated a mutual, shared responsibility for the war: "In great contests each party claims to act in accordance with the will of God ... God can not be for and against the same thing at the same time." That is, America does not know what God desires, and is better conceived as "an almost chosen people."[33] This more inclusive stance should be applied to many U.S. foreign adventures, moving away from the tradition of "my country right or wrong" toward "my country is the world." It encourages us to recognize both the reciprocal causes of violence and the humanity of our enemies. Indeed, this book concludes with an exploration into how peace educators might enable us to develop the imagination to create a national metaphor that facilitates a planetary consciousness. This goal appears to overlap in part with the National Council for the Social Studies' practical guidebook, *Expectations for Excellence*. The council encourages the construction of a "global perspective" with "concern for all people." This approach reaches for a "commitment to finding just and peaceful solutions to global problems."[34]

Some peace educators and readers might view my model of chosenness and unacknowledged guilt as a reverse projection. That is to say, my study may be charged with projecting my feelings of guilt on to the custodians of U.S. policy, while I accuse them of projecting their guilt in self-righteous attitudes and aggression toward adversaries. It should be said that this study in no way suggests that the United States is evil and incapable of good. Indeed, American strategists defeated Nazi fascism, helped to construct the United Nations, and brokered peace at Camp David. This study simply suggests that a single aspect of America — its foreign policy behavior — too often uses violence to solve global problems. This tendency toward violent intervention is also on the rise since 1991, exceeding its average from 1945 to 1991 as the previous figures document. The present study suggests that the United States has yet to address the root causes of its preference to use force. Understanding the role of unacknowledged guilt brings us closer to understanding these root causes of U.S. violence. This project does not seek to condemn U.S. leaders, but to change U.S. foreign policy behavior in order to reduce violence. Alas, this enterprise is largely a critical indictment of U.S. foreign policy, but one that emphasizes reconciliation, in the spirit and commitment of Dr. King's vision of redemptive love, which invites "constructive tension." The reader should keep in mind that the critical evaluation of U.S. foreign policy presented in this text does not pretend to be the final word on the topic; instead, it is an invitation to begin the reconstruction of the "whole story" of America foreign policy.

2

The Contours of U.S. Foreign Policy: A Critical Peace Education Perspective

This conjunction of an immense military establishment and a large arms industry is new in the American experience. The total influence-economic, political, even spiritual-is felt in every city, every state house, every office of the Federal government. We recognize the imperative need for this development. Yet we must not fail to comprehend its grave implications. Our toil, resources and livelihood are all involved; so is the very structure of our society. In the councils of government, we must guard against the acquisition of unwarranted influence, whether sought or unsought, by the military-industrial complex. The potential for the disastrous rise of misplaced power exists and will persist.
— President Dwight D. Eisenhower, 1961.[1]

There will be no peace. At any given moment for the rest of our life-times, there will be multiple conflicts in mutating forms around the globe. Violent conflict will dominate the headlines.... The de facto role of the U.S. armed forces will be to keep the world safe for our economy and open to our cultural assault. To those ends, we will do a fair amount of killing.
— Major Ralph Peters.[2]

All Members shall refrain in their international relations from the threat or use of force against the territorial integrity or political inde-pendence of any state, or in any other manner inconsistent with the Pur-poses of the United Nations.
— Charter of the United Nations, 1945

One significant figure who incited the nonviolent, creative tension that this book reaches for was General Smedley Butler. As a former U.S. Marine (and eventually a conscientious objector), I first discovered Butler's name while in boot camp at Parris Island, South Carolina. Part of our training included the rote memorization of rifle specifications and Marine Corps history. An important item that we were required to know included the names of the only two marines to win two Congressional Medals of Honor. They are Dan Daly and Smedley Butler. Later in his life, Butler became more critical of U.S. foreign policy during the 1930s. According to his biographer, Butler complained that the United States manipulated elections in Central America. The general wrote that

> I spent 33 years and 4 months in active service as a member of our country's most agile military force — the Marine Corps. I served in all commissioned ranks from second lieutenant to Major General. And during that period I spent most of my time being a high-class muscle man for Big Business, for Wall Street and for the bankers. In short, I was a racketeer for capitalism. I suspected that I was part of a racket all the time. Now I am sure of it.[3]

That this esteemed military hero would denounce U.S. warfare deserves investigation. Over thirty years later Martin Luther King, Jr. echoed Butler's sentiments. The civil rights leader explained that the United States' drive "to maintain social stability" for "investment accounts" had led to a problematic series of interventions, which made King's country the "greatest purveyor of violence in the world."[4] Although King did not call U.S. foreign policy a racket, he did point to the "unwarranted influence" of corporate imperatives on U.S. policy that has indeed led to a "fair amount of killing."

These two historical voices saw a connection between corporate priorities and U.S. policy, a link that compromised human rights and democracy. There is something of a taboo in raising the issue of economic influences on American foreign policy. Scholars have worked assiduously to jettison such connections as the purview of anarchists, Marxists and radicals. The economic motives behind U.S. interventionism were nevertheless noticed by an esteemed military officer and the nation's leading civil rights figure, both of whom articulate a generalized version of what an American president called the military-industrial complex. It was also noticed in its early form by one of the nation's leading philosophers of education, John Dewey. "A centralized government has been built up by war necessities," Dewey wrote, "and that such a state is necessarily militaristic in its structure." After visiting Latin America in the early twentieth century, Dewey observed that "Even widespread popular desire to the contrary is no obstacle. The natural movement of the business enterprise ... suffices to bring about imperialistic undertakings."[5]

A publication from the American Historical Association that seeks to clarify the meaning of the convoluted phrase, military-industrial complex, explains that it is most simply "an alliance between the defense industry and the Department of Defense to shape public policy." In other words, the military-industrial complex refers to the confluence of the arms industry with a national government. One irony is that Eisenhower's administration was very much responsible for accelerating the link between the government and the arms industry. But, it was not until the Vietnam War that Eisenhower's concept created any fanfare as critics of that conflict used it disparagingly to denounce the "corporate liberals" who engaged in imperial expansion. Defenders of military spending argue that Eisenhower felt that the military-government alliance was necessary. Even if true, Eisenhower clearly warned against its "grave" consequences, and pleaded that the country guard against its "unwarranted influence." In his private communications, Eisenhower described the complex as the "delta of power." Congress, the defense industry and armed services "pressured him relentlessly" to increase military spending.[6] Part of this chapter details how corporate and government ties exert pressure on U.S. foreign policy decision making, leading to choices and actions that contradict the nation's values of freedom and democracy. The purpose of this type of critique is to raise awareness about such behavior and to see the "weakness of our own condition,"[7] as King put it, so that a new policy can be envisioned. Changing negative behavior requires an acknowledgment of that behavior.

However, critiques of U.S. foreign policy are too often met with denial, an evasion that hinders our ability to develop more humane policies. As General Telford Taylor, the U.S. chief prosecutor at Nuremberg observed regarding the United States' denial of war crimes in Vietnam, "It is surely incumbent on us to engage in hard self-scrutiny, and to conform our actions ... to the principles we profess."[8] The purpose of the following chapter is to encourage this collective self-examination by outlining how corporate agendas have shaped U.S. foreign affairs since the end of World War II with little concern for freedom, democracy and basic human rights. Economic forces alone cannot explain U.S. policy, but they play a significant role. Pecuniary drives also intersect with national images of the United States as the benevolent superpower, which propels cycles of military interventions. Therefore, we must first locate the contradiction between corporate avarice and the United States' altruistic self-image to fully comprehend American diplomacy. This self-image often finds expression in chosenness rhetoric or the belief that the United States was destined or selected to lead the world. The inspection of specific interventions and their role in hampering democracy is explored alongside contradictory policy statements regarding the United States as the beacon of freedom on a global mission to protect democracy.

This underlying contradiction arises from America's belief that it is a staunch supporter of human rights overseas. U.S. membership in the United Nations and repeated endorsements of the Universal Declaration of Human Rights reinforces such attitudes. From its establishment in 1948, U.S. leaders continually confirm the UN's mandate to "maintain international peace." In 1976, the U.S. Congress enacted human rights policies into the International Security and Arms Export Control Act. The statute states that, "a principle goal of the foreign policy of the United States is to promote the increased observance of internationally recognized human rights."[9] Both international law and congressional legislation obligate the United States to bolster peace and human rights.

The United States reaffirmed this commitment in 1993 at the World Conference on Human Rights in Vienna, Austria. Grassroots activists, nongovernmental organizations, academics and national diplomats gathered to validate international human rights. During the conference, then deputy secretary of state Warren Christopher declared that the United States opposes any nation that violates the Universal Declaration of Human Rights.[10] We must observe these universal principles as they have "been advocated for millennia by each of the world's great cultural and spiritual traditions," U.S. ambassador Bill Richardson confirms. President George W. Bush holds similar beliefs. "Defending human rights," the president remarked during Human Rights Week in December 2001, "is a core tenet of civilized people." U.S. leaders rightly assert that a concept of universal human rights restrains the arbitrary abuse of citizens across the globe. In fact, Richardson mirrors this book's assertion that the UN Declaration sets "a yardstick of humanity's best principles, against which we all must be judged."[11] Should one judge the United States against its own stated standards, one discovers that it has regularly violated them since the end of the Second World War.

Radical scholar Noam Chomsky argues that U.S. leaders could not adhere to the standards written into the Nuremberg Laws after the Second World War. The laws were used to convict Nazi war criminals, while setting norms for crimes against humanity and related offenses. In some cases, commanders of forces in the Second World War whose regiments engaged in war crimes were hanged. "If the Nuremberg laws were applied," Chomsky caustically notes, "then every post-war American president would have been hanged."[12] Some may argue that Chomsky has gone overboard here, but this dramatic observation can be of use to peace educators. Students might study and learn the Nuremberg Laws and then examine a specific intervention and determine whether or not Chomsky's remark is accurate. Again, students are free to disagree with Chomsky's assessment, but it provides a provocative and thought-provoking way to study U.S. interventions. The following section examines U.S. foreign policy and argues that the United States has violated its own standards. Whether or not these cases constitute war crimes under Nuremberg (or Geneva Conventions in effect since 1949) is left to the reader and further research.

Holistic educator Dale T. Snauwaert adds that the international norms set forth under Nuremburg call for "citizens to actively oppose acts of state that are criminal in character."[13] This section subsumes the difficult task of challenging the behavior of one's own nation. Given that the United States deployed troops over fifty-five times since 1945, it would be impossible to document each case. Some key examples shall illustrate that postwar U.S. interventions increased global instability, while repeatedly undermining human rights, a tendency that increased sharply after the Second World War. What appear to be reckless, inconsistent campaigns in places such as Iran, Guatemala, Cuba, Vietnam, Afghanistan, and elsewhere are remarkably consistent in serving corporate needs. As one informed observer notes, if U.S. interventions are driven by the desire to expand freedom and human rights, then:

> The Batista regime in Cuba would have been intervened as much as the Castro regime; the Somoza regime in Nicaragua as much as the Sandinista regime; the military dictators in Guatemala as much as Arbenz in 1954; the Jimenez regime as much as the Chavez regime in Venezuela; the Saudi Wahhabite regime as much as the Taliban Wahhabite regime in Afghanistan; Israeli actions against the human rights of Palestinians as much as any Palestinian/Arab act; Libya under King Idriss as much as under Qaddafi; Kuwait under the al-Sabahs as much as Iraq under Saddam Hussein; the Shah Reza Pahlavi as much as Mossadeq in Iran; and so on and so forth, there are many such paired comparisons.[14]

It should be made clear that this chapter does not argue that U.S. policy is propelled simply by economic greed. Interventions are not undertaken for the sole purpose of generating lucrative contracts for the defense industry. U.S. strategists hold an uncritical allegiance to capitalism as the route to freedom and democracy. American planners develop strategies based on a wide, structural understanding of world politics. They wish to maintain and expand a neo-liberal, global economy that is conducive to "free" markets. National governments that advocate economic policies that are incompatible with the neo-liberal order are frequently confronted. In some cases, it might be perfectly sensible for the United States to frustrate governments with economies that are incongruent with global capitalism; in other cases, the commitment to "free" markets lends itself to supporting authoritarian, antidemocratic governments.

As the Second World War unfolded, the United States was setting the stage for this global order, which found expression in State Department policy plans about the "Grand Area." Mainstream scholars suggest that talk of the Grand Area was designed to calculate the minimum amount of territory needed to maintain U.S. political and economic strength. Yet, the Grand Area stretched across Western Europe, parts of Asia and the so-called Third World, which would "fulfill its major function as a source of raw materials and a market." Diplomatic historian Bruce Cumings notes that the Grand Area was "bound by the reach of the world market."[15]

Jeane Kirkpatrick, a U.S. ambassador to the United Nations under President Reagan, articulated the inclination to protect the "Grand Area" at all costs some thirty-five years later. She advocated support for Somoza in Nicaragua and the shah of Iran, two leading human rights abusers. These anti-democratic strongmen were "positively friendly to the United States" and had "many friends in Washington" as they "regularly" supported "U.S. interests." Authoritarian governments were acceptable when they "preserved traditional societies and encouraged capitalism and the profit motive."[16] There is a long history of backing authoritarian regimes when they are amenable to the global economic order. Peace educators confront a broad system, whose planners "think in the large and have a long-term trajectory. We too need a big picture analysis."[17] The following section ultimately reaches for a structural analysis of U.S. foreign policy as a balance against the prevailing grand narrative that the United States spreads liberty by means of upholding "free" markets.

The United States, the Cold War and Human Rights

Although Cold War tensions animated relations with the Soviet Union during the time period under discussion, the Soviet threat was deliberately magnified. Such exaggerations accelerated the arms race and created a permanent war economy. Despite repeated proclamations about protecting the "free" world from Soviet "slavery," a close inspection of U.S. interventions demonstrates that they were often influenced as much by corporate priorities. To avoid misunderstanding, Cold War tensions and the possibility of nuclear war were valid and troublesome concerns. However, U.S. statecraft frequently intensified rather than de-escalated these worries. "The growth of military expenditures and the readiness to use military force in foreign affairs," Betty Reardon wrote in 1982, "indicate to many that the U.S. is now more seriously threatened by militarism than by Communism or Soviet aggression."[18] While Moscow was equally culpable in propelling the arms race and militarism, this work focuses on the United States' misbehavior because such an analysis is largely missing from peace education endeavors.

Following the Second World War, a popular college textbook, *A People and a Nation*, explains that the United States was in the throes of a victory culture. The conviction that "unending triumph was the nation's birthright and destiny," swept the nation as many Americans viewed their country as "the greatest in the world, not only the most powerful but the most righteous."[19] A nation that emerged victorious after four years of global war against a totalitarian foe was understandably captivated by its success. Historians routinely characterize the postwar years in terms of this victory culture, the sense that it was the United States' destiny to spread freedom and prosperity. These descriptions surely raise the specter of self-righteous chosenness discourse. In 1945, the United States, if not ordained by God, certainly seemed God-like: omnipotent and benevolent.

Films such as *The Best Years of Our Lives* and slogans such as the "greatest generation" reflect this mood of endless progress and destiny. A postwar economic boom was yet another success to celebrate. The United States produced over half of the world's steel and nearly 50 percent of its electricity in the years after the Second World War. Even race relations appeared to improve. Jackie Robinson broke the color barrier in baseball and President Truman outlawed racial discrimination in the federal government. The triumphalist spirit incorrectly led many U.S. citizens to believe that racial tension would ease. On the domestic scene, the burgeoning civil rights movement would gradually shatter that myth as it dismantled and recast the very notion of U.S. chosenness.

On the global stage, the darker side of the grand victory still haunted the United States. That the Second World War was terminated by means of dropping atomic bombs on Hiroshima and Nagasaki in August 1945 was most traumatic. The trauma of exterminating over 100,000 Japanese required explanation. Chosenness rhetoric helped to convert this dreadful event into a holy cause. One the one hand, President Truman explained that it saved U.S. lives by avoiding a bloody land invasion of Japan. The veracity of this argument has been challenged by the U.S. government's own strategic bombing survey that estimated the number of casualties in the neighborhood of 50,000. On the other hand, according to a study by Jewett and Lawrence, Truman said, "thank God that [the bomb] has come to us ... may He guide us to use it in His ways and for His purposes." Phylis Schlafly, a conservative activist, concurred that, "The atomic bomb is a marvelous gift that was given to our country by a wise God."[20] U.S. leaders claimed that the Second World War and the dropping of the atomic bomb received God's blessing to reassure a self-congratulatory, yet anxious, nation.

Such massive destruction is more bearable when the United States is seen as God's ambassador. The atomic bomb delivered victory and power, but at a price. Fears of nuclear extermination combined with the developing Cold War attenuated victory culture. Although U.S. notions of chosenness contributed to the triumphant mood, it ironically constrained it as well. That is to say, U.S. wars are often construed as apocalyptic struggles or epic confrontations between the forces of good (democracy) against evil (totalitarianism). In the end, the good defeats evil to usher in an age of peace, and progress. The Second World War certainly falls within this pattern. The realization, however, that such wars are not the final battle against evil gradually sets in and stirs a certain despair and anxiety. After the Second World War, the diabolical Kremlin appeared as evil incarnate in a new form. The emerging Cold War transformed this celebratory mood into a more alarming dichotomy of good versus evil, democracy versus communism. Yet, the sense that U.S. decency and destiny shall prevail still moderated much of the rhetoric surrounding the Cold War. Victory culture stumbled, but it did not yet collapse. The United States was in the meantime busy fulfilling its duty to constrain the spread of evil, Godless communism.

President Truman articulated a policy of containment, identifying Greece and Turkey as trouble spots in 1947. He warned that Communist "terror and oppression" threatened "free peoples" in what became known as the Truman Doctrine. Thomas Dewey, who ran against Truman for the presidency in 1948, was equally convinced of the U.S. messianic mission against Marxism. "Wherever America has been," Dewey argued, "there is ... an increase in freedom.... It is the blessed proof of freedom under God." After a surprising victory over Dewey, Truman reassured the nation in his 1949 Inaugural Address that communism will be defeated because we are "steadfast in our faith in the Almighty" and "with God's help" the United States shall create a world of freedom and justice. According to the Truman Library, the president placed his hand on two open Bibles when he took the oath of office at the inauguration. One Bible was open at Exodus, chapter 20, the other displayed Matthew, chapter 5. The Exodus chapter was open at the pages of the Ten Commandments or the section of God's covenant with Moses and the Israelites. The selected chapter from Matthew, of course, includes Jesus' Sermon on the Mount, which is an offer of the Kingdom of God to believers. Was Truman attempting to send a message that he was recovering the biblical roots of John Winthrop's city on a hill to stress his feeling that the United States was a unique and special nation? Consider that Matthew 5:14 states that, "You are the light of the world. A city set on a mountain cannot be hidden." One cannot help but conclude that Truman turned to these passages to underscore his fanciful belief that "the American people stand firm in the faith which has inspired this nation from the beginning."[21] In 1949, the Soviets detonated their first atomic bomb and China fell to the Communists, requiring U.S. strategists to remain resolute in their faith that God would save them from this new menace.

The official blueprint of the Cold War, NSC-68, articulated the gospel of God's chosen people in April 1950. Conflicts were expressed in polarized, dichotomous terms in the memorandum. Moscow's "new fanatic faith" and "slave society," the document asserts, presents a "momentous" conflict, "involving the fulfillment or destruction, not only of this republic, but of civilization itself." Since the United States is the "principal center" of the "free" world, it is obligated to defend it "with a firm reliance on the protection of Divine Providence."[22] It is revealing that an official planning document trumpets the United States' self-anointed status as God's people. Equally important is the lasting impact of NSC-68. Leading historians have argued that the memorandum is one of the defining documents of Cold War policy. Consider that Paul Nitze, author of NSC-68, was an advisor to several U.S.

presidents, each of whom embraced the missionary impulse of his national security strategy. William Appleman Williams sarcastically called NSC-68 "the definitive City on a Hill document,"[23] one which was not designed for public consumption, suggesting that providential notions carry at least a certain degree of truth for U.S. strategists. The author of NSC-68 likely embraced these U.S. myths of benevolence, but the rhetorical swagger of NSC-68 held pecuniary implications. Historian Eric Foner notes that NSC-68 "issued a clarion call for a permanent military buildup to enable the United States to engage in a global crusade against Communism."[24]

Private communications among U.S. officials are consistent with Foner's suspicion that economic interests lie behind some of this Cold War rhetoric. In 1948, State Department head George Kennan wrote:

> We have about 50% of the world's wealth but only 6.3% of its population. This disparity is particularly great as between ourselves and the peoples of Asia. In this situation, we cannot fail to be the object of envy and resentment. Our real task in the coming period is to devise a pattern of relationships which will permit us to maintain this position of disparity without positive detriment to our national security. To do so, we will have to dispense with all sentimentality and day-dreaming; and our attention will have to be concentrated everywhere on our immediate national objectives. We need not deceive ourselves that we can afford today the luxury of altruism and world-benefaction.... We should dispense with the aspiration to "be liked" or to be regarded as the repository of a high-minded international altruism. We should stop putting ourselves in the position of being our brothers' keeper and refrain from offering moral and ideological advice. We should cease to talk about vague and — for the Far East — unreal objectives such as human rights, the raising of the living standards, and democratization. The day is not far off when we are going to have to deal in straight power concepts.[25]

Diplomatic historians dismiss this now-famous remark as an aberration, a single comment at odds with the general tenor of U.S. foreign policy. Others wish to argue that Kennan's statement is insignificant insofar as it applies only to the Far East. Considering that the United States engaged in two major conflicts in the region following Kennan's appraisal, it seems disingenuous to reduce its significance. Only two years later the United States was embroiled in the Korea War, and it was providing assistance to France's efforts to retain colonial control of Vietnam. Moreover, a Report of the Special Study Group of the Central Intelligence Agency (CIA), exhibits the same disregard for democracy and human rights.

> There are no rules in such a game. Hitherto acceptable norms of human conduct do not apply. If the United States is to survive, long-standing American concepts of "fair play" must be reconsidered. We must develop effective espionage and counterespionage services and must learn to subvert, sabotage and destroy our enemies by more clever, more sophisticated and more effective methods than those used against us. It may become necessary that the American

people be made acquainted with, understand and support this fundamentally repugnant philosophy.[26]

Whereas Kennan heralds the economic motives of U.S. foreign policy, the CIA advocates a distasteful military strategy. Notably absent from the plans of these key policymaking agents is the need to uphold freedom, democracy and human rights. Instead they focus on how the United States can maintain worldwide power and domination, which is the "real task" according to Kennan. If we compare these private statements with actual U.S. behavior, a disturbing pattern emerges, one which illuminates the financial pressures that sometimes compromise U.S. military interventions.

Economic pressures on American officials became increasingly strong after the allied victory in the Second World War, as evidenced by historian Frank Kofsky. Many of the leading officials in the Truman administration, such as James Forrestal and Stuart Symington, had close ties to big business. Such connections included aerospace manufacturing, a defense industry, which depended on government contracts for its survival. During the war, 92 percent of its contracts came from the government. The defeat of totalitarianism and the end of war translated into possible bankruptcy for the airline industry. "If we have lasting peace," explained Robert Gross, Lockheed's president, "the demand for airplanes will be limited," but if we have an "armed truce" the demand shall be "very considerable." The political influence of the industry led to a seemingly confused and contradictory foreign policy.[27]

One such policy occurred two weeks after the Truman Doctrine. It was discovered that U.S. airline manufacturers continued their sales to the Soviet Union. When the deals were made public, Truman responded that, "Russia is, at present, a friendly nation."[28] This shocking assessment contradicts Truman's belief that aid to Greece and Turkey was urgently needed to halt Communist "terror" and "outside pressures." Outrageous discrepancies require explanation. Perhaps corporate agendas outweighed national security in Truman's defense of the airline industry. Consider that the aerospace business encompassed steel, petroleum and other major industries. As the treasurer of Standard Oil explained in 1946, "our foreign policy will be more concerned with the safety and stability of our investments than ever before."[29]

Gradually this concern would cloud the nation's regard for human rights abroad. In the meantime, Truman's contradictory policies were not without opposition. Congressional leaders questioned the efficacy of aid to Greece; its government sided with Hitler's Germany during the war, while the Communists resisted Nazi infiltration. Facing a reluctant Congress, one adviser told Truman that it would be necessary "to scare the hell out of the American people." The project was approved after Truman apparently scared U.S. citizens regarding Communist "terror and oppression," hyperbole heightened by

Secretary of State Acheson, who claimed that, "like apples in a barrel infected by one, the corruption of Greece would infect Iran and all to the east."[30]

The Korean War and U.S. Culture in the 1950s

When the Korean War broke out in 1950, U.S. leaders offered their alleged providential freedom as an elixir against Communist terror that spread all the way to the East. Here was Truman's chance to assert the United States' mission and advance the cause of victory culture. Shortly before the war, Truman argued that "George Washington sought guidance from Almighty God as he faced these tasks in his time; let us be guided today by divine providence as we strive for lasting peace." And, early in the Korean conflict, he spoke before the nation on radio and television:

> There will be no profit for any people who follow the Communist dictatorship down its dark and bloody path. Against the futile and tragic course of dictatorship, we uphold, for all people, the way of freedom — the way of mutual cooperation and international peace. We assert that mankind can find progress and advancement along the path of peace. At this critical hour in the history of the world, our country had been called upon to give of its leadership, its efforts, and its resources to maintain peace and justice among nations. We responded to that call. We will not fail. The task which has fallen on our beloved country is a great one. In carrying it out, we ask God to purge us of all selfishness and meanness, and to give us strength and courage in the days ahead.[31]

Facts surrounding the war contradict Truman's belief that the United States was protecting sacred values of peace and freedom. The United States backed Syngman Rhee in the South, who was as brutal as the Communists in the North. He jailed dissidents, raided the National Assembly and killed 600 men, women and children at Koch'ang, among other atrocities. Nor did Korea usher in a great victory. It was a stalemate and the nation remains divided to this day. Nonetheless, then secretary of state Dean Acheson curiously noted that "Korea saved us."[32] What the Korean War likely "saved" was the defense industry and the nation's capitalist consensus. The war vastly increased the national security state, accelerating the military-industrial complex. Congress was somewhat reluctant to increase the defense budget and the Korean crisis erased this resistance. In 1949, the annual U.S. defense budget was $59.2 billion. At the end of the war in 1953, the defense budget soared to $189.2 billion.[33]

Several scholars have noted that the lack of victory in Korea weakened feelings of the United States' destiny to triumph over evil forces, so it was cast as the "forgotten war." Foreign policy failures risk open analysis and the questioning of U.S. motives. Hollywood blacklists, McCarthyism, the Internal Security Act and general anticommunist hysteria mobilized to protect

America's divine image. The Alger Hiss case, the harassment of scholar W.E.B. DuBois and the Hollywood Ten are well known examples of quieting those who challenged national myths. No one was immune from appearing as a Communist sympathizer. Some believed that the Truman administration was infiltrated by Communists, allegedly accounting for "losing" China in 1949 and failing to save Korea. Mounting U.S. casualties coupled with a soaring national debt and inflation eventually eroded Truman's popularity. The nation needed a new vision, perhaps a heroic leader who might revive the victorious spirit of the Second World War.

General Dwight D. Eisenhower performed that role in his 1952 presidential campaign against Truman. After defeating Truman, Eisenhower wound down the protracted war, negotiating a cease-fire in 1953. Unconditional surrender simply did not fit the complicated situation in Korea. Although Korea ended in a stalemate, the United States' mission allegedly remained unscathed. President Eisenhower reminded the nation that such challenges meant "strengthening our dedication and devotion to the precepts of our founding documents, a conscious renewal of faith in our country and in the watchfulness of divine providence. The enemies of this faith know no God but force."[34] Secretary of State John Foster Dulles also sought to restore the United States' pride and glory, noting some success in the Korean conflict. First, he maintained that the United States exists principally to "help men develop their God-given possibilities," which is "unique" insofar as the nation empowers people "everywhere" to acquire liberty and prosperity. Dulles pointed to Korea, where the 38th parallel divided "the free" and the "Communist-parts" of Korea, "but the line did not demarcate the hopes and aspirations of the people." While in Korea, the Secretary of State says he witnessed thousands of refugees at a religious meeting in Seoul, who fled from the Communist North "in the hope of finding the freedom of religion which they cherished." Finally, American institutions are "endowed by their Creator with certain inalienable rights and duties," a duty that the United States allegedly did not shirk as it protected those refugees in the South.[35]

That foreign policy rhetoric was saturated in religious metaphors was not new in U.S. history. But the 1950s was a time of heightened popularity for religion on the home front, which bolstered the United States' sense of chosenness. Membership in religious groups grew from 71.7 million in 1945 to roughly 116 million in 1960. The Bible appeared on the best-seller list, and filmmaker Cecil B. DeMille's remake of *The Ten Commandments* raked in some $40 million. Scholar Glenn Whitehouse reminds us that DeMille appeared in the overture to connect the cinematic extravaganza to the Cold War. "The theme of this picture," DeMille announced, "is whether men ought to be ruled by God's law or whether they are to be ruled by the whims of a dictator.... This same battle continues throughout the world today."[36] Apparently, Moses' divinely inspired liberation of Egyptian slaves foreshadows the United States' mission to free those held in Soviet bondage. Whereas NSC-68 and presidential addresses depicted the Cold War as a spiritual struggle, the film pointed to the biblical roots of this conflict: Moses' covenant with God, the spiritual wellspring that nourishes the nation's myth of chosenness. In brief, Moses symbolizes the birth of freedom for humankind much like the formation of the United States supposedly signifies birth of freedom for the modern world, according to the logic behind DeMille's introductory remarks.

The advent of television amplified these religious sensibilities. For instance, evangelical Billy Graham, whom one U.S. president later dubbed "America's pastor," was introduced into millions of American households. He gained great popularity, attracting over 100,000 people to his "New York Crusade" at Yankee Stadium in 1957. Then vice president Richard Nixon sat on stage with the pastor, and offered a welcome message from President Eisenhower. Graham had close relations with almost every Cold War president and described Richard Nixon as a close friend. From the start, Eisenhower recognized the importance of religion and Graham as a transmitter of religious sentiment in U.S. political culture. He met with Graham before his election and followed the spiritual leader's advice to join a formal church. Eisenhower allegedly told the minister that "I think one of the reasons I was elected was to lead this country spiritually.... We need a spiritual renewal."[37]

A spiritual renaissance of sorts spread across the nation in the 1950s. The National Committee for Christian Leadership, largely through the efforts of Abraham Vereide, lobbied for a National Prayer Breakfast. Hotel mogul Conrad Hilton offered financial support, and Senate chaplain Richard Halverson contributed to the movement's growth. Senator Frank Carlson, an adviser to Eisenhower, was another important figure in organizing the proposed prayer meetings.[38] These efforts were remarkably successful. On 5 February 1953, Eisenhower held the first Presidential Prayer Breakfast, which some critics charged was a clear infringement of the Constitution's church-state separation. Whether or not the prayer gatherings violate the Constitution, these government-sanctioned religious receptions eventually became institutionalized as the National Prayer Breakfast, a tradition that survives into the Bush II era. The spiritual rebirth in the United States at this time is not the object of this study, but the means by which this religious sentiment was conflated with U.S. power and identity is of special relevance to the present study.

The merging of religion and patriotism was evident in the movement to include the phrase "under God" in the Pledge of Allegiance. In support of this revision, the Reverend George M. Docherty, who ministered to Eisenhower, delivered his Under God sermon at Washington's New York Avenue Presbyterian Church on Sunday, 7 February 1954. The preacher's homily, which unambiguously accents America's so-called spiritual destiny, was read into the *Congressional Record* shortly thereafter. Reverend Docherty argued that

> Puritans ... did not realize that in fleeing from tyranny and setting up a new life in a new world, they were to be Fathers of a Mighty Nation. These fundamental concepts of life had been given to the world from Mount Sinai, where the moral law was graven upon Tables of Stone ... they heard in the words of Jesus of Nazareth, the Living Word of God for the world. This is the "American Way of Life." Lincoln saw this clearly.... The providence of God was being fulfilled.... What, therefore, is missing in the Pledge of Allegiance ... [is] the one fundamental concept that completely and ultimately separates Communist Russia from the democratic institutions of this Country.... "Under God" are the definitive words.... We face, today, a theological war.... It is Armageddon, a battle of the gods ... the issue of the Pledge of Allegiance is that it seems to me to omit this theological implication that is inherent within the "American way of life." ...To omit the words "Under God" in the Pledge of Allegiance is to omit the definitive character of the "American way of life."[39]

The minister weaves together God and country in a manner that constitutes the fabric of civil religion. Should we apply Johan Galtung's chosenness model (CMT) that was discussed in the introduction, we find in Docherty's homily all of its distinctive features (details of which are outlined further in chapter three). In short, this syndrome revolves around the belief in Chosenness, which is reinforced through various myths and traumas. Docherty offers a direct reference to (C)hosenness, both the Puritans and Lincoln had God's blessing. Docherty adds the attendant (M)yth that the Puritan's religious blessing contributed to the spread of God's justice that eventually culminated in the United States of America. Lincoln embodied this chosenness, the pastor believes. The (T)rauma of Civil War was a test, but ultimately the "providence of God was being fulfilled." The pastor's conviction that the nation holds a providential heritage (or in his words it "came down from the Judeo-Christian tradition") leads to his conclusion that the Cold War was a "holy war," an "Armageddon." Here Docherty blends together all the elements of the chosenness syndrome that we examine in chapter three. Suffice it to say, the problem here is that God and country are conflated, stirring nationalist sentiments rather than spiritual reflection alone. In short, the reverend's message is that a chosen nation would be remiss to exclude its definitive character in its pledge. "America," after all, is "under God."

Another troubling aspect of this thinking is that Eisenhower was purportedly inspired by the sermon to follow through with the "Under God" provision. In Eisenhower's 1954 Flag Day speech that codified the "under God" addition to the Pledge, he asserted that, "In this way, we are affirming the transcendence of religious faith in America's heritage and future; in this way we shall constantly strengthen those spiritual weapons which forever will be our country's most powerful resource in peace and war."[40]

The popular and influential evangelical Billy Graham launched these spiritual weapons at the Communists. He pontificated that, "We are dealing with a treacherous and vicious enemy who has the supernatural forces of evil behind him."[41] We might expect such spiritual ruminations from an evangelical preacher, but his belief that Satan incarnate resided in Russia fits all too neatly with presidential and popular beliefs that the Soviet Union's evil nature stood against the United States, which was "under God." Again we find an influential public figure confusing national dilemmas with spiritual conflicts.

Iran

In the case of Iran, it is difficult to argue that the United States protected oppressed peoples or upheld democracy. Specific examples of U.S. interventions enable peace educators to unravel the various devices that conceal the bellicose side of U.S. policy, which allows for the consideration of more peaceful solutions. The spiritual conflicts that Graham imagined cannot be easily applied to the case of Iran, where crude material interests seemed far more important to U.S. policymakers than upholding alleged providential freedoms. In 1953, Truman's successor, Dwight Eisenhower, authorized the overthrow of the Iranian premier, Mohammad Mossadegh. Most historians agree that the coup is especially important as it marked the first postwar significant covert operation, and one which ended Iran's last democratic regime. It also served as a model for future covert missions across the globe. Mark Gasiorowski, a leading expert on the affair, explains that the coup was an "important precedent" for interventions in places such as Guatemala and elsewhere. He argues that the coup was motivated by fears of a communist takeover rather than economic interests alone, but he does note that the arguments over monetary influences "cannot be entirely refuted."[42]

The Iranian crisis began when Mossadegh nationalized oil fields in May 1951, a decision that irritated the British owned Anglo-Iranian Oil Company. The British had been enjoying almost three decades of lucrative profits from the refineries. While Mossadegh offered a modest compensation package, the disgruntled Brits refused to negotiate, preferring to pressure Iran through economic sanctions and an oil embargo. Western powers supported the boycott, thrusting Iran into economic chaos. The upheaval bolstered the Tudeh (Communist) Party in Iran as diplomats searched for solutions to an increasingly difficult situation. Meanwhile, the British Secret Service drafted plans to oust Mossadegh on the pretext that he tolerated the growth of communism inside the oil-producing nation.

Tensions erupted in September 1951 when Mossadegh learned about the planned coup and resigned in protest. Widespread demonstrations demanded Mossadegh's return, and he was restored to power. The British turned to the United States to hasten the prime minister's removal. Initially hesitant, the CIA eventually launched Operation TJAJAX to topple Mossadegh. Under the command of Kermit Roosevelt, the first phase of the operation entailed a propaganda campaign designed to erode Mossadegh's popular support. The United States favored General Zahedi to serve as prime minister under Shah Reza Pahlavi, both fervent anticommunists. Zahedi was imprisoned during the Second World War due to his pro–Nazi leanings, but the unsavory politician agreed to fight communism. "The holy religion of Islam," Zahedi once argued, "is being threatened by infidel Communists."[43]

With Zahedi committed to unseating Mossadegh, Kermit Roosevelt organized anti–Mossadegh crowds in the streets of Tehran, including a CIA-staged riot that ended with 300 deaths. The well-choreographed mob brought Mossadegh's surrender in August 1953, marking the agency's first successful coup. Zahedi was awarded U.S. aid, while the Shah regained his throne, purportedly telling Roosevelt that, "I owe my throne to God, my people — and to you."[44]

While this adventure satisfied the authoritarian shah, it risked instigating a conflict with the Soviet Union, which borders Iran. U.S. leaders maintained that this dangerous operation was necessary to avoid a Communist takeover in Iran. Such arguments are questionable for several reasons. That Russia shares a border with Iran, yet failed to intervene during the coup belies the argument that it was necessary to contain Communist expansion. True, the Soviets occupied northern Iran during the Second World War, but they withdrew troops long before the coup. Another problem with this argument was that Mossadegh was not a Communist. Stephen Ambrose, an establishment historian, acknowledges that such charges were "quite ridiculous," owing principally to Mossadegh's suppression of Iran's Communist Party.[45] If Mossadegh enjoyed support from the Communists, it was likely inspired by the Western oil embargo, a punishment imposed by foreigners that united disparate elements within the country.

It seems that the "unwarranted influence" of oil companies better explains why the United States undertook such a risky operation. With no ties to Moscow, Mossadegh petitioned the United States for help during the oil embargo. Eisenhower responded that "it would be unfair to the American taxpayer for the United States to extend any amount of considerable aid to Iran so long as Iran could have access to the funds derived from the sale of oil."[46] Notice that Eisenhower's rebuff is concerned mainly with oil sales, not Communist penetration. If the United States feared a Communist takeover, Eisenhower might have mentioned this significant detail at the moment of negotiation. Not only did Eisenhower fail to mention the Communist question to Mossadegh in this instance, Secretary of State Dulles told a Senate committee that there was "no substantial evidence" that Iran was working with the Communists.[47] After Mossadegh's overture to Washington was dismissed, and with an oil embargo destroying the Iranian economy, Mossadegh mistakenly appealed to the Soviets for economic support. Two weeks later the Iranian premier was violently expelled on the grounds that he was a Communist conspirator. In short, U.S. policy moved Iran closer to communism rather than away from it, gaining little in the struggle to contain Marxism.

U.S. oil companies, however, gained much from the coup. They received roughly 40 percent of Iranian oil concessions, previously controlled by the British and seized by Mossadegh. These same oil conglomerates were involved in an antitrust suit for monopolizing petroleum production in the Middle East and elsewhere. In June 1952, the U.S. Justice Department ordered a grand jury investigation into Exxon (Standard Oil), Texaco and Gulf—each of whom joined the Iranian oil concession after Mossadegh's dismissal. Curiously, around the same time the State Department met with oil companies to assess the possibility of selling Iranian oil, having consulted those firms involved in the antitrust violations.[48]

The antitrust case was dismissed in January 1953, only months before the coup. No longer hampered by antitrust legislation, Standard Oil entered the Iranian oil consortium. Sullivan and Cromwell, the law firm that represented Standard Oil, once employed Secretary of State Dulles and his brother, Allen, director of the CIA in the early 1950s. Recall the oil executive who asserted that U.S. foreign policy would become "more concerned" with the stability of its global investments. To be sure, the Dulles' brothers central role in formulating foreign policy helped to stabilize Standard Oil concessions, yet destabilized relations with the Soviet Union. Similar observations hold for another consortium member, Gulf Oil. They hired Kermit Roosevelt, the mastermind behind the coup, who brokered deals directly with the shah. He also received $75,000 from Northrop, an aerospace giant that sold hardware to Iran. These deals exemplify the misplaced power of big business in shaping U.S. policy.[49]

Various commercial interests profited from their power to mold U.S. policy during the shah's twenty-five-year reign. By the 1970s, Iran was perhaps the world's leading weapons importer, purchasing hundreds of fighter planes from U.S. manufacturers, such as Grumman, General Dynamics and McDonnell-Douglass.[50] The shah's preoccupation with arms purchases devastated Iran's economy, leading to widespread protest. Dissenters were routinely tortured by the secret police, SAVAK, a group once trained by General Norman Schwarzkopf, father of the Gulf War hero. Iran earned one of the worst human rights records under the shah, yet remained a U.S. ally. In effect, the overthrow of Mossadegh terminated Iran's experiment with democracy and introduced almost thirty years of repression. This case is important to peace educators because the Western media frequently casts the Middle East as a region that is either incapable of democracy or in need of Western tutors to assist its people in building democratic institutions. However, Iran was in the throes of a democratic experiment in the 1950s that was derailed by Western powers. Equally noteworthy is that the Iranian adventure served as an exemplar for future U.S. interventions and demonstrates that the United States disregards peace and international cooperation under certain political and economic conditions.

Guatemala

That the Iranian coup was hailed as a successful example for future invasions further demonstrates the "disastrous" influence of big business on U.S. policy. In 1954, the CIA orchestrated the overthrow of Guatemala's democratically elected president, Jacobo Arbenz. Fears of Communist infiltration in Guatemala date back to 1944, when a student revolt ended the dictatorship of Jorge Ubico Castañeda. During Ubico's rule, 2 percent of the population controlled more than 60 percent of the land, most of which was held by the U.S. company, United Fruit. The company also held a monopoly over the nation's banana, utility and railroad industries and controlled significant portions of the country's shipping center and activities at Puerto Barrios. Secretary of State John Foster Dulles negotiated this favorable arrangement while doing legal work at the firm of Sullivan and Cromwell in the 1930s. Following the defeat of Ubico's government, Guatemala's first elected president, Juan José Arévalo, threatened to reverse these profitable trade agreements.[51]

Part of the threat entailed mild land reform measures and the 1947 Labor Code, which gave nonunion workers the right to organize, to bargain for increased wages and to strike. These activities had been forbidden under Ubico's dictatorship. Given that United Fruit employed over 40,000 workers, such reforms unsettled the company's management. The fruit conglomerate reportedly funded a CIA coup of the Guatemalan government, code named Operation Fortune. The Truman administration eventually aborted the operation.

With the change of leadership in both the United States and Guatemala in the early 1950s, plans of a coup heated up. In 1951, Jacobo Arbenz defeated Arévalo in the presidential race, and the new leader promised to implement agrarian reforms. The incoming Eisenhower administration was bristling with confidence in its ability to thwart communism after the Mossadeq operation. Arbenz's pledge to nationalize all arable land coupled with the close ties of the newly appointed secretary of state, John Foster Dulles, to United Fruit provided fertile soil for another coup plot. That scheme came to pass in 1954 after Arbenz passed Decree 900, which called for the government seizure of all uncultivated land. Although United Fruit owned more than 40 percent of the arable land in Guatemala, it cultivated only 10 percent of it. Arbenz seized about 200,000 of the company's unused acres and offered the company $127,000, an amount equal to United Fruit's own estimate of the land for tax purposes. U.S. officials viewed the offer as an underhanded political maneuver. To U.S. observers, Arbenz appeared to be a Marxist dupe. As Eisenhower explained in his memoirs, the land measure constitutes a "discriminatory and unfair seizure," clearly the work of "a puppet manipulated by Communists."[52]

Dulles underscored the president's accusation, characterizing Arbenz as a ruthless Communist. These charges proved difficult to sustain. Shortly after assuming office, Arbenz vowed to transform Guatemala from its depleted economic condition into a modern capitalist state. Many of his programs resembled the free-market economics praised by U.S. leaders, such as constructing a highway to compete against United Fruit's transportation monopoly. As it became increasingly clear that Arbenz was not a Communist, U.S. policymakers instead charged that Arbenz tolerated Marxist penetration in his government. Communists held four seats out of fifty-one in the Guatemalan Congress, and twenty-six out of 350 administrators in the National Agrarian Department were socialists.[53] Nevertheless, the toppling of Arbenz appears to have been motivated largely by his policies toward United Fruit, rather than by his tolerance of communism.

According to Stephen Schlisinger and Steve Kinzer's highly regarded study, *Bitter Fruit: The Story of the American Coup in Guatemala*, many of the U.S. officials involved in the overthrow of Arbenz had ties to United Fruit. Not only did Dulles once serve as its counsel, he invested in United Fruit. Another major shareholder, John Moors Cabot, was appointed Assistant Secretary of State for Inter-American Affairs at the time of the overthrow. His brother was once president of the fruit company. Senator Henry Cabot Lodge, a significant stockholder, was U.S. ambassador to the United Nations. Finally, CIA director Walter Bedell Smith was seeking employment with the company during the plot and was later appointed to its board of directors.

The intricate connection between Washington, D.C., and United Fruit helps to explain why the United States removed Arbenz from power. For example, E. Howard Hunt, a key U.S. agent in Guatemala during the coup who was later embroiled in the Watergate scandal, expressed some resentment that his duties appeared to be more in the way of missionary actions for United Fruit than a legitimate instance of fighting communism. Given Arbenz's rather tenuous connection to communism, American strategists resembled corporate mercenaries in their zeal to oust the Latin American leader. Consider that

Eisenhower later acknowledged that Arbenz's "expropriation in itself does not prove Communism."[54]

Agrarian reform was not an adequately alarming pretext to justify Arbenz's removal. The *Alfhem* incident provided the needed justification. Arbenz had ordered a shipment of weapons from communist Czechoslovakia, which sailed into Guatemala aboard the *Alfhem* in May 1954, under the eyes of anxious CIA agents. Secretary of State Dulles overstated the significance of the weapons shipment, telling reporters that the weapons were part of a larger strategy to create a communist base at the Panama Canal. Reports soon appeared in U.S. newspapers regarding Guatemala's design to spread communism throughout Central America. Missing from these embellished reports was the fact that the United States had initiated an arms embargo against Guatemala before the shipment arrived. Such restrictions led Guatemala's foreign minister to suspect that the United States was searching for an incident to rationalize its planned invasion. That the coup was already planned before the arms shipment confirms this suspicion.

Armed with a reason to remove Arbenz, the CIA launched Operation PBSUCCESS in June 1954. Bombings accompanied fabricated radio reports that a massive internal uprising was taking place. In reality, the United States relied on outside forces, particularly Nicaraguan dictator Anastasio Somoza, to organize what was very much an external invasion. The air assault and psychological warfare successfully undermined Arbenz, who fled to Mexico City in July. The United States installed Castillo Armas to replace the democratically elected Arbenz.

Armas cancelled Decree 900 and returned all of the confiscated land to United Fruit. The authoritarian regime soon outlawed over 500 labor organizations, including the Banana Workers' Federation, from which seven labor leaders were missing under questionable circumstances. While U.S. leaders celebrated Guatemala's liberation, Armas also prevented 75 percent of the population from voting and formed the National Committee of the Defense against Communism at the request of the CIA. The group prevented the formation of political parties, blocked newspaper stories and burned books. Dostoyevsky's works, Victor Hugo's writings and those of Miguel Angel Asturias, a Nobel Prize recipient who chastised United Fruit, were among the books set ablaze. Despite Armas's record on human rights, U.S. leaders supported his regime. Then vice president Richard Nixon considered him "a good man," who "really desires to do what the United States wants him to do."[55]

Critics across the globe felt differently about Armas's rule. The British Labour Party described U.S. actions as a naked act of aggression, and anti–American protests swept across Latin America. Che Guevara was among these protestors. He traveled to Guatemala in the hope of witnessing Arbenz's reforms. Instead he watched the CIA dismantle Guatemala's social progress.

According to Guevara's wife, it was the Guatemalan experience that influenced him to engage in armed struggle against imperialism. Guevara fled to Mexico City, where he met Fidel Castro. The two men traveled to Cuba to overthrow the government in 1959.

Cuba

Sailing on Castro's yacht, they left Mexico City in November 1958 and by New Year 's Day defeated Cuban dictator Fulgencio Batista. Castro's new revolutionary regime instantly captured the United States' attention. U.S. businesses controlled most of Cuba's sugar, railroad and utility industries. In August 1959, Castro seized the U.S.–owned utility company and reduced electricity costs by over 30 percent. As in Guatemala, agrarian reforms were implemented, including the nationalization of 35,000 acres owned by United Fruit. Since land reform was the hallmark of Marxism, the United States refused to negotiate a settlement with Cuba. Italy, France, Spain and Mexico each reached an agreement with Castro regarding their property holdings.[56]

Underestimating Castro's popular support, the United States preferred bombings over negotiation. United States' planes firebombed Cuban sugar fields in October 1959, severely hampering its economy. Consider that Castro was not at first aligned with the Communists; a 1958 CIA study clearly distinguished Castro from the nation's Communist Party. It seems that the United States' aggressive stance once again pushed a Third World leader toward the Communist camp, although Castro was more inclined than others to arrive there. Rather than deterring communism, the United States' initial hostility toward Cuba stems from the island nation's attempt to operate outside the global economic system. As the U.S. ambassador to Cuba, Philip Bonsal, explains,

> They felt that the reciprocal tariff arrangements were working very much against them, that the tariff which they had granted us prevented them from protecting their own industries and from diversifying their own agriculture, all in the interest of our exports.... It was the degree to which major industries were under foreign control. In the case of sugar 10 years ago we controlled 50 percent of production.... We own and manage the two major public utilities, electric power and telephone.... We own and the British own and manage the oil refineries.... All of these things building up ... are the things which gave Dr. Castro his tremendous support.[57]

The United States worked assiduously to erode that popular support. By 1960, Eisenhower approved plans to assassinate the Cuban leader, everything from exploding cigars to poisoned coffee was considered. Plans to remove Castro were also pursued by the Kennedy administration. A more serious strategy involved establishing a base in Guatemala to train exiled Cubans, mainly disgruntled businessmen from the Batista government. At least 1,400 exiles assembled in Guatemala in preparation for a secret plot to overthrow Castro called Operation Pluto. Overblown with confidence, U.S. intelligence grossly miscalculated Castro's ability to resist an invasion. The attack was crushed at the Bay of Pigs causing much embarrassment to the Kennedy administration.

Politicians feared that the illegal invasion was a potential scandal. In anticipation of such failures, adviser Arthur Schlesinger, Jr., submitted a damage control plan to President Kennedy one week before the attack. It advised the president to mislead the press, "because the alleged threat to our national security will not seem to many people to justify so flagrant a violation of our professed principles," Schlesinger reports. People "will assume that we are acting, not to protect our safety, but to protect our property and investments," Schlesinger worried.[58]

When Castro captured the exiles, he discovered a collection of former factory and sugar plantation owners from the Batista regime, which intensified U.S. concerns that the invasion might appear as an imperial adventure. Castro seized the opportunity to deride U.S. foreign policy, stating that, "they are the ones who are bringing the world to the brink of war through their warlike spirit ... which cause them to provoke a series of crises in order to maintain their war economy."[59] Castro's overblown rhetoric drew attention to Schlesinger's private concern that the failed adventure might appear as an instance of economic avarice. For this reason, the United States first denied involvement in the attack, but Kennedy was later forced to acknowledge the blunder.

Blame was placed on an overzealous Central Intelligence Agency. Kennedy ordered an investigation, and it was decided that the president would rely on the more moderate and stable Joint Chiefs of Staff for future covert plans. Within a year, the group's chairman, General Lemnitzer, proposed a plan equally daring and imprudent as the Bay of Pigs debacle. Designated as Operation Northwoods, the report suggested sinking boatloads of Cuban refugees, staging a plane hijacking and assassinating Cuban rebels to create "pretexts which would provide justification for U.S. military intervention in Cuba."[60] Such audacious plans were rejected, but they mirrored the concerns of high-ranking officials such as Attorney General Robert Kennedy, who publicly spoke of sparking a "Remember the Maine" incident. U.S. officials needed a pretext to attack Cuba because it violated international law and the desires of the U.S. population. Since the United States was unable to intervene directly in Cuba, it pursued aggressive tactics such as economic embargoes and maintaining military bases at Guantánamo Bay. These punitive measures were largely driven by Cuba's refusal to acquiesce to the neo-liberal economic order. All of these actions clearly intensified Cold War tensions, providing an excuse for the Soviet Union to extend its power in Latin America.

The United States' failed attempt to kill Castro, its economic embargo and its occupation of Cuba's Guantánamo Bay provoked conflict. Such provocations were met by equally irresponsible Soviet behavior during the Cuban Missile Crisis in late 1962. Soviet premier Khrushchev placed nuclear warheads and missiles in Cuba. Kennedy threatened to invade Cuba if they were not removed. Khrushchev responded that the United States must first remove missiles from Russia's neighbor, Turkey, and pledge nonintervention in Cuba. With the world on the brink of nuclear war, Kennedy agreed to these terms and the crisis was averted. All parties involved in the missile crisis share the blame for bringing the world so close to a nuclear catastrophe, yet the United States failed to learn any serious lessons from the incident.

One possible lesson that might be derived from these interventions rests in Eisenhower's farewell address in 1961. Recall that Eisenhower identified a central problem of U.S. foreign relations that was related to economic interests. Failure to address this complex would inevitably lead to "plundering" resources and damaging our "spiritual heritage" for future generations. Despite Eisenhower's trenchant critique, he too embraced a civil-religious framework for articulating modern dilemmas. Eisenhower maintained that "we still face a hostile ideology," one that is "atheistic in character." Unfortunately, Eisenhower's successors failed to heed his warning about the economic forces influencing foreign policy; instead, they uncritically adopted the task of defeating an atheistic, hostile enemy. Eisenhower handed over a contradictory legacy, one that warned against military crusades and one that engaged in deep entanglements indicative of such crusades across the globe.

Successive administrations joined what might be sensationally characterized as the military crusaders. John F. Kennedy professed that he was "guided by the standard of John Winthrop," who also confronted a "perilous frontier." Whereas the Native Americans occupied Winthrop's frontier, Kennedy faced the evil Kremlin, which infiltrated Vietnam and Cuba. In light of these dangers, the United States remains a "city upon a hill" with a "great responsibility" to fulfill its historic destiny of "national greatness." After Kennedy's untimely assassination, Lyndon Johnson also reinvigorated the nation's imagined covenant. "Our enduring covenant" with justice and liberty, Johnson exclaimed, makes America "great and mighty." Images of divine election indeed saturate the speeches of almost every Cold War president.[61]

Vietnam

The great John F. Kennedy was no exception; his foreign policy discourse and behavior comported with his immediate predecessors and successors. He also cast the world in the simple good and evil framework. The only "useful lesson" from Cuba, Kennedy suggested, was that its "message" of communism spread to Vietnam. "Whether in Cuba or South Vietnam," the young president explained, "the message is the same" and "we must combat it."[62] Kennedy's successors, Johnson and Nixon, agreed that we must contest communism in Vietnam, escalating what became the most contentious war in U.S. history. This protracted nightmare provided a far different lesson than the one Kennedy offered. The message of Cuba was not simply the message of socialism; it was the notion that Third World peoples could successfully resist the U.S. Empire. From Truman to Nixon, five consecutive presidents failed to appreciate this message as they sent aid and then countless young soldiers into the jungles of Vietnam.

Escalating the conflict cost 58,000 American lives and entailed several deceitful schemes as well as outright atrocities. The initial strategy dates back to Harry Truman, who ignored Ho Chi Minh's appeals for self-determination. Instead, the United States supported the French colonization of Vietnam. After the Vietnamese defeated the French, the nation was divided between the Communist North and the non–Communist South at the 1954 Geneva Accords. At this time, Eisenhower feared that Ho Chi Minh might win elections and unite Vietnam under the Communist banner. The United States backed the unpopular Ngo Dinh Diem to control the South and prevent a Communist takeover in Southeast Asia. Diem cancelled the elections and was later removed due to his harsh, authoritarian rule. After Diem's installation in the South, Kennedy sent 16,000 advisers in violation of the Geneva agreements, thereby expanding the conflict. A few years later President Johnson committed 500,000 troops following the Gulf of Tonkin incident. After so-called unprovoked attacks on the USS *Maddox* in the Tonkin waters, Congress authorized the president to "take all necessary measures" against North Vietnam. However, the first attack was hardly unprovoked, and the second attack that led to the Tonkin Gulf Resolution likely never occurred.

The Johnson administration maintained that Communist North Vietnam launched an "unprovoked attack" on the USS *Maddox* on August 2, 1964. This first attack was not unprovoked; declassified documents demonstrate that the United States engaged in raids and intelligence gathering against the North before the August 2 clash. It was the second attack on August 4, one which probably never occurred, that led to a congressional resolution that greatly expanded the Vietnam War. During the morning of August 4, Defense Secretary McNamara told President Johnson that "this ship is, uh, to be attacked tonight." National Security Advisor McGeorge Bundy questioned whether there was clear evidence to confirm the August 4 attack before they presented the matter to Congress. Staff member Douglas Carter wondered if the congressional resolution should be postponed until more data had been gathered. According to the National Security Archive: "Bundy, in reply, jokingly told him perhaps the matter should not be thought through too far ...

he welcomed the recent events as justification for a resolution the administration had wanted for some time."[63]

Alongside these manipulative actions were outright atrocities. The most infamous case was the My Lai massacre in 1968, where U.S. soldiers murdered some 500 unarmed civilians, including the shooting of a young child who climbed out of a mass grave. Similar carnage was practiced by the CIA. Agent William Colby testified to Congress regarding Operation Phoenix, a program that detained Vietnamese "Communists," some allegedly confined in tiger cages and others thrown from helicopters.[64] The operation eliminated some 20,000 Vietnamese. As the U.S. public became aware of these offenses, Nixon was forced to withdraw U.S. forces in 1973. The point is not to isolate and condemn the United States; North Vietnam also engaged in atrocities. Almost all wars include large numbers of civilian casualties and a host of nefarious acts committed on both sides. The problem is that the United States rushed to war on faulty grounds, devoting more attention to finding reasons to engage in war than to exploring possible alternatives. Not only did this posture ultimately lead to military defeat, but it also temporarily shattered America's benevolent image.

A tidal wave of self-doubt spread across the nation. No longer confident that the United States was governed by noble intentions, people began to challenge American interventionism. The most cherished values of the American character were dramatically called into question. Radical dissidents, such as Noam Chomsky and Daniel Ellsberg, produced scholarly studies that revealed U.S. offenses in Vietnam. Distinguished historian Henry Steele Commager further aroused a public examination of U.S. behavior with the publication of his renowned essay, "The Defeat of America." He summoned the nation to examine its hypocrisy, to come to terms with the glaring discrepancy between its stated goals and actual behavior. For example, Commager argued that U.S. leaders rightly denounced German aggression in World War II as a war crime, "but when we wipe out defenseless villages ... or engage in massacres as brutal as that at Lidice, these are mistakes or aberrations that do not mar our record of benevolence." The pensive, widely respected Commager echoed the dissident scholars in calling U.S. behavior in Vietnam "demented."[65]

Activists of this time provide an inspiring example for how peace educators can both critique foreign policy and open channels of understanding. Discussions in respect to international malfeasance can include how citizens should not succumb to alienating stereotypes. Peace educators, like activists of the Vietnam years, can help move the national dialogue beyond simple frameworks of "evil" villains and "good" Americans. Peace educators have long ago demonstrated that understanding one's adversaries helps to reduce violence. In 1965, Yale University historian Staughton Lynd along with Communist scholar Herbert Aptheker and activist Tom Hayden traveled to Vietnam so as to understand the "other side." Lynd's description of the impact of this trip is essential to understanding the wider context of U.S. aggression, while grasping that enemies are part of the human community. The fears that disciplined and dispassionate Vietnamese Communists would spread Marxism throughout the region later proved to be false. At the height of the war, Lynd attempted to break through the stereotypes to generate a more balanced view of the world and reduce anxiety that often contributes to aggressive action. After his trip to Vietnam, Lynd wrote:

> To make war the modern administrator requires stereotypes. All Germans must be seen as "Huns" ... all Japanese must be regarded as little, yellow bucktoothed fanatics ... all Vietnamese [are derided as] faceless schemers in black pajamas and conical hats who can live for a week on a ball of glutinous rice — whatever that is — and don't mind being tortured because they are stoical Asiatics. But if you and I can talk to people directly that stereotype may crumble. My personal experience, for example, was to observe a museum director, an interpreter, a factory manager ... break down and cry in public, as they tried to describe the suffering of their country.... It means that they are human just as we are, that their feelings are close to the surface as are our own. In Prague, a [National Liberation Front] interpreter said to us: "We know you say that we are faceless. But as you see we do have faces."[66]

Several activists would follow with their own trips into the so-called Communist darkness. These travelers reported back to the American people that the Vietnamese were not simply "gooks" in black pajamas but human beings with fears and concerns. The sojourns into Southeast Asia are a form of peace education insofar as they helped people to understand their enemies rather than simply demonizing them.

Of special interest to peace educators was the massive antiwar movement among military personnel. Too few U.S. history textbooks give a prominent place to this dissent. Providing specific examples of antiwar GIs and evaluating the moral implications of their dissent can enrich a classroom, while providing some balance against discussions of the battles and outcome of the war. The widespread GI resistance cannot be properly ignored or reduced to a footnote when studying the Vietnam War. Consider Colonel Robert D. Heinl's 1971 article, "The Collapse of the Armed Forces," which appeared in a military journal. The colonel wrote that "sedition, coupled with disaffection within the ranks ... infests the armed services." The "army that now remains in Vietnam," he continued, is "approaching collapse" as "individual units" have "refused combat." Actions by the Fort Hood Three, who refused deployment to Vietnam should be further explored in this context. After completing basic training, these three soldiers held a press conference to publicize their resistance, and eventually they received three-year prison sentences. By the late 1960s and early 1970s the GI antiwar movement proliferated. There were "widespread rebellions" in the armed services as well as significant discontent among the U.S. populace. The desertion rate steadily rose as the war dragged on: in 1966, the rate was 14.7 per 1,000 soldiers; in 1970, the rate had sky-rocketed to 52.3 per 1,000. One study finds that between 1967 and 1972, over 350,000 military personnel abandoned their duty stations. By the early 1970s, the Vietnam Veterans against the War (VVAW) emerged as a significant movement. Thousands of these GIs marched on Washington and held "Winter Soldier" hearings denouncing the U.S. war in Indochina. Most notable among them was future senator and presidential candidate John Kerry. David Cortright's *Soldiers in Revolt: GI Resistance during the Vietnam War* carefully catalogs the prevalence of military dissent through his study of GI newspapers and government documents.[67]

Another interesting element of this resistance is that some soldiers offered an alternative to American chosenness mythology. In April 1967, five soldiers organized a "pray-in for peace" in Fort Jackson, Tennessee. Marine Corps reservist Stephen Fortunato, Jr. refused to carry and rifle and later wrote an essay "Thou Shall Not Kill," arguing that the New Testament prohibited killing. An even more challenging critique came from heavyweight boxing champion Muhammad Ali. He applied for conscientious objector status, which means one is morally opposed to war because of religious training and belief, as the military describes it. Ali explained that he became "a conscientious objector the hour that I first heard the teachings of the honorable Elijah Muhammad." Alice Lynd reminds peace educators of the essential lesson that these various war resisters made heroic efforts to build peace and they were for the most part everyday people. "Rather than measure ourselves as less worthy we need to have faith that there is something in humanness or in relatedness which has tremendous untapped resources and that when circumstances require it ordinary people with hang-ups and quirks may be able to act with a dignity of which [humankind] can be proud."[68]

During the 1960s, the Civil Rights and the anti–Vietnam War movements advanced an alternative spirituality that sought to preserve the U.S. republic rather than the empire that was wrapped in the fabric of chosenness rhetoric. In particular, the Vietnam conflict and the Civil Rights movement profoundly altered America's mission during the 1960s. Following the defeat in Vietnam, U.S. leaders and the general public seemed to question whether or not the United States was a unique country with the duty to spread God's democratic ideal across the globe. Under these circumstances, the United States' blessing from God was transferred temporarily from international issues to domestic affairs, particularly the Civil Rights movement's emphasis on renewing sacred rights of liberty and equality in the journey of blacks to the "Promised Land." U.S. leaders still evoked the God's New Israel idiom, but with greater caution. The failure of the Vietnam War coupled with white terrorism inflicted on African-American citizens begged for a reevaluation of

U.S. notions of destiny. Even President Nixon acknowledged this crisis. "To a crisis of spirit," Nixon announced, "we need an answer of spirit ... we are torn by division." One solution that Nixon offered was that "We must work as if everything depended on us ... recognizing that America is a nation under God."[69] Chosenness rhetoric conceals the deep and dark traditions that haunt the U.S. Empire. The "crisis" Nixon identified was simply that marginalized groups demanded their God-given right of freedom that was denied them by the U.S. Empire. The myth of a united nation was impossible to sustain in the 1960s as war crimes and white brutality were daily broadcast on television. In this time of "crisis," previously silenced citizens began to have a voice. This voice often carried spiritual undertones that challenged U.S. chosenness. Dr. Martin Luther King, Jr. best exemplifies this tradition. The spiritual leader warned:

> Don't let anybody make you think that God chose America as his divine messianic force to be a sort of policeman for the whole world. God has a way of standing before the nations in judgment and it seems I can hear God saying to America, "You are too arrogant. If you don't change your ways, I will rise up and break the backbone of your power."[70]

King represents a spirituality that promotes democratic values against a U.S. Empire that often erodes those values. It was during the crisis of Vietnam that the nation was forced to reckon with its mythology. Charles Long explains that these events might be understood as "centennial cycles of violence," where the ritual performance of U.S. providential destiny is openly challenged. During these moments, marginalized groups who are normally rendered invisible appear on the scene, a presence that challenges the national religion. The result of these challenges are the "centennial cycles" of violence that Long identifies: American Revolution (1776), Civil War (1861), and Vietnam War (1961) and the associated civil rights and protest movements.[71] The purveyors of the dominant culture often modify the ritual performance of America's civil religion to incorporate at least some of these "invisible" voices, as evidenced in the temporary expansion of black political participation following the Civil War and Dr. King's "dream." Consider also the emergence of Black Theology or Vine Deloria's God is Red in the 1960s; these protest movements are firmly embedded in the dominant language even as they challenge it.

Middle-class college students also found in their political rebellion an alternative to chosenness rhetoric and the City on a Hill discourse. Consider Paul Potter, who served as president of the Students for a Democratic Society (SDS). Potter said that "I am attracted to religious images like love and communion and soul and spiritual and church.... Not of any church that I have directly known or experienced, but ... the early revolutionary church, whose followers lived in caves and shared their bread, their persecution and their destiny."[72] As Gregory Calvert, a national secretary for SDS, has observed, "the marriage of spiritual values and democratic convictions that had inspired the advocates of participatory democracy was animating movements as apparently diverse as liberation theology and Buddhist political activism in the Third World and Green Politics in the First."[73] The 1960s brought to the fore a plethora of spiritual-political voices that challenged the dominant U.S. civil religion. Recall the long and diverse roster of spiritual resisters: Fathers Daniel and Philip Berrigan; Yale chaplain William Sloane Coffin; Dorothy Day and the Catholic Workers Movement; the National Committee of Black Churchmen; Malcolm X and Muhammad Ali; activist Rennie Davis's New Age spirituality; Paul Goodman's *New Reformation*; the emergence of a womanist theology; and so on. The Civil Rights movement and portions of the 1960s New Left activism represented a prophetic civil religion rooted in values of participatory democracy. It was much more representative of the longing for community than any formal or even informal religion. Unfortunately, dogmatic Marxist-Leninists and a fixation for violence coupled with significant government repression suffocated many of these voices.

In this time of moral examination, U.S. presidents turned the theme of chosenness to support the U.S. Empire. American civil religion is often employed by elite classes to deflect attention away from class division, poverty, racism, etc. Yet, it is also promoted by oppressed groups to galvanize the country to live up to its professed ideals. Here was the moment to assess U.S. priorities in the Cold War and temper its enthusiasm for violence. The tragedy in Southeast Asia provided the opportunity to pursue a more restrained and rational foreign policy.

The custodians of U.S. foreign policy resisted any such possibility. To avoid accountability, U.S. leaders continued to evoke American mythology, particularly its benevolent superpower image. Guiding myths of U.S. destiny and innocence obscured the reality of abuses in Vietnam, gradually transforming the bully into a victim of his own generosity, as Tom Englehardt's brilliant text, *The End of Victory Culture*, reveals. He traces how the United States emerged from Vietnam as a victim of its own nobility, an unjustly restrained hero whose virtuous efforts were undermined by a shiftless enemy and unreliable allies.[74] Although they failed, U.S. officials cannot be blamed for undertaking a well-intentioned crusade against communism in a distant, exotic land. U.S. leaders tried to help Vietnam, the story goes, but were "constrained" by antiwar activists and misled by incompetent strategists. While the United States made mistakes in judgment, its intentions were noble and decent according to the dominant narrative. Former secretary of defense Robert McNamara's apology embodies this mood.

> I want to be clearly understood: the U.S. fought in Vietnam for eight years for what it believed to be good and honest reasons.... Although we sought to do the right thing — and believed we were doing the right thing — in my judgment

hindsight proves us wrong. We both overestimated the effect of South Vietnam's loss on the security of the West and failed to adhere to the fundamental princi-ple that, in the final analysis, if the South Vietnamese were to be saved, they had to win the war themselves.... In the end, we must confront the fate of those Americans who served in Vietnam and never returned.... That our effort in Vietnam proved unwise does not make their sacrifice less noble.[75]

Wrong is understood here in terms of pursuing flawed strategies, not the moral mistake of bombing Vietnamese villages and destroying a tiny nation. Although we should not downplay the significance of McNamara's apology, he remains captive to a parochial image of America. Despite killing some 2 million Vietnamese and disfiguring countless others with napalm sprayings, U.S. officials mourn the nation's shattered image rather than the victims of air raids. As Nixon exclaimed, "we are a pitiless, helpless giant."[76] Such depic-tions portray America as a victim and serve to relieve the haunting memory of widespread human rights abuses and war crimes in Vietnam.

President Ford further encouraged U.S. citizens to forget such uncom-fortable historical facts. "The lessons of Vietnam have already been learned," Ford claimed in 1975, "and we should have our focus on the future."[77] Oper-ating here is the government's desire to put to rest the notion that U.S. aggres-sion is a moral problem in need of correction. It turns out that Ford's assessment satisfied few citizens. A concerned public demanded the establish-ment of the Senate Select Committee to Study Governmental Operations in 1975. Headed by Senator Frank Church (D–Ida.), the committee acknowl-edged that, "revulsion at the Phoenix program which took at least 20,000 lives in south Vietnam ... created the climate for a thorough Congressional inves-tigation." Indeed, Ford's attempt to minimize the lessons of Vietnam did not relieve the shock of the war. America's foreign policy consensus evaporated and U.S. officials could not readily solidify public opinion. In light of this critical climate, the Church Committee exposed the improper and illegal actions of the U.S. government. Yet, it also worked tirelessly to consolidate America's benevolent image. Even as the highly critical Church Committee exposed countless U.S. abuses, its aim was to "restore ... our reputation in the world for decency, fair dealing and moral leadership."[78] In brief, maintaining America's pristine image was a difficult task, but one which took priority over self-examination.

One way that Washington opinion makers worked to restore the United States' image was to declare that anyone who criticized U.S. interventions suffered from a disease, labeled the Vietnam Syndrome. Those who could not easily forget massive human rights abuses and "focus on the future" were afflicted with this ailment. It now appears that the malaise was nothing more than an accurate historical memory and a dislike for violence, a condition that lingered for decades. President George H. Bush's 1989 inaugural address mimics Ford's concern that "the final lesson of Vietnam is that no great nation can long afford to be sundered by a memory."[79] Remembering U.S. misdeeds and questioning policy is akin to tearing the nation apart in Bush's view. Such an attitude disavows any reflection upon U.S. guilt, promoting instead an uncritical acceptance of U.S. war goals. U.S. leaders' attempts to dismiss the vital and vibrant critiques of U.S. power that spread across the country in the Vietnam years reveals their inability to come to terms with guilt, a topic that is fully analyzed in chapter 3. Suffice it to say that America's unacknowledged guilt operates alongside economic forces in explaining its penchant for widespread military violence. Denying guilt allows the United States to uphold its decent and noble image, but the haunting memory of these misdeeds looms just beneath the surface. Under these strained circumstances, U.S. foreign policy remains embedded in a contradiction between its cherished values and its moral misdeeds.

At the outset of this chapter it was suggested that corporate needs endangered the United States' commitment to human rights. The reader may wonder exactly how these business priorities shaped military intervention in Southeast Asia. Some researchers have demonstrated that the Vietnam War "opened up commercial opportunities" for companies that "profited directly from operations in Vietnam," including the construction company Brown and Root, petroleum businesses and banks. Chase and the Bank of America set up branches in Saigon. But the war was not waged simply to enrich private corporations. U.S. officials certainly wished to contain the spread of communism, and they also wanted to make sure that nationalist governments that did not conform to the capitalist world order would be eliminated. In 1974, Assistant Secretary of State Robert Ingersoll was asked by a congressional representative if the U.S.-supported government of South Vietnam was any better than the North Vietnamese Communists. Ingersoll replied that it was no better, but it "has deliberately chosen, at least from the standpoint of economics, a free market system rather than a completely controlled system."[80] Free markets are ironically defended at all costs.

Afghanistan: Russia's Vietnam

Rather than reflecting on U.S. moral transgressions, they are both denied and projected onto the United States' enemies. A good example of this phenomenon concerns U.S. aid for Afghanistan's "freedom fighters" in 1979. Shortly after the end of the Vietnam War, the United States supported Afghan militants to prevent a Soviet takeover of that country. Congressman Charles Wilson, a leading advocate of assisting the rebels, explained that "There were 58,000 dead in Vietnam and we owe the Russians one. I have a slight obsession with it because of Vietnam. I thought the Soviets ought to have a dose of it."[81] Carter's National Security Advisor, Zbigniew Brzezinski, was also preoccupied with "the opportunity of giving to the USSR its own Vietnam."[82] U.S. strategists' obsession with demoralizing the Soviets, rather than confronting their own failed adventures and associated guilt, contributed to unsound U.S. foreign policy decisions in the late 1970s.

Consider Carter's daring policy of funding the mujahideen, or Afghan holy warriors, the largest covert program since Vietnam. Among the mujahideen was Osama bin Laden and much of the Taliban leadership that the United States would wage a war against in 2001. The CIA constructed camps, provided antiaircraft missiles and awarded the radicals large sums of money, despite their repeated record of violating human rights. Rapes, summary execution, torture and blowing up schools were tactics employed by the freedom fighters in Afghanistan. Many of these rebels later turned their weapons against the United States, including attacks on the World Trade Center in New York, a topic that is assessed in chapter five. Nevertheless, many observers uncritically celebrate and defend this clandestine operation.

Assistance to the Afghan rebels is defended for two main reasons. First, it is argued that the United States protected the Afghan freedom fighters right to self-determination only after the Soviets invaded that nation in 1979. Absent from these arguments is that the United States armed the Islamic militants before the Soviets attacked Afghanistan. Brzezinski proudly explained that "it was a plot to induce the Soviet invasion." In reality, Carter approved aid to the Afghan extremists in July 1979, five months before the Soviet invasion, a story corroborated by former CIA director Robert Gates in his book, *From the Shadows*. Classified documents confiscated after the 1979 U.S. embassy siege in Iran confirm that the Soviet invasion was partly a reaction to these secret CIA operations. Although the Soviet offensive is indefensible, it is inseparable from the United States' aim to assemble and equip Islamic warlords to ignite a war against Moscow. Asked if he regretted this action, Brzezinski reportedly said, "Regret what? That secret operation was an excellent idea." What is most troubling here is that an operation that left over 1 million dead, and one that included giving over $3 billion to Muslim terrorists, causes little regret.[83]

Part of the reason why policymakers fail to regret the operation stems from their belief that it facilitated the breakdown of the Soviet Union and the end of the Cold War. This conclusion, while not completely implausible, is still far from conclusive. Consider Mikhail Gorbachev's attempt to thaw the Cold War by way of glasnost, or opening up to the West. Soviet desires to cut back its military and reduce Cold War rivalries were undermined by hard-line U.S. policies. For instance, in March 1985 Gorbachev repeated an earlier peace offer concerning Afghanistan. Moscow agreed to withdraw if the U.S. weapons pipeline to the Muslim guerrillas was terminated. Instead of considering this peace offer, Reagan approved National

Security Decision Directive 166, advocating the removal of the Soviets from Afghanistan "by all means available." One could argue that such aggressive policies may have prolonged the collapse of the Soviet Union rather than accelerate it. George Kennan, the dean of U.S. foreign affairs, notes that "the general effect of Cold War extremism was to delay rather than hasten the great change that overtook the Soviet Union by the end of the 1980's."[84] The question of whether or not the funding of Islamic militants contributed to the end of the Cold War awaits future scholarship. But surely, funding Islamic terrorists undermines the United States' stated goals of ensuring human rights and international cooperation.

Nicaragua and Beyond in the 1980s

Whereas Islamic reactionaries were the United States' "freedom fighters" throughout the 1980s, Latin American clergy were viewed as Communist villains. The year 1979 was a tumultuous one in international relations. Not only did the Russians invade Afghanistan but the shah of Iran was also overthrown, both actions weakening the U.S. intention of containing communism. Those fears mushroomed after the Sandinista revolt defeated the Somoza dictatorship in Nicaragua. With two loyal dictators on opposite sides of the globe eliminated, the United States relied on illegal arms deals to contain communism. In Nicaragua, this meant funding the Contras, a group that supported the Somoza dictatorship against the Sandinistas, socialist rebels who seized power and appointed several priests to key government posts.

Since Congress banned aid to the Contras in 1984, the Reagan administration brokered illegal weapons sales with Iran to gather money to funnel to the Nicaraguan warriors. Known as the Iran-Contra affair, the United States sold sophisticated weapons to Iran, despite its classification as a terrorist state. The profits from these illegal sales were distributed to the Contras, who waged an illegal war against the Nicaraguan people. In 1986, the International Court of Justice denounced the United States for supporting the Contras. The Court found that the United States mined Nicaraguan harbors and distributed murder manuals to the Contras, actions "contrary to the general principles of humanitarian law." The World Court reached an unprecedented conclusion that the United States represented a threat to international peace in dealing with Nicaragua.[85]

As for selling arms to Iran, President George H. W. Bush somehow defended it as "patriotic." A congressional investigation concluded otherwise, indicting several high-ranking officials, Defense Secretary Casper Weinberger, Assistant Secretary of State Elliott Abrams and Deputy National Security Advisor John Poindexter among them. This far-reaching scandal is frequently downplayed as the actions of a few rogue officers within the National Security

Council, such as Lieutenant Colonel Oliver North. Congressional investigators concluded that "it was the president's policy — not an isolated decision by North or Poindexter — to sell arms to Iran."[86] Few investigators followed up on this startling conclusion. Independent prosecutor Lawrence Walsh charges that such inquiries were frustrated by high-level officials, who were part of a "disturbing pattern of deception."[87] This pattern was buttressed by President George H. W. Bush's pardon of those indicted by Congress. Instead of wrestling with the root causes of American misconduct, U.S. leaders once again shielded themselves from responsibility.

Despite the disturbing dealings noted above, scholar Paul Kengor's book, *God and Ronald Reagan: A Spiritual Life*, relates the former president's religious convictions behind his anticommunism. Reagan's spiritual principles, the reader is informed, aided him in the fight against communism. In a chapter titled, "That Shining City: America as a Chosen Land," Kengor argues that Reagan noticed "a special quality and special duty ... of America as a nation chosen by God." Kengor proffers a series of quotations to support this observation. "I believe that God in shedding his grace on this country has always in this divine scheme of things kept an eye on our land and guided it as a promised land," said Reagan.[88] Perhaps no U.S. leader better symbolizes the rhetoric of providential destiny than Ronald Reagan. "Can we doubt that only a divine Providence placed this land, this island of freedom, here as a refuge to all those people who yearn to breath free?" the charismatic president asked.[89] With unending enthusiasm, Reagan classified the United States as the "beacon of freedom" against Moscow's "Evil Empire." He went so far as to charge that the Russian language did not contain a word for freedom. In his farewell address, Reagan underscores the alleged connection between God and the United States. "I've spoken of the shining city all my political life," Reagan says, because "America is God blessed." Similar hyperbole is scattered throughout Reagan's speech, which the *Washington Post* chastised as a series of "fables and mythology." True, but those fables carry great ideological potency.

One reason for Reagan's (somewhat inaccurate) reputation as a great communicator stems from his understanding the power and appeal of these myths. His rhetorical strategies were constantly criticized, yet these melodramatic exaggerations did not diminish Reagan's status as a great communicator. Heroes and exalted leaders can employ this fundamentalist ideology, but they are still susceptible to disapproval, as the *Washington Post*'s assessment indicates. The key to acceptance is to employ the national legends during crises or with occasional humility. For example, before announcing that America's divine providence entails a "crusade," Reagan admitted: "I confess that I've been a little afraid to suggest it." Part of the reason why Reagan is viewed as a great communicator does not stem from his repeated use of national archetypes, but rather his use of them at times of distress and with periodic caution.

Indeed, Reagan's handling of American myths enabled him to achieve popularity regardless of his administration's role in such offenses as the Iran-Contra scandal. Evoking the language of chosenness helped the Reagan administration to present itself as a defender of freedom and democracy, despite its role in illegally funding terrorists. The media's role in what Noam Chomsky calls the manufacture of consent accounts for some of Reagan's acceptance, but we should not ignore the power of chosenness folklore in this regard. As Reagan confessed, "I wasn't a great communicator, but I communicated great things ... beliefs and principles that have guided us for two centuries."[90]

Reagan's public discourse on religion is largely a variety of civil religion that attempted to engender patriotism and loyalty to the state. This loyalty was required in dealing with the Soviets and Communists in Latin America. According to Kengor, Reagan believed that "communist ideology posed a danger to religious practice not only in the Soviet Union but around the world [including] Central America."[91] Citing a Puebla Institute report by a journalist who traveled to Nicaragua, Kengor relays the story that the Sandinistas engaged in the "mocking of God" and a general "persecution of believers." These comments are a bit odd. Daniel Ortega, a member of the Sandinistas and the president of Nicaragua, openly spoke about how the revolution was consistent with Christ's message. Many Sandinista government posts were held by Roman Catholic priests such as Ernesto Cardenal (minister of culture) and Miguel D' Escoto (foreign minister). The revolution was also supported by the many Christian base communities throughout the countryside. Countless journalists traveled to Nicaragua to witness the revolutionary government and they did not find the religious persecution outlined in the Puebla stories. Although the revolution was certainly Marxist, it was also profoundly influenced by religion and the progressive strand within the Catholic Church. One problem with the Puebla Institute is that it has been accused of working with the anticommunist Contras and the CIA. Former Contra Edgar Chamorro claimed that the Puebla Institute had received money from the CIA and one of its leaders was part of the Contra forces.[92] There is good reason to believe that the accusations that the Sandinistas persecuted the faithful were inaccurate. Whatever one wishes to conclude about the Sandinistas, it is a bit of a stretch to chastise them for being antireligious because a significant slice of the movement was profoundly religious. For the Nicaraguan poor and priests like Father Miguel D'Escoto, Reagan's City on a Hill was not a beacon of freedom but a sinister darkness defined by actions like the Iran-Contra affair. Reagan, the priest said, was "possessed by the demons of manifest destiny." D'Escoto continued, "I pray that God" will "forgive him for having been the butcher of my people."[93]

Another case of the United States evading responsibility concerns El Salvador. Here U.S. strategists backed the ARENA party against various united factions of guerrillas in the 1980s, charging that Nicaragua exported its Communist revolution to El Salvador. A number of witnesses challenged this claim, while documenting the cruelty of the Salvadoran armed forces. International human rights groups and church leaders urged the United States to terminate its support of the brutal Salvadoran military. Most notably, Archbishop Oscar Romero of San Salvador sent a letter to President Jimmy Carter on February 17, 1980. He wrote,

> I am very concerned by the news that the government of the United States is planning to further El Salvador's arms race by sending military equipment and advisers to train these Salvadoran battalions in logistics, communications, and intelligence ... your government's contribution will undoubtedly sharpen the injustice and repression inflicted on the organized people, whose struggle has often been for respect for their most basic human rights.[94]

The Carter administration failed to act on the archbishop's appeal, and the incoming Reagan administration accelerated aid to these battalions. In the month following Romero's letter, he was assassinated while saying mass at the La Divinia Providencia Hospital chapel. It turns out that a United Nation's truth commission considers Roberto D'Abuisson the mastermind behind the murder, a graduate of the U.S. Army School of Americas at Fort Benning, Georgia. Six Jesuit priests and their housekeeper were also brutally executed in 1989. Again, the United Nations reports that several of the officers involved in the killing were trained at the U.S. Army facility in Georgia. Similar events led the former U.S. ambassador to El Salvador, Robert White, to describe U.S. interventionism in Central America as "a campaign of terror."[95]

These startling and unsettling aspects of U.S. foreign policy are merely a small sample. One might expand the list of U.S.-supported atrocities to the Congo (1960), Chile (1973), East Timor (1975), Guatemala (1980s), Panama (1989) and it would remain incomplete. That the U.S. government undertook such egregious actions across the globe undoubtedly evokes intense emotions in the reader. Some readers denounce this critique as "left-wing rubbish"; others rightly demand further documentation and analysis. The purpose of chronicling these troubling events is to raise awareness regarding the role of the United States in international affairs. Raising awareness is the first small step in a long journey toward constructing a more peaceful and restrained foreign policy, a task of pivotal importance to peace educators.

Indeed, as Senator Tom Harkin (D-Iowa) explains, "We can continue to conduct disinformation campaigns and court military despots," but "it only fosters an insecure world." It is time to question U.S. tactics abroad, the senator notes, as the United States has "earned a reputation around the world as hostile to human rights."[96]

3

Unacknowledged Guilt and U.S. Militarism*

We did not recognize that neither our people nor our leaders are omniscient. Where our own security is not at stake, our judgment of what is in another people's or country's best interest should be put to the test of open discussion in international forums. We do not have the God-given right to shape every nation in our own image.

— Former defense secretary Robert McNamara[1]

It is not really the point to say simply that if all of us are guilty, then no one is guilty. The trouble is that when all of us are guilty we much prefer to shovel it off on a few so that we can go on with business as usual. It is time that we recognize the potential health of honest guilt, acknowledged our mistakes, and healed ourselves through political action to create an America that will no longer be hated and feared. That is, incidentally, the only sure way to solve our problems of the military. And, also, the problem of law and order.

— William Appleman Williams[2]

Those of my generation who were saved from the altars of infanticide in the service of the American war against Vietnam often found ourselves seeking messianic hope wherever we could find it. The American Dream, John Winthrop's City upon a Hill, collapsed under the weight of the shameful and macabre spectacle of the wanton destruction of Vietnamese villages, body bags containing our dead friends and neighbors, as well as pompous and unrepentant nationalism paraded daily on national television.

— the late James Melvin Washington, professor of church history, Union Theological Seminary[3]

Introductory Framework

American foreign policy behavior in the Cold War period was frequently inimical to human rights. Whether this phenomenon was the result of trying

*A shorter version of this chapter appeared as "Guilt and Sacrifice in U.S. Warfare" by C. Mirra in *Peace Review*, 17, no. 1. Copyright ©2005; reproduced by permission of Taylor & Francis Group, LLC.

to contain communism or pecuniary interests, it was rarely acknowledged in the United States that its foreign policy undermined human rights. Instead, U.S. interventions have been portrayed as nearly a religious mission, where the United States always tries to save or protect others. The eminent historian William Appleman Williams once wrote that if the United States grasped that its, "self-righteousness was the hallmark of inner guilt, it would cease to embark on crusades to save others."[4] What Williams suggests is that U.S. expansionism is driven by a distorted national identity that masks its criminal conduct. American national consciousness is a *Weltanschauung* or worldview of moral supremacy; a guiding myth of benevolence that shapes its purpose in the world. Part of the appeal of this self-congratulatory image is that it conceals a deeper national shame and guilt. The American inclination for violent conquest — from the extermination of the Native Americans to killing some 6 million souls since 1945 — evokes a sense of guilt. When these negative facts remain unacknowledged, it produces a skewed national identity. This identity crisis manifests itself in three main ways. First, unpleasant facts are hidden behind a veil of self-righteousness. This strategy is inseparable from a second, related tendency to project the unflattering qualities of oneself onto enemies. And third, in rare moments where self-aggrandizement is untenable as it was for the United States during the Vietnam War, a country beset by unacknowledged guilt evades accountability by portraying itself as a victim of its own innocent desire to rescue others. Therefore, the following chapter traces how the self-righteous national narratives that were outlined in the previous chapter are symptoms of unacknowledged guilt. It also demonstrates that these fabricated national myths are maintained through the mechanism of projecting one's pernicious behavior onto foes, which perpetuates aggression and war. The chapter concludes with an examination into how the "victimhood" model further protects national honor and arises from unacknowledged guilt.

The Link Between Unacknowledged Guilt, Self-Righteousness and Violence

Modern society generally shuns guilt as misguided and enfeebling. We should remember, however, that serial killer Ted Bundy also dismissed guilt as an "unhealthy" form of "social control."[5] Although guilt has gained a poor reputation in modern culture, its role in facilitating positive behavior is well documented. Guilt is understood here as an unsettling sense of responsibility for one's actions. Shame, on the other hand, deals with unpleasant feelings about one's overall character. Repressing guilt usually heightens feelings of shame, while acknowledging guilt can heal the psychological scar of shame. Accepting guilt for a particular transgression paves the way for rebuilding the self by means of avoiding a repeat of negative behavior. As psychologists Tangney and Dearing document, denying guilt leads to "ugly feelings" that give rise to "resentful anger and hostility."[6] Similarly, peace educator Betty Reardon reminds us that violent behavior has much to do with projecting our guilt on to others. Riitta Wahlström, a peace educator in Finland, adds that in militarized societies the creation of enemy images permits "undesirable cognitions and emotions" to be projected onto the other. "Weakness and failures are transferred to an external target," Wahlstrom concludes.[7]

While unacknowledged guilt is often relieved through violence, it can also be released through genuine acceptance and apology. "Moderately painful" guilt inspires people to act in a "socially responsible manner," concludes a major study on the subject.[8] Robert Jay Lifton, a former U.S. Air Force psychiatrist and medical doctor who has done extensive work with combat participants, similarly finds that an "animating guilt" can heal. He discovered that Vietnam veterans were capable of articulating their own misdeeds without slipping into a paralyzing sense of overall failure. These Vietnam veterans accomplished this by accepting responsibility to resist the war, exposing its "grotesque details," and demanding that U.S. citizens and leaders take responsibility for the devastation that was inflicted on Southeast Asia. They illustrated "an impressive capacity to transform guilt feelings into expressions of responsibility in seeking to redirect their society toward a more humane path," Lifton summarizes.[9] Despite its role in promoting moral behavior, it is difficult to come to terms with guilt, both for individuals and for groups. That the United States sees itself as benevolent is an example of this denial. In fact, the United States' role in international affairs and its self-image are so incongruent as to approach "the modes of psychopathological experience."[10] As long as the United States remains trapped in a web of unacknowledged guilt, it will reveal itself in false pride and violence. To forge a more humane foreign policy, we must locate how unacknowledged guilt and economic avarice foment U.S. global aggression. To avoid misunderstanding, guilt is not the only emotion involved in violent behavior, but one that is generally overlooked, especially in terms of U.S. foreign policy.

Emphasizing guilt as a factor in U.S. policy at first glance appears as an inappropriate application of individual psychology to international relations. Solid evidence for the role of unacknowledged guilt in the outbreak of the First World War is documented in Thomas Scheff's magnificent study, *Bloody Revenge: Emotions, Nationalism and War*. Bertrand Russell's *Why Men Fight* draws a similar conclusion that the Great War was, in part, sparked by pride and honor, emotions closely tied to evading shame. Researchers James and Ilsa Halpern also note that the denial of guilt leads to the projection of one's repressed feelings onto enemies and, "plays a powerful psychological role in the development of [international] conflict and the willingness of people to enter combat." Historian Franklin Ford adds that the role of unacknowledged guilt in violent combat is also present in ancient warfare, particularly in the battles between the Romans and Zealots in ancient Palestine. All of these studies illustrate that the connection between shame, pride and violence applies to both personal and international disputes. Operating in many quarrels is what Helen Block-Lewis calls, "humiliated fury," or cycles of shame and violence. When guilt is submerged, it surfaces as shame that finds relief in furious, violent outbursts.[11]

It should again be said that the United States is hardly alone in masking its crimes behind self-righteous aggression. As the aforementioned studies indicate, repressive regimes since ancient times view themselves as noble and their victims as wholly evil. None of these exemplary studies, however, extends its findings to the United States. Recall that Johan Galtung's penetrating lecture, "Global Projections of Deep-Rooted U.S. Pathologies," is perhaps the only study that connects U.S. repressed guilt with its combativeness.

Galtung's basic hypothesis is that Americans share a collective unconscious through shared archetypes. Swiss psychologist Carl Jung first popularized the theory of archetypes, or deeply embedded images that arise from an original creative source common to all humanity. They are models of behavior such as the "great mother," "hero" and the "supernatural warrior" images found in religion, poetry, and fairy tales. On the American terrain, these archetypes are experienced in the United States' self-congratulatory image as a benevolent superpower, the global policeman who defeats evil foes. This national narrative arouses the collective appeal of archetypical myths regarding divine heroes who protect us from danger. That Americans share this collective, unconscious image should not be interpreted as an "ironclad law," as Galtung cautions. U.S. national images are distortions of deeper human prototypes that are fluid and flexible, and should not be confused with an essentialist claim that they are fixed models of behavior. These images should also not be confused with a consensus paradigm that suggests all Americans are united behind these noble principles, thereby erasing the contentious class and racial struggles among U.S. citizens who have been denied the "blessings" of U.S. democracy. Most ordinary citizens, particularly those denied access to the American dream, are less enthralled by the notion of the United States as a benevolent power. Archetypes are merely one significant factor among several psychological and economic forces that propel U.S. interventionism.

Galtung simply organizes enduring U.S. myths into archetypes, placing them under the seemingly obscure label, "The CMT/DMA/RP Complex." CMT represents America's collective feeling of "chosenness," with a unique set of myths and traumas. The DMA symbolizes the tendency among "chosen" people to organize reality into sharp contrasts associated with dichotomy, Manichaeism, and Armageddon. The crucial element in the equation is the

"RP" axis, which signifies repression and projection. In short, these archetypes reflect a mental landscape where reality is divided into sharp categories of us versus them, a basic feature of all "chosen" people. Everything that is good is embodied by us, and everything that is bad is subsumed by them, which adds a Manichean perspective to this thinking. So, when violence erupts it is understood as an epic, Armageddon-like battle among the forces of good and evil, god and Satan.[12] Modern phrases such as "total victory" or "total defeat," and "you are either with us or with the terrorists" reflect this mental model. U.S. self-righteousness seems to be inextricably linked with these deeper archetypes, especially the collective perception that the United States is a unique and God-ordained nation.

Galtung's model intersects with definitions of civil religion. Donald Jones and Russell Richey organize these collective perceptions into five broad definitions of civil religion. The first is civil religion as folk religion, where the nation and its heroes are spiritualized; creating an "American religion" that competes with traditional faiths. A second meaning is the "transcendent universal religion of the nation," which is not tied to any particular denomination, but a sort of ecumenical sensibility that comprehends the U.S. national experience in terms of a universal reality. Under this framework, the civil religion can subsume a prophetic quality, where it judges and corrects the nation's transgressions. Lincoln's conception of the country as "an almost chosen nation," and his admonishment that "God has his own purposes" are expressive of this transcendent understanding of the American experience. The third meaning is civil religion as "religious nationalism"; it is the worship of U.S. institutions. Martin Marty categorizes Nixon's religious rhetoric in this vein and I consider at least some of Bush's public theology to fall under the rubric of religious nationalism. The fourth meaning is "democratic faith," which casts democratic virtues, with or without a transcendent quality, as a civil religion. The final meaning of civil religion is a "Protestant civic piety," which restricts the nation's theology to the Puritan and Revivalist traditions; it is civil religion as the dominant culture, the Anglo-American tradition of missionary expansion.[13]

Robert Bellah suggests that civil religion it is not simply a patriotic fervor, but an understanding of the U.S. experience "in light of universal reality."[14] In other words, civil religion offers a vague set of metaphors and symbols that provide a sense of social cohesion and meaning to anyone who might identify themselves as "American." The distinctive features of these symbols are that America is a unique geographic space where God-given liberties are spreading in a progressive, unfolding drama. It is not a sectarian church, denomination or even a Christian tradition, but an understanding of the United States in terms of a universal reality that finds expression in Judeo-Christian metaphors. Civil religion subsumes two conflicting forms, according to Bellah. The first resembles a religious nationalism and the second is a prophetic vision. Under religious nationalism, the nation takes on a transcendent quality and offers itself as "God" or the supreme representative of God on earth. This approach is often expressed by the dominant culture, particularly presidents at times of war and is what Galtung calls the "chosenness syndrome." As the noted religious scholar C. Eric Lincoln observes, "Presidential politics is clearly the arena in which the implicit religion of the people is made explicit."[15] On the other hand, civil religion contains a prophetic element; the idea that values of equality, freedom and justice are endowed by God or a "higher law" and that America is obligated to fulfill them.

Scholars Robert Jewett and John Shelton Lawrence in their magisterial text, *Captain America and the Crusade against Evil: The Dilemma of Zealous Nationalism*, categorize these traditions as "zealous nationalism" versus "prophetic realism." Philosopher Cornel West similarly identifies these oppositional elements of America's religion as "Constantinian Christianity" and "prophetic Christianity."[16] This chapter emphasizes the role of civil religion as a "chosenness syndrome" that accelerates violence. While religious vocabulary informs this syndrome, some readers may wish to think of these metaphors as an existential craving for community. It should be stated loud and clear that this book is not promoting religion, but universal values of equality and dignity that are experienced in community and often expressed in religious language.

The self-righteous attitude that the United States stands for the good has become an almost indisputable "patriotic code." Galtung suggests that most peace-education and conflict-resolution programs reinforce this patriotic code as they are "unable or unwilling" to document the behavior and "function of the key actor in the world system, the USA."[17] Although the tendency among American peace educators to elude U.S. policy is changing, this chapter still fills an enormous gap in peace education by examining how U.S. sanctimonious attitudes represent a massive denial of its violent behavior (i.e., unacknowledged guilt) in international affairs. It expands Galtung's hypothesis by illuminating the role that these archetypal myths play in post–World War II policy, particularly the war on terrorism.

Chosenness and Civilization: The Self-Righteous Hallmarks of Inner Guilt

Chosenness archetypes, or the collective myth of being selected by God to lead the world, permeate U.S. history. This covenant is precisely the brand of self-righteousness that is the hallmark of inner guilt. Eric Hoffer's highly respected study, *The True Believer*, makes a similar point about individuals attracted to mass movements. Although he includes nationalism under the banner of mass movements, Hoffer oddly exempts U.S. patriotism. Setting aside this omission, Hoffer rightly notes that, "there is a guilty conscience behind every brazen word and behind every manifestation of self-righteousness." He writes that the, "contrast between the loftiness of profession and the imperfection of practice" creates a "guilty conscience."[18] The United States of America, of course, is predicated upon a most conspicuous contrast between the practice of slavery and professions of equality. Given the endless selection of brazen words by U.S. leaders, it is remarkable that Hoffer's study is not applied to the United States' patriotic code. It seems that the self-righteous posture of the United States as God's chosen nation is ample evidence for the presence of a guilty conscience.

From the Plymouth colony in the seventeenth century to Manifest Destiny in the nineteenth century, scholars have long ago noted the imprint of chosenness on the American character. While historians recognize the missionary impulse of early U.S. expansionism, few link it to later periods. Revisionist scholars such as William Appleman Williams have argued that the ideology of Manifest Destiny, or the God-given right to expand, shaped U.S. thinking throughout the twentieth century. Feelings associated with Manifest Destiny have not only contributed to American thought, but they have also played a pivotal role in justifying and accelerating U.S. violence into the twenty-first century. While divinely inspired imperialism is generally understood as an ideological relic of the distant past, it animates the thinking of post–World War II strategists almost as much as their Puritan forerunners.

The theological foundation of the Plymouth colony is a familiar story, yet it is worth briefly repeating to illustrate how deeply embedded divine election is in the U.S. psyche. Exiled Puritans successfully recast the Jewish notion of chosenness. For Puritans fleeing English persecution, the journey to the New World was an exodus, complete with its own traumas and myths. After arriving in the New World, it was viewed as the Promised Land and properly named New Canaan. The geographic space of America became the sacred place of God's new covenant, "the Lord make it like that of New England, for we must consider that we shall be as a City on a Hill," proclaimed Governor John Winthrop.[19]

This self-righteous stance quickly translated into violence and massacre. God's chosen people encountered challenges from the dark forces lurking in the wilderness — from the Native Americans. When tension erupted into war with the Pequot in 1636, it was a matter of the elected souls fulfilling God's plan. Take, for instance, William Bradford's account of the burning of a Pequot village: "it was a fearful sight to see them frying ... but the victory seemed a sweet sacrifice, and we gave the prayers thereof to God, who had enclosed the enemies in [our] hands." Around the same time, Winthrop welcomed the smallpox epidemic among Amerindians as a sign that "God hath consumed the Natives."[20] From the start, atrocity and violent conquest are conflated with God's will on America's shores.

Winthrop's rhetoric is well known and several colonial groups understood their journey to the New World in similar biblical terms. Consider William Penn's "holy experiment" in Pennsylvania, which he described as an "example to the nations"; or, the Georgia colonists who arrived in their "promis'd Canaan." Even the dissenting Roger Williams described his experiment as "Providence" in Rhode Island. In short, New England Puritanism most clearly exemplifies the spirit of God's New Israel that was experienced by early settlers in search of paradise in the New World. While we should not overemphasize the importance of the Plymouth and Massachusetts Bay colonies in propelling images of God-ordained expansionism, we should not ignore it. Early New England Puritanism alone cannot explain the development of America's national character. It does, however, provide enduring images and symbols, particularly the theme that history is a progressive, unfolding narrative under God's design with the New World ("America") as the central, chosen actor.

This cultural archetype was further cemented in the American psyche in the Revolutionary era. The Puritan legacy informs early civic identity and influences the images employed during the American Revolution, when the forging of a self-conscious national identity occurred. Robert Bellah has explained that the Founding Fathers put to use Puritan imagery and symbols in forging an American identity/nation-state. He has argued that the United States' formation is a "strategic point of departure," owing to scholarship in comparative religion that illustrates that where people locate their origins is where they discover their most basic self-conceptions. These self-conceptions are deeply ensconced in chosenness symbols. To illustrate, Thomas Jefferson and others proposed that the Great Seal portray Moses parting the Red Sea. John Adams went so far as to argue that the early settling of America was part of a "grand scheme in Providence," a theme echoed in the Declaration of Independence.[21] America's Founding Fathers were unquestionably embedded in Puritan symbolism of divine election, periodically tested through traumatic events, such as the American Revolution.

It is important to avoid conflating the Founder Fathers' use of religious metaphors with the belief that they sought a unified, Christian state. Some commentators would have us believe that the United States is indeed God's Christian land. To provide one example among many, Mark Beliles and Stephen McDowell's text, *America's Providential Heritage*, includes a chapter "How God Defends Christian Liberty." The authors explain that "God providentially protected the Continental Army on numerous occasions. God was more than just supporting Christian individuals.... He was supporting the entire cause of liberty."[22]

Many of the founders were Deists, who did not believe that God directed all human events. Thomas Jefferson was attacked by religious zealots as a "red-haired deist," and he dismissed Jesus' divinity. Although Jefferson edited a volume of Jesus' sayings, he did so in the context of the 1800 presidential election, during which he was sometimes charged with being an atheist.[23] That Jefferson did not recognize Jesus's divinity clearly suggests that he did not seek to create a Christian nation. Frank Lambert's *The Founding Fathers and the Place of Religion in America* reminds us that the federal Constitution does not mention Divine Providence or God as did earlier political declarations. In fact, the First Amendment sets the tone: "Congress shall make no law respecting the establishment of religion." More importantly, a Senate proposal to establish a Christian Commonwealth was explicitly rejected at the time.[24]

Casting the Founder Fathers as creators of a Christian country propels the myth of the United States as God's chosen nation. It perpetuates the view that there was clear consensus regarding religion and who should rule at home, when no such consensus existed. James Madison's *Notes on the Constitution* contributed to this popular myth. He wrote that Benjamin Franklin addressed the delegates at the Constitutional Convention, pleading for a daily prayer before deliberations, a motion that was seconded by Roger Sherman. Later accounts of this event in two books that sold some 800,000 copies claim that the delegates declared three days of fasting and prayer. As one leading scholar of U.S. religious history has demonstrated, "Franklin's motion was not approved but tabled; there was no three day recess; and the Convention never did begin its sessions with prayer."[25] The story contributes to a founding myth that the nation was unified under the banner of a Christian God. It ignores the diversity of religious and political views among Native Americans, slaves and the various, competing Christian sects. In short, the Founders employed a civil religion to preserve and promote a harmonious national consensus, one that never truly existed.

The United States' self-proclaimed status as God's favored nation gradually climaxed in the Great Seal of the United States in 1776: "God has blessed this undertaking, a new order for the ages." Placing the seal on U.S. dollar bills alongside the slogan, "In God We Trust" further imprints the feeling of divine election on the American character. America's Founding Fathers assumed it was their right and duty to spread God's will and forge a new order for the ages, or at least make it appear as such to dissenters and doubters.

By the nineteenth century, that new order was brazenly described as "our manifest destiny." It was the United States' destiny to spread freedom across the continent, enthusiastically expressed by one expansionist: "Yes, more, more, more! ... till our national destiny is fulfilled and ... the whole boundless continent is ours." President McKinley's explanation for conquering the Philippines in 1898 is an unequivocal example of this divinely inspired imperialism. "I went down on my knees and prayed," McKinley dramatically explained, "and it came to me." It was our task to "civilize and Christianize them and by God's grace do the very best we could by them." Some scholars have questioned the accuracy of McKinley's remark, but it is consistent with what leading politicians articulated at the time. Senator Albert Beveridge (R–Ind.) agreed that the Lord blessed this undertaking as he "has marked us as a chosen people."[26] In reality, the Spanish-American War and the conquest of the Philippines accelerated the expansion of commerce and the American empire. Such crude goals are difficult to justify, but more easily digested if viewed as a fulfillment of God's will.

In the modern era, however, McKinley and Beveridge risk appearing as fundamentalist fanatics. As scientific rationality and technical reason gained wider currency at the turn of the twentieth century, the language of divine providence required secular alternatives. Chosenness, which is simply a religious metaphor for superiority, finds expression in the modern vocabulary of civilization. Nowhere is the Manichean nature and mythic appeal of chosenness more pronounced than in its secular substitute, civilization. Recall Carolus Linneaus's *Systema Naturae* (1735), which classified Europeans as "gentle and inventive," and Africans as "crafty, indolent and negligent."[27] Europeans, according to so-called objective scientific inquiry, were supposedly civilized and Africans were uncivilized. Under this framework, civilization embodied Western progress and so-called primitives were incapable of modern political institutions. We can see how the language of civilization is predicated upon a dualistic mind-set. It separates civilization and primitives in the same rigid manner that theological dogma divides good and evil.

Theological metaphors of chosenness and discourse on civilization share a fundamentalist quality. They are informed by a literal-mindedness, as Owen Barfield calls it, which dogmatically carves reality into rigid, fixed categories. Modern idolatry of rigid laws often replicates the reified images of religious doctrine. To illustrate, the popularity of Charles Darwin's evolutionary theory in the late nineteenth century seems to undermine God-ordained mythology, yet it frequently reinforces it. The logical extension of divinely inspired superiority is the distortion of the survival of the fittest. If God did not endorse Western hegemony, then the blind logic of nature did. The natural world is simply divided among the civilized and uncivilized, according to this thinking.

As it gradually became unfashionable to describe the United States' ascendancy as God's mission, natural selection and "civilization" served the same purpose. It is no wonder that scholar Charles Long discovers that the exact word civilization emerges during the age of imperialism. Along these lines, Owen Barfield finds that the words category, classify, and arrange take on their modern meanings around the same time.[28] The ultimate category, or classification, is civilization. The dualistic apparatus that is necessary to sustain the subjugation of whole cultures finds a home in the discourse on civilization. The chosenness complex fits neatly with the secular image of the civilized (fit) in an inevitable struggle against the uncivilized (unfit). To be sure, U.S. officials employ the rhetoric of civilization and chosenness interchangeably in the modern age.

This discussion regarding how civilization sometimes serves as a surrogate for theological metaphors does not mean that the chosenness metaphor was altogether abandoned. Civilization and natural selection make the delicate concept of God-ordained conquest more acceptable to modern skeptics, yet the religious myth still carries influence. Galtung reminds us that those with power, such as U.S. presidents, are able to draw upon both divine election and civilization mythology throughout the twentieth century. Rhetoric that revolves around providential destiny continues to mask guilt in the modern age.

God's People or a Guilty People?

The sober former secretary of state Colin Powell is also intoxicated by the myth of divine providence. At the 2000 Republican National Convention, Powell extolled the United States as a "trusted nation" that seeks only to share all that it has been given "by a generous God." America reigns as "that shining city on a hill that Reagan spoke of and the world looks up to," Powell insisted. According to a White House press release, the speech "sent a jolt" through the auditorium, indicating that Powell's theological musing matched the general mood of the Republican constituency. Recognizing the potency of this metaphor, Senator John McCain's address to the convention mimicked Powell's remarks. McCain announced that, "we are part of something providential," and "meant to transform history."[29]

The United States has transformed history, but sometimes for the worst. U.S. interventions since 1945 frequently subverted democracy and bear little resemblance to a "trusted nation" seeking to spread God's gifts. Contrary to the myth of American decency, a Department of Defense study admits that, "Historical data show a strong correlation between U.S. involvement in international situations and an increase in terrorist attacks against the U.S." Amnesty International adds that, "on any given day," someone is likely to be "displaced, tortured or killed ... more often than not, the United States shares the blame." The United States routinely assists governments that commit "gross violations and unspeakable offenses." It follows that the U.S. government "must accept widespread responsibility," the respected human rights agency concludes.[30] A central concern of this chapter is exactly this glaring denial of responsibility. All of the flamboyant rhetoric regarding the United

States as God's favored nation is indeed a hallmark of inner guilt, a basic avoidance mechanism. Unless we accept that the United States is God's providence, we must question the intensity and severity of this rhetoric. Evidence strongly suggests this self-congratulatory mood arises from the denial of guilt.

When one's practices flagrantly contradict one's principles, it creates tension. Anxiety accompanies fabricated self-images as they are in constant need of protection. Psychology teaches us that the best defense for vulnerable self-images is to overcompensate for shortcomings with "narcissistic feelings of self-righteousness and superiority."[31] For example, where human rights groups locate U.S. support for "unspeakable offenses," American leaders see themselves as the greatest force for peace on earth. Simply put, violent leaders and nations tend to "overrate themselves." Adolph Hitler and Saddam Hussein, for instance, were confident and self-righteous concerning their imperial adventures, as Roy Baumeister demonstrates.[32] It is easy to find this trait among one's opponents; few observers dispute Hussein or Hitler's inability to acknowledge their misdeeds. The challenge is for peace educators to facilitate a conversation that permits Americans to locate this tendency among themselves. It might be well to open discussion on how statements such as "the world looks up to us" and that "we're the natural leaders of the world" point to a guilty conscience.[33] As Eric Hoffer ironically reminds us, beneath such self-righteous proclamations resides a guilty conscience.

However, this avoidance of guilt sometimes rises to the surface in unmistakable terms. Recall that following the accidental bombing of an Iranian passenger jet that killed 290 people in 1989, then–vice president George H. Bush opined, "I never apologize for the United States of America. I don't care what the facts are."[34] Such a deliberate refusal to apologize is at first glance baffling. Because the United States sees itself as benevolent and infallible, a simple apology jeopardizes the nation's identity. When national myths are endangered, leaders may resort to denying even the most obvious error. American slogans such as "My country, right or wrong" and "love it or leave it" arise from this same dynamic. Like Bush's denial, these phrases silence discussion and impede any possibility of acknowledging guilt.

Psychologist Ervin Staub underscores the dangers of these denials. He proposes a model to identify societies that are prone to mass killing and genocide. The United States, owing principally to its narcissistic superiority complex, exhibits predisposing factors. There is a "sense of superiority" alongside "an underlying insecurity about worth and moral goodness," Staub notices, "a dangerous combination."[35] This concern about "moral goodness" emanates from repressed guilt that expresses itself through self-righteousness, which Staub believes is a cultural prerequisite for mass killing. He in no way suggests that the United States is likely to engage in an internal genocide (although one may wish to discuss the treatment of Native Americans from the seventeenth century through the late nineteenth century here). Staub does suggest that the United States' self-righteous attitude toward its foreign neighbors does lead to the mass killing of external enemies.

Overcoming this penchant for violence involves the development of a more "balanced view of the self," one which recognizes its violent disposition. To impede the evolution toward greater and greater violence, the United States must acknowledge its guilt. The purpose in outlining American expressions of divine election is to underscore how this incredibly unbalanced view of the nation is inextricably bound to insulating itself from this process of accepting guilt. Until the world's sole remaining superpower comes to terms with its self-deception, it will continue to seek violent solutions to international disputes. The first step in opening this process of acknowledgment is for nations to evaluate their own behavior before "deflecting self-blame to others," as Staub writes.[36]

Projection: Protecting Us from Them

Unfortunately, the most effective way to avoid guilt is to project it onto others. Projection simply means to attribute the repressed, unwanted qualities of the self to others, which distorts the perception of that other. Bellicose, imperialist nations normally displace their aggression onto their victims. Where we find expansionist empires casting themselves as peaceful and their victims as malicious, we are likely to locate the projection of guilt. A clear example of this denial is Hitler's comment in 1939 that, "I have not conducted any war [and] I have expressed an abhorrence of war."[37] A less extreme example involves Reagan's statement that, "We always seek to live in peace. We resort to force infrequently"; it is the "barbarous assault" of the "Evil Empire" that erodes peace.[38] Whether or not the Soviets are barbarous, Reagan's forays into Nicaragua, Afghanistan, Libya, Grenada and elsewhere are anything but a peaceful, infrequent use of force. His self-deceptions are part of the broader chosenness syndrome that propels this pattern of repression and projection. If God sides with the U.S.A., then it must be peaceful and good. Conversely, anyone who challenges God's people must be deranged and demonic, the story goes. U.S. national myths are an ideal framework for projections.

Melanie Klein calls this process "projective identification." Feelings of guilt that accompany violence are avoided through "splitting." The good and bad selves are divided or split, the good is retained and the bad is exported. With the unwanted qualities located safely outside oneself, it is possible to destroy these painful feelings. Since the other subsumes those violent emotions, in an inflated form, it is seen as demonic and worthy of destruction. The shadow side is never acknowledged, it is projected and destroyed. This procedure inspires an almost endless spiral of violence as there is a continual struggle to find "containers" for our projections, objects that will hold our undesirable qualities.[39]

Much controversy surrounds Klein's work, but its key component is a commonly accepted feature of "scapegoating." History is replete with scapegoats, targets who carry other people's unwanted emotions. Hitler projected his shortcomings onto the Jewish people. The United States' scapegoats include Native American "savages," African "half-devils," Communist "tyrants," Vietnamese "gooks" in "black pajamas," narco-terrorists and terrorists. History confronts us with this ongoing struggle to label enemies, the search for scapegoats to carry the burden of guilt. In fact, the origin of the word scapegoat comes from a religious ritual of guilt projection. In the Old Testament Book of Leviticus, a "goat for Azazel" is sacrificed to atone for the sins of the Jewish people. The ceremonial belief that guilt can be transferred to animals (goats) translates into the contemporary proclivity to demonize adversaries. Just as it was cathartic to toss the biblical goat of Azazel from a cliff, it is psychologically satisfying to reject and annihilate our scapegoats.[40]

Few observers can deny that this centuries-old tradition of scapegoats surfaces in almost every war. Lawrence Leshaun's study, *The Psychology of War*, finds that the projection of unacknowledged feelings figures centrally in militaristic attitudes. As nations enter war, a "mythic reality" consumes people's thinking; concepts of good and evil quickly become oversimplified illusions of us versus them, Leshaun says. This bifurcation of reality mirrors Klein's theory of "splitting," good qualities are reserved for us and bad for them. Such thinking is normally associated with fairy tales, but becomes believable during wartime.[41] The crusader mentality behind U.S. interventions matches this fairy-tale picture of good against evil. America as a God-like figure always defends against evil forces; it is never the perpetrator of aggression according to the legend.

Many problems grow out of this mythic, fairy-tale splitting of reality. When the myths are taken literally, it intensifies the idea that it is "we" who are correct and "they" who are immoral. It gives the impression that "we" have the right to violently subdue "them," as the conflict worker Else Hammerich observes.[42] Essentially, the mental framework for the projection of guilt is the mythic dichotomy of good against evil, where we are good and they are evil.

To provide a practical example, both sides of the Persian Gulf War in 1991 conform to this skewed picture. After invading Kuwait in 1990, Saddam Hussein claimed that it was the United States who was the aggressive devil. "This is the mother of all wars. It is led by the Satan, Bush," Hussein declared. George H. Bush responded with a similar distortion, "Hussein is an evil villain and America will lead a crusade against the Saddamites."[43] Each party displays a guilt projection. The selfish goal of seizing the region's petroleum plagues both actors, yet they only see aggression in the other. Despite Hussein's slaughter of Kurds and his military capture of oil fields, it is Bush who is "Satan." In spite of Bush's desire to control the oil-rich region, he depicts Iraq as evil, inhabited by fairy-tale villains known as "Saddamites." Again, when one depicts one's enemy as wholly evil, it is easy to overlook one's own guilty behavior.

This avoidance mechanism is also found in the euphemisms surrounding the Gulf War. The United States claimed to use "smart bombs" and "surgical strikes" in Iraq. Whereas Iraqi soldiers were rapists and torturers, U.S. forces were humanitarian. *ABC News* correspondent Ted Koppell was so impressed with the American military's "humanity," he called the Gulf War a "work of art." Koppel's masterpiece was later blemished, as former attorney general Ramsey Clark has explained, by the Pentagon's confession that 93 percent of the bombs dropped on Iraq were conventional missiles. Nor was the U.S. engagement "surgical," as evidenced in the Basra Road killings, where an unspecified number of people were the victims of a crude U.S. air raid.[44] We should not underestimate the power of terms such as smart bombs, surgical strikes and collateral damage. They provide a safe psychological distance from killing, thereby restricting feelings of guilt. Both combatants and civilians are less apt to feel responsible for deaths if they are convinced that "smart" bombs targeted only "Saddamites."

The Challenge to Overcome Guilt Denial and Psychological Projections

As we have seen, the acceptance of guilt normally halts violent behavior. Contrary to the belief that soldiers are natural born killers, they must be convinced to overcome feelings of guilt before they can kill. Dave Grossman cites a once unknown study conducted by the U.S. Army during the Second World War, which finds that only fifteen to twenty percent of soldiers would fire on enemies. Its chief investigator, Brigadier General S.L.A. Marshall, concluded that, "the average healthy individual will not of his own volition take a life." To overcome this inhibition, the army "manufactured contempt," namely, the "psychological denial, and contempt for, the victim's humanity."[45] To accomplish this task, military planners consciously turned enemies into scapegoats. The Army convinced soldiers who were preparing for battle that the world is split between friend and foe, a mental landscape ripe for killing insofar as it precludes the formation of guilty feelings. According to Sergeant Martin Smith, who served in the U.S. Marine Corps, "dehumanization is central to military training." Training exercises include bayonet training and fighting with pugil sticks, where Marines are instructed to "imagine the enemy"; its "educational method is based on" a "structured form of cruelty," the marine sergeant concludes.[46] After the Second World War, this militarized pedagogy stimulated a dichotomous mind-set in soldiers and contributed to an increased firing rate. If the army understands the value of suppressing guilt in killing, peace educators should emphasize the importance of acknowledging it.

This possibility was greatly diminished immediately after the events of September 11. "Bush's bombastic odes [are] dedicated to," critical educator Peter McLaren quips, "defining the war as a way of cleansing the world of evil — an evil projected onto others, so we can have our own sins expiated."[47] President Bush rushed to divide the world between good and evil, setting the stage for intense scapegoating and projection. Bush warned that, "you are either with us, or with the terrorists." New York City mayor Rudolph Giuliani parroted Bush's threat, "you're either with civilization or you're with the terrorists. We're right, they're wrong, it's as simple as that."[48] Although the September 11 attacks are grotesque and inexcusable, U.S. leaders seek to shut off any possibility of guilt and dialogue. They oversimplify reality, offering only two choices: good or evil. This simple picture precludes us from investigating whether or not the U.S. role in funding Islamic militants or threatening to strike Afghanistan only months before September 11 may have contributed to this cycle of violence. To evaluate U.S. policy is "to blame America first" and side with evil, according to this thinking. One could be both against terrorism and critical of the United States, but the paradigm does not permit it. Ironically, Osama bin Laden adopts a similar rigid and dogmatic worldview, reversing the agents of good and evil. For him, the United States is the "head of the serpent," while he believes that his jihad is blessed by God. Their warrior logic, according to Johan Galtung, is so alike that, "George bin Laden and Osama Bush could exchange speeches."[49] While Bush's rage is understandable, he mimics bin Laden when denying any accountability and projecting all that is evil onto vague enemies. Because each party is committed to guilt projections, s/he is unable to see any possible cause of the other's grievances.

Another example of psychological projections among U.S. strategists and intellectuals involves the "West versus Islam" dichotomy. Dinesh D' Souza argues that America creates "tolerant" people, whereas "Islamic societies" supply "servile, fatalistic and intolerant" individuals. Perhaps the most formidable expression of the West versus Islam demarcation is Samuel Huntington's *The Clash of Civilizations*. "The central theme of this book is that culture and cultural identities," Huntington writes, "are shaping patterns of cohesion, disintegration and conflict in the post–Cold War world." European culture "differs from other civilizations," its "distinctive character" includes "liberty, political democracy, the rule of law and human rights." Other civilizations are different, such as "Islamic culture," which "explains in large part the failure of democracy to emerge in much of the Islamic world." These very different cultural identities, we must assume, are "shaping patterns" of "disintegration and conflict."[50]

Although the Bush administration shies away from the clash of civilizations thesis, it is the natural extension of Bush's rhetorical strategies. The president's monumental struggle against evildoers coupled with the Muslim background of the September 11 criminals is likely to encourage such divisions. Saxby Chambliss (R–Ga.) who served on the House Subcommittee on Terrorism, further invited a cultural conflict when he suggested that the sheriff of Georgia should "arrest every Muslim that crosses the state line."[51]

Chambliss's comments are overdrawn and unappealing, but the clash of civilizations thesis is much more sophisticated and seductive. After all, bin Laden ceaselessly discusses a jihad against the United States and has endorsed the idea of a clash of civilizations. But it is disingenuous to ascribe bin Laden and other extremist's values to over a billion people. It ignores the great diversity of Muslim attitudes. Another problem with the Islam versus the West picture is that the United States maintains an alliance with the world's largest Muslim country, Indonesia. America also has several postwar alliances with Islamic countries and groups, including Pakistan, Jordan, the Kosovo Liberation Army and the Islamic Front for the Salvation of Afghanistan. Moreover, a world opinion study of nearly 250,000 people, including nine Muslim countries, concludes that there "are striking similarities in political values in Western and Islamic societies."[52] It is tempting to see a historical clash between Islam and the West, but a close inspection of reality reveals that it is an exaggeration and perhaps a psychological distortion.

Consider Huntington's contribution to a study, *The Crisis of Democracy*, prepared for the Trilateral Commission. The commission included Jimmy Carter, Zbigniew Brzezinski, Walter Mondale, Warren Christopher, Cyrus Vance, David Rockefeller as well as several corporate executives and academics. The report discusses models of effective democratic governance. An effective administration, the report tells us, "need have little relation to the electoral coalition." Hence, a worthwhile model occurs under President Truman, who "was able to govern the country with the cooperation of a relatively small number of Wall Street lawyers and bankers." This arrangement unraveled in the 1960s, owing to the political participation of "marginal groups" in the political process. The system became "overloaded," Huntington writes, because "the effective operation of a democratic political system usually requires some level of apathy and noninvolvement." Evidently, the increasing involvement of blacks, women and students during the 1960s prevented "Wall Street lawyers and bankers" from running the nation. Authority was undermined by the "democratic distemper," as Huntington puts it.[53] In effect, Western politicians, corporate executives and professors endorse an authoritarian perspective. Many of these same people have classified Islamic culture as inherently "undemocratic," despite polls that show otherwise. Such a blatant reversal of attitudes seems to have much to do with psychological projections.

There are alternatives to this paralyzing paradigm. Following the Oklahoma City attack in 1995, no serious observer responded that you are either with America or you are with the militia extremists. Instead, sheriffs met with militia groups to discover the root causes of their misguided anger. The either/or worldview prevents such constructive and effective measures. As for international conflicts, Iran proposed a meeting of Islamic and Western states after the September 11 massacre, a move that because it deflates the easy "for us or against us" perception was ignored in the West. American planners' commitment to a Manichean creed suggests that they crave an outlet for their aggressive tendencies.

A more general example of American officialdom's repression of obvious facts concerns the United States as an empire. "We refuse the crown of empire," then governor George W. Bush assured an audience at the Ronald Reagan Presidential Library in 1999. Driving the point home Bush continued, "America is a peaceful power.... All the aims I've described today are important. But they are not imperial. America has never been an empire. We may be the only great power in history that had the chance, and refused — preferring greatness to power and justice to glory." Instead of empire, Bush explained, the United States pursues a "distinctly American internationalism." After assuming the presidency, Bush repeated at West Point in 2002 that "America has no empire to extend." Former defense secretary Donald Rumsfeld is also in denial regarding America as an empire. In 2003, a reporter from *Al Jazeera* asked Rumsfeld if the United States held imperial ambitions. "We don't seek empire," Rumsfeld snarled, "We're not imperialistic. We never have been. I can't imagine why you'd ask the question." This evasion is not unique to the Bush administration. During the Clinton presidency a State Department official explained that, "We are a benevolent power. We don't seek empire."[54]

Despite these denials, the fact that the United States is an empire is no longer avoidable. Establishment scholar Niall Ferguson has gone so far as to claim that the United States is an "empire in denial." Andrew Bacevich, a conservative professor of international relations, urges us to discard "hoary old axioms" and view American policy through the lens of empire.[55] Indeed, with over 700 military bases in some 130 nations, few can deny the existence of an American Empire. Think tanks and conservative writers have responded creatively to the increasingly open acknowledgment of empire. They advance descriptions that might be loosely classified as sophisticated secular versions of chosenness discourse. Many now claim that the United States is an "empire of liberty" or "liberal empire" that imposes democracy abroad for the betterment of humankind. Columbia University professor and former president of the American Political Science Association Robert Jervis explains that this "imperial temptation" to spread Western values abroad makes the United States a "compulsive empire."[56] Rather than connecting the United States with economic exploitation, these descriptions suggest America seeks to impose democracy and modernity in foreign lands.

This narrow conception of empire has led to some rather crude suggestions. Max Boot, for instance, believes that the United States needs a "colonial office" in Iraq, while Charles Krauthammer insists that an "American global dominion is a good thing." However, not all establishment writers are enthusiastic about American hegemony. C. Boyden Gray, a Washington insider and counsel in the first Bush administration, has endorsed a group that seeks to warn the public regarding the dangers of empire. Meanwhile, the rather temperate journal, *Foreign Affairs*, openly denounced the Bush administration's "bullying and inflexibility."[57]

Part of this debate concerns whether or not the United States properly qualifies as an empire. Scholars typically define empire as a relic of the past, namely, nation-states that dominated others through direct rule and territorial conquest. The old direct rule of empire has been supplemented with terms such as neo-colonialism, where one state dominates others without establishing colonies. In recent years, it has become fashionable to label imperialism as primacy, supremacy, and most often, hegemony. Theorist Graham Evans has pointed out that such terms are "politicized," and that imperialism has come to indicate any form of domination of one group over another. While the nuanced debate over definitions is important, it tends to obfuscate uncomfortable realities. Whatever our preference for calling the United States — empire, hegemon, or neo-imperialist — America exploits foreign markets for the benefit of a domestic elite. J. A. Hobson's understanding of imperialism from his 1902 book *Imperialism: A Study*, rereleased in 2005, remains useful. Imperialism "is a depraved choice of national life, imposed by self-seeking interests, which appeals to the lusts of quantitative acquisitiveness." This avarice takes many forms, creating confusion over definitions of empire. Johan Galtung's definition of empire captures its various manifestations. Empire is a "trans-border Center-Periphery system," Galtung writes, "with a culture legitimizing structure of unequal exchange between center and periphery."[58] Unequal exchange militarily, economically, politically and culturally is at the heart of empire.

The intricate network of American military bases across the globe maintains U.S. hegemony, an unequal exchange whereby America is the sole superpower that protects allies and punishes foes. This unequal exchange surfaces in a variety of ways. For example, U.S. disdain toward the United Nations, coercing weaker states into treaties or imposing structural adjustment programs through so-called neutral bodies such as the International Monetary Fund. Bush administration hard-liners represent an audacious form of this imperial dominance. The open, public debate over empire is bound up in the longstanding imperial ambitions of the key architects of Bush's foreign policy that were put in motion following the September 11 catastrophe. To follow Ferguson, the United States is quite simply an empire in denial.

The U.S. Empire as a Victim

Intellectuals and politicians excite public emotions by way of masking U.S. guilt and projecting it onto enemies. This process also lends itself to the "victimhood" motif. When a country that perceives itself as morally virtuous is attacked, it follows that it is the victim of another group's evil nature. A noble nation does not invite attack, only evildoers would harm such a pristine state.

Occasionally, however, this illusion is shattered. "Some accident of life will deny us the privilege of avoidance," writes psychiatrist Donald Nathanson, a "ruthless foe" may strip us of our comforting self-deception.[59] The Vietnam War, for example, peeled away America's veneer of benevolence. Under such circumstances, an aggressive nation often presents itself as a victim to insulate itself from guilt and uphold its false image. While such an attempt was only partially successful for the United States after the Vietnam debacle, it nonetheless prevented the United States from accepting any genuine guilt. The Gulf War, however, enabled the United States to bury any lingering guilt from the Vietnam War in the sands of Desert Storm. Doubts about U.S. decency faded and America once again flexed its imperial muscles, while simultaneously celebrating its "kindler and gentler" role in world affairs.

On September 11, the privilege of avoidance was again challenged. Americans wondered why they hated us. Many observers asked what the United States might have done to incite such a vicious attack. If America is uncritically viewed as the victim of evil forces alone, there is no need to investigate how American military and economic dominance might have contributed to the attack. One's behavior and actions do not matter when you are the victim of an unprovoked attack, according to this framework. Regardless of U.S. support for "unspeakable" violence, according to the illusion, "September 11 changes everything." This sweeping dismissal of U.S. actions opens the way for the release of emotions associated with guilt projections. We are "good" and they are "bad." Therefore, as an innocent victim we have every right to punish "them" with a vengeance.

Indeed, the sudden loss of innocence and pride on September 11 mobilizes the desire to demonize others as outlined in this chapter. The underlying shame surfaces under such circumstances and is defended against in two main ways, the first is to denying any wrongdoing and project it onto one's enemies. The second avoidance mechanism entails assuming the role of the innocent victim, who must avenge such unprovoked assaults.

The earlier discussion regarding aggressive nations that split reality into good and evil to absolve themselves of guilt also serves as the foundation for perpetrators to portray themselves as victims. In most conflicts, violent nations view themselves as innocent victims of nefarious foes. The myth of good and evil, Baumeister notes, shields people from the reciprocal, shared causes of violence.[60] This dichotomy, then, enables aggressors to transform almost any attack upon itself as entirely undeserved. These assertions of victimhood, or what historian John Dower calls "victim consciousness" carry several benefits.[61] For one thing, it provides a potent avoidance mechanism, while generating sympathy. If a violent nation is seen as an injured victim, it frees it to pursue an expansionist agenda with much less scrutiny. Historians Omer Bartov, Atina Grossman and Mary Nolan observe in *Crimes of War*:

> Efforts at documentation invariably set off a competition to avoid being counted among the perpetrators and to secure one's place among the victims. Surely, one might object, even if the full circle of perpetrators may be hard to pinpoint with accuracy, the victims are an easily identifiable group.... But the politics of memory are precisely about contesting and confusing that seemingly self-evident category.... Those seen as perpetrators are most likely to insist that, on the contrary, they are victims.... This scramble reflects in part a simple desire to repress the consequences of one's own actions while dwelling on one's sufferings. In part it reflects a belief, held individually and collectively, that one's suffering and the suffering of one's nation were quantitatively and qualitatively greater than that of any others.[62]

In the following section, we shall see how the United States utilizes this victimhood model in its representations of the Vietnam War and the September 11 disaster to conceal its imperial agenda.

Many commentators have noticed the United States' attempt to depict itself as a victim after the failed Vietnam adventure. H. Bruce Franklin and Tom Engelhardt argue that the American prisoners of war narrative lends itself to America as the victim, a captive held hostage in dark jungles. Not only were U.S. soldiers victims of Communist abduction, but American diplomats were held hostage by a liberal media and bewildering war strategies. James C. Thomson, a State Department analyst in the Vietnam era, expresses an interesting variant on this victim mentality. In an otherwise thoughtful essay, Thomson wonders how "men of superior ability, sound training and high ideals" could create such misguided policy. It turns out that the "tired" policymaker, who was "short on sleep," fell victim to "confusion." As victims of fatigue, these superior leaders were unable to fulfill their "high ideals."[63] Thomson's description reflects a broader tendency to cast U.S. officials as victims rather than accomplices to an expansionist agenda.

Language surrounding the Vietnam conflict bears on this victimhood theme. For example, American leaders maintain that they defended against Communist aggression in Vietnam. Despite sending 500,000 troops to Indochina, U.S. strategists consider it a defensive engagement. This understanding turns the Vietnamese into invaders of their own country, while the United States was defending itself thousands of miles from its shores. As Martin Luther King, Jr. quipped, it requires a "sense of humor" to listen to the world's strongest nation discussing Communist aggression as it "drops thousands of bombs" on a tiny country. Nevertheless, it sounds "odd" to say that the United States invaded South Vietnam.[64] It appears strange because national images present the United States as a victim of Marxist aggression. On the one hand, the Vietnam War cannot be viewed as an instance of U.S. aggression insofar as it implies guilt. On the other hand, denying U.S. aggression preserves the victim myth, enabling the United States to see itself as an injured party after it destroyed a poor nation.

The Vietnam Veterans Memorial also illuminates U.S. suffering, yet downplays the Vietnamese victims. The monument, as important and valuable as it is in facilitating the healing process, also appears to help the perpetrator to feel like the victim. Incidents such as My Lai are rarely remembered, or are dismissed as tragic mistakes that are unrelated to the systematic plan to demoralize Vietnam. In fact, the National Park Service states that the memorial seeks to "separate the issue of sacrifice from U.S. policy on the war."[65] In this regard, the monument rightly laments the soldier's deaths, but incorrectly buries U.S. guilt. It asks visitors to divorce the soldier's suffering from the very policies that produced it. Few will remember that these policies led to some 2 million Vietnamese deaths as they mourn the loss of 58,000 U.S. service members. Remember that Lifton's studies found soldier's who accepted responsibility for the war's ugly details were able to steer their guilt into productive activities. While the memorial offers necessary relief to those who lost loved ones, it also encourages a national denial of responsibility. This denial hinders America's ability to heal the wounds of the war as it does not acknowledge the underlying sources of the grief, especially the psychological scar of harming others. That is to say, it hinders America's ability to see the Vietnamese as victims of U.S. aggression. By framing America's attention on its own pain and ignoring Vietnam's, the memorial risks serving as a national symbol that suppresses guilt. In subtle, yet potent ways, it tells an aggressive nation that it is really a victim.

However, the September 11 catastrophe dramatically transformed an aggressive nation into a hapless victim. The difference between September 11 and the Vietnam crisis is that the United States was clearly the victim of a verifiable attack in the former. And U.S. officials did not hesitate to take full advantage of this victim status.

The appeal of victimhood, in part, explains the inflated casualty figures following the disaster. New York Newsday declared that 6,500 were dead or presumed dead, an observation supported by Mayor Rudolph Giuliani, who announced that, "they slaughtered 5,000 6,000 people."[66] Reports surfaced that the mayor's office ordered that 6,000 body bags be sent to the site. It was later discovered that the actual death toll was near 3,000, a traumatic figure by any measure. The initial figures were exaggerated for several reasons, ranging from shock to confusion. It seems to me that these inflated numbers have something to do with the emotional satisfaction of victimhood. Victims are blameless and warrant support. The more one is victimized the more worthy one is of sympathy and support. The present study does not wish to suggest that officials deliberately inflated the death figures to generate sympathy, but that such exaggerations follow the natural tendency to seek sympathy after one is attacked. The most responsible and cautious leaders might minimize the damage to protect an already traumatized population. That U.S. leaders repeatedly reported massive death tolls is indicative of a nation searching for victimhood status.

The same observation holds for the remembrance of national traumas. Following the September 11 attacks, media reports and politicians ceaselessly compared it to Japan's surprise assault on Pearl Harbor in 1941. President Bush said that this nightmare reminded him of "one Sunday in 1941." The American Council of Trustees and Alumni, founded by Lynne Cheney, charged that some radical scholars failed to appreciate the severity of the attacks, urging them to recall that after Pearl Harbor there was a "swell of patriotism."[67] That September 11 was a catastrophe is beyond dispute. The point here is that the ongoing, persistent comparisons to other national calamities heightens the feeling that the United States is an innocent victim.

Although the United States is a victim, it is not an innocent one. A nation-state embroiled in cycles of violence is rarely a pure victim. Recall that the United States was an active party in several violent disputes at the time of the September 11 attacks, including sanctions in Iraq and the protection of Saudi Arabia's despotic rulers. Few innocent victims contribute to the killing of tens of thousands of Iraqis or defend Islamic extremists. To illustrate, the 1996 attack on the U.S. Air Force towers in Saudi Arabia, while unjustified, cannot be considered an attack upon an innocent victim. The military base protects violent rulers, serving as part of a global U.S. military program that aids autocratic regimes. To pretend that the United States is a pure victim when it operates under these conditions is a distortion.

What happened on September 11 also allows U.S. planners to distort the grief of those who perished. American leaders ignore their own violent provocations and co-opt the suffering of the true victims. U.S. strategists make the suffering of innocent citizens trapped in the crossfire between U.S. military violence and global terrorism their own. When the American Empire pretends it is a victim, it obfuscates the underlying causes behind the real victim's deaths. While President Bush believes that in our grief we have found our mission to destroy terrorism, many of the families of the September 11 victims disagree. They charge that the president appropriates their pain. Phyliss and Orlando Rodriguez, who lost their son in the World Trade Center, write that "our government is headed in the wrong direction of violent revenge.... It will not avenge our son's death. Not in our name." Amber Anderson, who lost her husband in the Pentagon attack, also complains that "angry rhetoric by some Americans, including our nation's leaders" provides "no comfort." She adds that the U.S. military response to the assaults does not bring justice to her husband's death. Likewise, Peggy Neff, who lost a loved one on September 11, chastises Bush for exploiting her agony. Pictures of Bush at the disaster site, used for a fundraiser, constitute, "the exploitation of an event that should not be exploited," according to Neff.[68] To be sure, when the United States presents itself as an innocent victim, it appropriates the suffering of these genuine victims.

Another example of converting the American Empire into a victim is Jennifer Roback Morse's essay, "Battered America." An analyst at the Hoover Institute, Roback assails critics of U.S. foreign policy for behaving like someone who tells a female victim of rape that "you must have provoked him."[69] It is a bit disingenuous to equate a global superpower to a rape victim. More troubling is that the United States supports groups that tolerate or practice rape, such as the Northern Alliance and Saudi Arabian rulers. Or, consider the Pentagon contractors who operated a sex ring in the Balkans with near impunity. This attempt to transform a hegemonic empire into an innocent rape victim once again confuses and conflates the perpetrators of violence with those who happen to get in the way of its international policies. Portraying a nation that has indirectly supported rapists across the globe as a "battered" woman may be overdrawn, but it fosters the perception that the United States is an innocent victim.

The "blame America first" label depends on this feeling of victimization. This ideological battle cry presupposes that the United States is an innocent victim and to suggest otherwise amounts to blame. One does not blame innocent victims and seek to find the causes as to why they may have been assaulted. Take, for instance, Americans for Victory over Terrorism (AVOT), who insist upon U.S. innocence. Echoing President Bush, AVOT argues that, "We are not a target for anything we have done, but because of who we are." Since it understands the United States as a victim, the group vows to "take to task" anyone who "blames America first,"[70] presumably those folks who suggest that there are tangible causes behind the attacks. Operating here is an empty slogan that promotes a "victimhood" mentality to guard against the possibility that the United States might provoke violence. Alas, victim mythology works to conceal the complicated, mutual causes of violence.

The American Council for Trustees and Alumni (ACTA) report, "Defending Civilization: How Our Universities Are Failing America and What

Can Be Done about It," perpetuates this victim motif. The essay warns that, "the message of much of academe was clear: BLAME AMERICA FIRST." Additionally, it approvingly quotes Lynne Cheney, a former board member at the defense industry conglomerate, Lockheed-Martin Marietta. She says that, "to say it is more important now [to study Islam] implies that the events of September 11 were our fault."[71] That studying Islam constitutes blaming America borders on paranoia, but it appears sensible to those who see America as a pure victim. A better understanding of Islamic and Islamic extremist's interaction with U.S. policymakers will quickly dispel the victimhood myth. Such an examination reveals the reciprocal causes of violence. Therefore, it is jettisoned as somehow "blaming" America.

It seems to me that individuals and organizations that interpret specific policy critiques as an all-encompassing attack on America's character are in the throes of shame. Recall that shame is the feeling that one's overall character is morally flawed, arising from the inability to accept guilt for particular transgressions. Rather than accept U.S. wrongdoing in the international arena, the blame America first sloganeers pervert basic analysis into a personal degradation of America. Such cognitive confusion obfuscates the simple observation that elite U.S. planners, who regularly fund Islamic warlords, are responsible for stimulating violence. Such an observation does not negate the achievements of the American people, who struggled for the enactment of the Bill of Rights, fair labor conditions and civil rights. The heroic energies of the U.S. people and the institutions that they forged are not under attack by those who criticize U.S. foreign policy. Elite planners are the ones under attack, and they deserve blame for promoting global violence. The blame America first label insulates these elite strategists from guilt; it relies on the illusion that they are being victimized rather than simply criticized.

In conclusion, subsuming the role of the victim is an effective strategy to avoid guilt. When combined with enduring myths regarding American greatness, the victimhood motif suffocates serious analysis. A major aim of this study is to unravel this defensive posture and pave the way for the acknowledgment of U.S. misdeeds in the global arena.

4

George W. Bush and the Resurrection of the Chosenness Syndrome after September 11: A Unique Challenge for Peace Education

> Bush's defense of the war on terrorism works largely through arche-
> typal association.... Ever since the myth of America as God's chosen
> nation ingressed into the collective unconscious of the American people,
> U.S. politics has been primed for saviors and sinners.
> — Critical educator Peter McLaren[1]

After the trauma of September 11, President Bush took full advantage of the nation's victimization and breathed new life into centuries-old chosenness discourse. For those who wanted to explore the connection of America's global role to the attacks, Bush marshaled all the components of the chosenness pathology to quell any serious inquiry. Images of the United States as God's chosen nation resonate all too neatly with Bush's personal feeling of salvation. Consider that in his autobiography, *A Charge to Keep*, Bush argued that "a divine plan ... supercedes all human plans." One dimension of God's plan, Bush confessed, was to save him from alcoholism. "God sent his son to die for a sinner like me," wrote Bush.[2] As he catapulted to the White House, Bush's individual sense of mission intersected with divinely inspired national narratives. "For all its flaws," Bush noted on the 2000 campaign trail, "I believe our nation is chosen by God and commissioned by history to be a model to the world."[3] Bush's brazen response to the September 11 catastrophe resurrected this national religion in an especially intense way. The emotionally charged moment generated collective feelings of fear, anger and bewilderment. Tragically, the thousands of buried corpses beneath the rubbish that was once the World Trade Center seemed to scream for a divine warrior to stand up for the good in the face of such unimaginable evil. George W. Bush appeared to hear those cries as he proclaimed that a "crusade" has commenced and the forces of good will destroy evil. Such grandiose rhetoric is understandable under the circumstances. Bush publicly reassured the nation that the "evildoers" will be defeated, while he privately connected his personal mission with the nation's destiny.

Many critics argue that Bush's crusader mentality is a crude brand of propaganda, merely the work of an insincere president attempting to rally support for an aggressive foreign policy. There is significant temptation for Bush to cater to conservative, evangelical Christians. Bush's adviser, Karl Rove, acknowledges that evangelicals and Bible-belt Christians constitute an important voting block for the 43rd president. Meanwhile, a *Time/CNN* poll finds that 59 percent of U.S. citizens believe that the events described in the Book of Revelation will eventually come to fruition, while 36 percent feel that the Bible is the literal word of God. George W. Bush has long been aware of these trends; he worked assiduously in his father's presidential campaign to gain the evangelical vote. That George W. Bush as a political creature attends to religious voters is incontestable. However, scholar E. J. Dionne, chair of the Pew Forum on Religion and Public Life, cautions that although some 70 percent of U.S. citizens prefer a religious president, 50 percent say that they distrust a president who overemphasizes religion.[4] Americans are a spiritual people, but there are limits they place on the extent to which religion should enter the public sphere.

This chapter does not attempt to determine if Bush's public faith is sincere or if his religious rhetoric merely panders to evangelical Christians. Instead, it examines Bush's rhetoric as part of what Galtung identifies as the national chosenness syndrome. Doug Wead, a Bush family friend associated with the evangelical Assemblies of God Church, says that Bush's faith is authentic, but "there's no question that it is also calculated."[5] It is nearly impossible to determine whether or not Bush's religious discourse is genuine. Bush's calculated use of religious metaphors largely revolves around enduring themes of chosenness. The blending of God and country is often a political move designed to foster patriotic attitudes, employed by both religious and secular politicians alike. What this means in terms of Bush's faith on an individual level is largely irrelevant. The Bush administration's endless war on terror presents the country's civil religion as a destructive, violent redeemer nation that threatens the future of the planet, and warrants fresh approaches to this epochal topic.

Although Bush's personal convictions are not the central object of the present study, a brief discussion of his background and faith is in order. Bush's religious discourse has moved U.S. civil religion back to the center of American politics and his personal faith forms part of this conversation. Diverse commentators have noted this resurgence of civil religion. *The American Prospect* writes that, "Like no president in recent memory, George W. Bush wields his Christian righteousness like a flaming sword." Likewise, the liberal *Progressive* magazine warns of Bush's "Messiah Complex," which "can no longer be denied." Bush supporters, on the other hand, celebrate this revitalization of the nation's religion, while expressing the chosenness motif. Thomas M. Freiling, editor of *George W. Bush on God and Country*, goes so far as to claim that the president has "given us a renewed sense of our divine providence." Stephen Mansfield, author of *The Faith of George W. Bush*, similarly welcomes the Bush administration's "sense of divine purpose that propels the present to meet the challenges of its time."[6]

Reports regarding America's alleged providential heritage have appeared in the *New York Times, Newsweek*, the *Village Voice*, the *Christian Science Monitor, Business Week, Time* and elsewhere. Documentaries on Bush and God have also examined the proper role of religion in U.S. politics. PBS's *Frontline* featured a detailed program on Bush's faith called *The Jesus Factor*. After Michael Moore's *Fahrenheit 9/11* gained tremendous box-office success in its condemnation of Bush's integrity, a group of Bush supporters released an alternative program, titled *George W. Bush: Faith in the White House*. Regardless of Bush's personal convictions, each of these reports indicate that U.S. civil religion entered the public arena in full force during Bush's presidency. George W. Bush and his supporters often articulate the distinctive features of this quasi religion, as outlined by Galtung and Bellah. While George W. Bush consistently combined faith and politics throughout his career, it became a toxic mixture following the attacks on the World Trade Center and the Pentagon. This section briefly examines Bush's personal and political background as the seed that sprouted into a chosenness syndrome following the 9/11 catastrophe.

George W. Bush: Chosen to Lead?

Bush's background enables us to better understand the man who "broaches spiritual issues with a frankness and conviction that is unprecedented in modern times."[7] George Walker Bush was born on July 6, 1946, in New Haven, Connecticut, where the senior Bush moved following the Second World War. A decorated navy veteran, George Herbert Walker Bush married Barbara Pierce in 1945 and moved to Connecticut to attend Yale University. Bush senior would eventually serve as a UN ambassador, CIA director, vice president and president, following in his father's footsteps, Prescott, who was a U.S. senator.

When George W. Bush was two, the family moved to Midland, Texas, where the family attended the First Presbyterian Church. They relocated to

Houston when Bush junior was in seventh grade and he served as an altar boy at an Episcopalian church, his father's denomination. In 1961, Bush junior, now fifteen years old, was sent to the prestigious Phillips Academy in Andover, Massachusetts. The school stressed Christian teachings and held a 7:50 A.M. chapel service that the younger Bush "generally resented."[8] The priming at Andover led to Bush's acceptance at Yale in 1964, the same year of the Gulf of Tonkin incident and escalation of the Vietnam War. Bush says that the college unrest of the 1960s did not occur at Yale during his tenure, and he generally avoided politics.[9] Instead, he joined the Delta Kappa Epsilon fraternity that gained a reputation for holding superior parties. According to some of his peers, Bush drank heavily and partied often. He nevertheless graduated Yale in 1968 with a degree in history and joined the Texas Air National Guard that same year.

His entrance into the guard may have something to do with the assault on America's sacred values at this time. Surely, the repeated revelations of U.S. misbehavior in Vietnam and at home toward African Americans captured the attention of G.W. Bush. In fact, he recognized the erosion of what this text identifies as civil religion. Bush calls the late 1960s "the end of an era of innocence," highlighting that he was "horrified" by the nation's brutality toward blacks.[10] Like many of his generation, Bush probably had little desire to serve in Vietnam to spread God-given freedom that was denied to a significant portion of his fellow citizens. It was, as Bush admits, "a confusing and disturbing time." He further expresses this bewilderment in his decision to join the military: "We all knew that something was fundamentally, frighteningly wrong.... My inclination was to support the government and the war until proven wrong, and that only came later, as I realized we could not explain the mission, had no exit strategy."[11] This apprehension may account for his less-than-enthusiastic decision to enter military service, choosing a cozy National Guard position rather the regular army. According to the *New York Times*, it is during this difficult national crisis that Bush family friends secured him a placement in the guard's "Champagne Unit." Former Speaker of the Texas House Ben Barnes reportedly testified under oath that he was approached by a Bush associate to get Junior into the 147th Texas Air National Guard. Much controversy surrounds Bush's service, but it is indisputable that Bush served in a unit that was unlikely to serve in Vietnam.[12] Were the challenges to American civil religion, or the nation's cherished values, intense enough at the time to dissuade Bush from fully supporting the war effort?

In October 1973 Bush was honorably discharged from the guard and entered Harvard Business School, where he graduated in 1975 with an M.B.A. He resettled in Midland, Texas, and married Laura Welch in 1977, a Methodist who graduated from Southern Methodist University.[13] The couple soon had twin daughters in 1981, whom they baptized at the First United Methodist Church, which Bush subsequently joined.[14] During these years, Bush engaged in an unsuccessful congressional bid in 1978 and worked in the oil industry, including his company, Arbusto Energy.[15] Throughout these years, Bush remained a heavy drinker who had trouble with self-control.

Two significant "turning points," however, steered Bush away from the bottle and toward God. At the family's vacation home in Kennebunkport, Maine, in 1985, Bush reports that he firmly recommitted his "heart to Jesus Christ." During a private walk with Reverend Billy Graham, the religious leader asked if Bush was right with God. He answered that he attended a Methodist Church, but soon confided that he was not right with God, but desired to be so. The encounter with Graham, Bush says, was "like planting a mustard seed," a clear reference to Mark 5:30, which explains that the Kingdom of God is a small seed but one that is nurtured by God's intervention into a wondrous gift. In spite of the moment of deliverance with Graham, Bush's salvation had not yet blossomed as he continued drinking heavily.[16]

A trip to Colorado Springs to celebrate the birthdays of a group of friends who all turned forty the same year was the final "turning point" for Bush.[17] During a jog the next morning, Bush suddenly pledged to himself that he would drink no more. Although not quite as intense as, say, Martin Luther King, Jr.'s "kitchen table" encounter with Jesus, this experience was an epiphany for Bush. From that moment on, Bush stopped drinking. The Graham meeting and the jogging revelation were "defining moments" for Bush, that is, "Through the love of Christ's life, I could understand the life-changing powers of faith," explained Bush.[18]

Bush returned to Midland a new man, determined to nurture the seed that Graham planted in his heart. He began reading the Bible frequently and joined a Bible study group with his friend Don Evans. George and Laura also remained quite active in the First Methodist Church, participating in James Dobson's Focus on the Family series, which Bush briefly notes in his autobiography.[19] Dobson deserves special mention as he exemplifies a rather intense variety of civil religion, one which borders on promoting a theocracy. The Focus on the Family Web site argues that "a fundamental responsibility of government is to punish those who do evil," as "the Bible teaches us that governments are responsible to bear the sword." Furthermore, "the Bible also teaches us what kind of laws governments should have."[20] That Bush mentions Dobson favorably in his autobiography is interpreted by many as pandering to the religious right. Bush's vague connection to this zealous group seems to add a sense of authenticity to his quasi-religious speeches and enables him to navigate America's civil religion with a certain degree of comfort. Brief references to "hard" Christians like Dobson might appeal to evangelical voters, but it is sufficiently vague to avoid offending "softer" churchgoers and nonbelievers.

University of Chicago religious scholar Bruce Lincoln suggests that Bush's religious discourse constitutes, "double coding." It signals to his evangelical base that he follows the Lord, yet remains subtle enough to evade secular cries that he violates the constitutional separation of church and state. Bush employs linguistic "winks and nudges," argues Lincoln. Journalist Ron Suskind similarly views Bush's religious parlance as a signaling system. Bush desires to signal to religious voters that he is godly, but in swing states he wants to remain appealing to more secular-oriented voters.[21] Bush may indeed be mindful of this religious signaling procedure. In private meetings with family friend and evangelical preacher Doug Wead, who tape recorded the conversations, Bush alluded to this coding system. "As you said," Bush told Wead as he prepared for a meeting with Christian leaders, "there are some code words. There are some proper ways to say things, and some improper ways." Bush does go on to say that he will tell the Christian leaders that he had accepted Christ as it was true.[22]

The point is not to analyze Bush's theological sincerity, but to illustrate the degree to which he handles religious talk with discreet care. Wead warned Bush that too many meetings with evangelicals might backfire; it may distance him from secular voters. Bush replied, "I am just going to have one," and it will not be public.[23] In this conversation with Wead, Bush paid special attention to how he would attract religious and nonreligious voters simultaneously. Such attention strongly suggests that Bush places much thought into his use of religion in the public sphere. Whatever one concludes about Bush's public religion, the present study suggests that it amounts to a skillful use of civil religion. It is pointed enough to attract messianic types, yet sufficiently opaque to gently awake deeper archetypes that provide comfort in perilous times.

In 1993, Bush ran for governor of Texas, where his balancing act of religion and politics experienced its first real test. Bush won a surprise victory in 1994 over the popular Democratic incumbent, Ann Richards. Bush began his inauguration "with a church service," selecting Charles Wesley's Methodist hymn, "A Charge to Keep I Have," for attendees to sing together. The hymn praised a "God to glorify," and "a calling to fulfill," and a call "to do my master's will."[24]

Bush certainly signaled that religion would be part of his political leadership. Driving the point home, Bush displayed a painting inspired by the poem in his office, which was loaned by a friend. In case there was any doubt, Bush distributed a memo in 1995 explaining to staff members that the hymn "epitomizes our mission," particularly that "we serve One greater than ourselves." In 2000, Bush again affirmed this duty in an official memorandum that designated June 10 as "Jesus Day," urging Texans "to follow Christ's example."[25] Such provocative declarations risk appearing overly devout, but as a state governor Bush's religion for the most part did not capture national attention.

It was not until Bush entered the 2000 presidential race that his religious leanings received national scrutiny. Bush's autobiography intimates that the decision to run for the Oval Office arose from a divine source. Just as America is chosen to lead, Bush was allegedly elected by God to become president. This realization first came to Bush during a sermon by the Reverend Marc Craig, and according to those in attendance, the minister suggested that Bush's political ascendancy was similar to Moses' leadership. Craig noted that America was starved for leaders, people with strong values. Moses was the exemplar for the kind of leader that America craves, the minister proclaimed. Moses was hesitant, telling God that he is not a "good speaker." But, God called him to liberate the Israelites from Egyptian bondage and there was no turning back. Bush's mother told her son that the pastor was talking to him. Bush seemed to agree, having written that "the sermon spoke directly to my heart."[26]

Notice that Bush does not overtly state that God selected him to lead the free world. Comparing oneself to Moses would be pompous, even fanatical. Bush instead relays the pastor's message and his mother's belief that it was meant for George W. This move appears to be another example of Bush's signaling. It illustrates to right-wing Christians that Bush is a faithful servant while avoiding the appearance of being a megalomaniac. In fact, Paul Kengor, who is an informed observer of Bush's faith, notes that many religious conservatives believe that God elected Bush to exterminate terrorism.[27] Bush publicly walks the tightrope of religious zealotry in a secular democracy, usually offering subtle hints that God chose him to lead. Privately, however, Bush has made some rather grandiose claims about his leadership. Richard Land, president of the Southern Baptist Convention's Ethics and Liberty Commission, claims that a group of religious leaders met with Bush at the governor's mansion the day he was inaugurated for his second term. "And among the things he said to us," Land recalls, is that "I believe that God wants me to be president."[28] Elsewhere, a senior Bush administration official told the *New York Times* that Bush was asked if his leadership was part of God's design and Bush responded that, "I accept the responsibility."[29]

To be sure, Bush conflates faith, not simply with politics, but state power. In this way, Bush's religion lends itself to a destructive "Constantinian Christianity." Consider that Jesus, who Bush credits with saving him, was crucified by the Roman state apparatus. Jesus did not seek Roman office; instead, he traveled with the downtrodden. The difference between Bush's faith in this regard and a mature civil religion is genuine humility. No rational person can conclude that suggesting that God chose you to lead history's most powerful nation-state constitutes humility.

On the campaign trail, Bush's theology immediately drew the attention of the media. In December 1999, Bush was asked at a debate in Des Moines, Iowa, about the political philosopher who most influenced him. "Christ," Bush answered, "because he changed my heart." When asked to elaborate, Bush said that it would be hard to explain.[30] Whatever we conclude about Bush's answer, we can see that from his start in national politics Bush was sowing the seeds of his potentially explosive civil religion. Like his predecessors, Bush hoped to rally the nation behind him by way of theological cues that arouse deeper archetypes.

While we noted that the modern language of civilization is a vehicle for chosenness metaphors, the World Trade Center catastrophe revived both secular and religious vocabularies of superiority with increased vigor. "The enemies of civilization," Bush immediately responded, "attacked not just our people, but freedom loving people everywhere in the world." Consequently, Bush, who considers Jesus the philosopher who most influenced him, launched a "crusade" against the perpetrators. Advisers worried that talk of a crusade was too inflammatory, but they did not forsake religious metaphors. If September 11 did not constitute a crusade, it did ignite a "monumental struggle of good versus evil," and "good will prevail," the president informed us. Within hours of the attack, Bush instantly surmised that an epic conflict had commenced. Here Bush impersonated an Old Testament prophet, having articulated the dichotomy of "us" versus "them" alongside the Manichean assumption that the United States represents all that is good in the world.[31]

Equally revealing is Bush's emphasis on an Armageddon-like battle, a "monumental struggle" against "evildoers." Another example of Bush's nod to apocalyptic narratives involves the "Battle Hymn of the Republic." It is widely acknowledged that the Civil War song was inspired by the Book of Revelation. Before President Bush's remarks at a memorial service for the victims of the Pentagon attacks, a military chorus sang the battle hymn. The crowd reacted by standing and raising flags over their heads. It is rather curious that a war song, a battle cry, was performed at a memorial service. The lyrics state: "Mine eyes have seen the glory of the coming of the Lord: He is trampling out the vintage where the grapes of wrath are stored.... Let the Hero ... crush the serpent ... he has sounded forth the trumpet that shall never call retreat.... God is marching on." The hymn follows Revelation's theme of suffering, followed by a confrontation with evil that culminates in victory. Bush's speech also followed this script. He told the crowd of some 20,000 that, "The wound to this building will not be forgotten.... We have awakened to the evil of terrorism and we are determined to destroy it. We will continue until justice is delivered."[32] This allusion to revelation by way of the hymn was not an isolated event. On the sixth month anniversary of the

September 11 catastrophe, the Harlem Boys Choir performed the battle hymn at a speech by Bush in Washington, D.C.[33] The Harlem Boys Choir again performed the religious war song at the 2004 Republican National Convention.

The repeated use of the "Battle Hymn of the Republic" illustrates how U.S. civil religion merges the American experience with biblical myths. It brings the epic story of God's holy war against evil onto the U.S. battlefield. Several scholarly studies have noted that Armageddon literature is Western civilization's most spectacular example of good defeating evil; it is the "cosmic conflict" that reminds us that freedom prevails. In Western history, the lure of a cosmic holy war has seduced the masses at least since the medieval Crusades. More recently, James Carroll's important work, *Crusade: Chronicles of an Unjust War*, provides details into the Bush administration's use of this religious imagery.

Was Bush entranced by this eternal imagery after September 11? While answering a reporter's question on the south lawn of the White House just days after the attack, Bush asserted that, "This crusade, this war on terrorism is going to take a while."[34] White House aids immediately downplayed the remark as a broad statement that was in no way intended to convey a holy war. Others came to the president's defense, saying it was a knee-jerk response that should not be overblown. However, this is a president who has asserted that he makes "gut" decisions, relying on "instinct." Are we to believe, then, that Bush's "gut" tells him to wage a great holy war? Despite the fanfare over the crusader line, Bush again depicted the war on terror as a crusade two weeks later.[35] The more restrained Colin Powell also mentioned crusade: "No civilized nation dare not be part of this crusade against the evil of terrorism," the former secretary of state announced at the Kennan Institute. When meeting with Pakistan's President Musharraf, Powell said, "We need you as part of this campaign, this crusade."[36]

On the one hand, we should not overemphasize the administration's use of the word crusade. Neither Bush nor Powell adopts a millennial outlook. On the other hand, the term stirs the historical imagination. Crusade is unambiguously associated with holy war; the word itself comes from the Latin *cruce signati*, namely, those stamped with the Cross. Crusades are the well-known series of wars of the Roman Catholic Church against Muslims (and Jews) to capture the holy city Jerusalem. Pope Urban II issued a call for the first crusade in 1096 with apocalyptic overtones. Religious scholars argue that the pontiff did not foresee the coming of the Lord or view the Crusades as the literal unfolding of the Book of Revelation. Rather, the pope drew upon a legendary narrative to rally the European masses. *Deus Vult, Deus Vult*, or "God wills it, God wills it," was the Crusader's slogan. That Bush and Powell selected a term with all this historical baggage can not be ignored. As

Bush's former speechwriter David Frum puts it, "war has made him ... a crusader after all."[37]

We cannot blame Bush for relying on the durability and vitality of chosenness theology. Such extravagant expressions are cathartic and emotionally satisfying for a nation beset by disaster. People crave heroes who can articulate their frustration in moments of despair. There is a "wish that the president will be a strong father figure," the *New York Times* observes approvingly.[38] The president's discussion of good defeating evil is akin to a father reassuring his children that we shall prevail because God protects and favors us. The collective allure of the chosenness idiom empowers Bush to assume the role of the "hero," who righteously defends the bereaved.

The challenge for peace education is to funnel this deep-seated energy in nonviolent directions. One simple strategy is to challenge the slogan "war on terrorism," which instead should be labeled a moment of genuine defense and rebuilding, as several peace educators have indeed noted. The labels "war" and "national security" must be replaced with "mutual security" and "economic justice," as these peace researchers point out. And heroic energy can be spent on rebuilding America's foreign policy, with authentic steps toward a defensive military, rather than an aggressive one that failed to prevent the September 11 attacks in the first place.

While the American public finds comfort in their leader's self-righteous mythology, they are not warmongers. There are a broad range of opinions in the United States concerning its place in global affairs. We have seen how a catastrophe arouses national myths, but other emotions that lend themselves to peaceful solutions also exist. "The drumbeat for war," reports the *New York Times* shortly after September 11, "is barely audible on the streets of New York." The paper found that "even those directly affected by the destruction of the World Trade Center," are calling for nonviolent alternatives, but many are afraid "to buck the tidal wave of patriotism."[39] These silent peace advocates might speak out if leaders espoused nonviolent visions rather than apocalyptic ones. Even during times of crises, people crave peaceful metaphors. Hence, peace educators must help us to develop the moral imagination that kindles our capacities for decency, a topic that is fully explored in chapter seven. Seemingly antiquated notions that the United States is the embodiment of God's divine providence remain central to U.S. planners, but they are hardly insurmountable.

Friends and close advisers to the president report that the events of September 11 brought Bush "face to face with his life's mission," one which parallels the "country's destiny," according to a senior counsel. For Bush, the war on terror is a sign of his mission and the nation's destiny, it is "civilization's fight" and "God is not neutral between them." Remember that Bush says that he "accepts responsibility" for leading the free world as it is "part of God's plan." This messianic zealotry led to the *New York Times's* conclusion that Bush sees the war in "grand, even Manichean terms." Bush's remarks bear every indication of self-righteous theology. His "life's mission" is part of "God's plan" to embark upon an epic struggle against evil. It seems to me Bush borders on seeing himself as a modern-day Moses, someone who "restructures the world towards freedom."[40]

That segments of the Israeli press celebrate this crass comparison bears on the dangers that the chosenness pathology holds for international affairs. Bush's biblical stance, according to the Israeli newspaper *Yediot Achronot*, produces a "positive gut feeling" for Israel, making the United States its "special ally" against "mutual enemies."[41] What the Israeli periodical welcomes is the special connection between two nations that share the same Western Judeo-Christian God. The goal here is not to quarrel over Israel's theological claims to its land, but to illustrate how the chosenness archetype stimulates violence. No rational person can conclude that Israel's providential covenant attenuates violence in the region. This religious chauvinism, and similar ones promulgated by Israel's opponents, serves only to perpetuate animosity and attack. If Israel's claim of divine election teaches us anything about interstate conflict, it is that such views generate aggression. Bush's religious rhetoric resonates with those embroiled in a messianic confrontation, which underscores the pitfalls of this self-righteous enterprise.

Regardless of the danger of depicting Israel and the United States as religious and political partners, William Bennett aggressively promotes the comparison. In his book, *Why We Fight*, the former secretary of education argues that the two nations are blessed by "the same beneficent God." Remaining loyal to Israel in their "still unfinished confrontation with evil" amounts to "keeping faith with ourselves," Bennett says. These spiritual partners have special duties as they are "entrusted with the fate of liberty in the world." Hence, the war on terrorism is "all about" the "survival of liberty." Since freedom itself is at stake, we should not criticize Bush's "old-fashioned" biblical language, but embrace its "moral clarity," argues Bennett. On the one hand, Bennett is sensitive to the delicate nature of these symbols, noting that readers might find them old-fashioned. On the other hand, he carelessly promotes them. Bennett praises Bush, whom he labels a "cowboy president," precisely because he revitalizes the "language of good and evil," clearly articulating that America will rid the world of "evildoers."[42] Just as cowboys took on the Indians and God's people destroyed the heathens, the United States will stamp out the "enemies of civilization." Although Bennett's rhetorical strategy sounds a bit antiquated, it is consistent with almost every post–World War II president.

From the Truman doctrine to the Bush doctrine, the myth of chosenness survives. Some sectors of the knowledge industry also peddle the imagined sense of American destiny. Dinesh D' Souza's curiously titled book,

What's So Great about America, offers a sophisticated version of this perspective. A former Reagan administration official, D'Souza, explains that America was not only "founded on Divine Right," but also improved the very notion. Following the American Revolution, divine right was "transferred" from monarchs to the masses, creating a "new kind of human being." As a result, the United States developed into the "greatest" civilization on earth, fully prepared for the task of "redeeming humanity from a global menace" in the twenty-first century.[43] D'Souza follows the familiar theme that U.S. warfare spreads God's democratic ideal.

Notions regarding U.S. decency and benevolence informed much of the public discussion in the immediate aftermath of the destruction of the World Trade Center. The Bush administration's use of civil religion helped to mobilize public opinion in this renewed time of intense patriotism. But the demons of empire would slowly become exorcised as Bush's bellicose foreign policy raised questions about America's role in the world.

5

The War on "Terrorism," Iraq and the Challenges for Peace Education

Despite repeated statements since 11 September that it remains committed to international law and standards, the U.S. government is failing to match its actions to this rhetoric following the attacks on New York and Washington.

— Amnesty International[1]

If there is one overarching goal they share, it is the overthrow of what Islamists call the "apostate" regimes: the tyrannies of Egypt, Saudi Arabia, Pakistan, Jordan, and the Gulf states. They are the main targets of the broader Islamist movement, as well as the actual fighter groups. The United States finds itself in the strategically awkward — and potentially dangerous — situation of being the longstanding prop and alliance partner of these authoritarian regimes. Without the U.S. these regimes could not survive.

— Report of the Defense Science Board, September 2004, a federal advisory committee established to provide independent advice to the Secretary of Defense.[2]

The heinous act of terrorism on September 11, 2001, forever changed life as we've known it. It has made peace education more vital than ever.

— Cora Weiss, Hague Appeal for Peace, Global Campaign for Peace Education.[3]

Many pundits joined Bush in turning to the image of America as God's nation after the attacks on the World Trade Center and the Pentagon. We have seen how mainstream political analysts in the United States wished to ignore analysis concerning the United States' reputation for eroding human rights that was detailed in Chapter 2, arguing instead that it was somehow rendered irrelevant by the horrific acts of September 11, 2001. To recall these abuses was akin to "blaming America first" and served only to shore up support for international terrorism, we were told. Only the forces of evil would attack the world's bastion of liberty, or so the narrative goes. True, the ugly and earth-shattering events of September 11 forever changed the United States. While September 11 changed the physical and political landscape of America, it in no way absolves the country's responsibility for eroding human rights. The Defense Policy study above indicates that there is a connection between the U.S. disregard for human rights and the anger of Islamists who target the country. Moreover, the Defense Science Board study admits that "they do not hate us for our values, but because of our policies."[4] It is precisely those policies that lead to the repeated violation of human rights by the world's remaining superpower that contributes to cycles of violence.

This chapter documents how the Bush administration's war on terror exacerbates violence. It should be said again that the September 11 attacks were monstrous and without any justification. Peace education can discuss the causes of violence without excusing that violence. Like many acts of political aggression, these presumably incomprehensible attacks carry historical causes. American peace educators are in a unique position to evaluate these actions and offer nonviolent alternatives that create genuine security. Peace education can offer a proper understanding of U.S. foreign policy while creating appropriate curricular materials that enable students to grasp such politically charged subjects without instigating adversarial debates. One way to accomplish this task is to evaluate the military alliances of the U.S. government over the past two decades that many critics find contribute to cycles of violence. Tracing recent American policy enables peace educators to underscore how military strategies do not prohibit terrorism or provide lasting security. For this contentious pedagogical strategy to work, it must occur alongside an exploration into why foreign policy issues raise such powerful emotions in American citizens. Chapter 3 suggested that introducing emotions such as guilt into conversations regarding foreign policy may sometimes open channels of communication. In chapter 7 we explore how constructive metaphors might enable peace educators to affirm that which is valuable and worthy in the American tradition alongside our critique of U.S. policy.

The following arguments are offered to construct a concept of critical peace education as a form of "nonviolent tension" by way of critiquing how U.S. policy contributes to global aggression. What follows is directed at peace educators. As such, it presents a strong argument against the Bush administration's foreign policy. This approach is designed to expand the narrative framework of U.S. interventionism. In a classroom setting, responsible educators would likely proceed a bit more carefully than the review in this chapter in their presentations of U.S. diplomacy. However, peace scholars in their writings and activism must be willing to engage in sharp critiques of U.S. policy if they wish to reduce violence. Educators should counter what Henry Giroux labels the "pedagogy of terrorism" that shuts down democratic practices. "Educators have an important role to play in making their voices heard both in and outside the classroom as part of an effort to articulate a vibrant and democratic notion of the social in a time of national crisis," Giroux reminds us. Peace educators can help to "create the conditions for debate and dialogue over the meaning of September 11" and the war on terror.[5] For those critics tempted to equate this analysis with providing "aid and comfort" to the enemy, recall that it was U.S. policymakers who led the Islamic extremists to assemble in the first place and continue to support some of the world's most feared and hated dictators and warlords. The following is an invitation for discussion and debate regarding recent U.S. international behavior.

Indeed, this ongoing support for violent states and groups has made peace education more vital than ever. Evaluating recent U.S. policy enables peace educators to underscore how violent military strikes do not provide lasting security. When we compare U.S. military policies with peaceful alternatives, it elucidates the supremacy of nonviolent options. Instead of bellicose measures that contribute to threats and hostilities, this chapter points to practical alternatives that are more likely to provide both security and peace. "When you look at the shock of 9/11," former U.S. Army colonel Andrew Bacevich observes, "it's really remarkable that there was virtually no debate about plausible alternative responses."[6] Finally, this chapter argues that an effective approach to peace education must foster a civic dialogue about U.S. militarism and alternatives to global war, with special emphasis on the U.S. invasion of Iraq.

Peace Education Is Not Indoctrination

Civic dialogue in the United States was temporarily stifled following the September 11 attack. Those concerned with accuracy were often accused of being biased or "unbalanced." Consider the following personal anecdote, which illustrates how demands for balance often obfuscate open discussion, an essential feature of democracy. Before the United States invasion of Iraq in March 2003, the author was chastised after a public lecture by one community member for bias. A comment that it was unlikely that Iraq possessed WMD that constituted a threat to the United States was derided as "lefty, anti–Americanism," by an irate audience member. This person demanded a more balanced presentation, one which took into account all sides. The Bush administration's own teams, under David Kay and Charles Deufler, eventually reported that Iraq had no weapons of mass destruction. When the author opined that Iraq likely did not have weapons of mass destruction in March 2003, the CIA had already reported in October 2002 that Iraq "probably does not yet have nuclear weapons." Mohamed ElBaredi, a director at the International Atomic Energy Agency, publicly announced that the agency had not located any evidence that Iraq advanced its weapons program.[7] A so-called balanced analysis in early 2003 would demand that the author include at least some level of government deception, such as a plagiarized British report that Iraq could launch WMD in days. Stating that Iraq probably did not pose a threat to the United States in March 2003 was an accurate assessment, but one that became obscured by the call for balance and countervailing views. Should one call Osama bin Laden a murderous villain, will those calling for balance demand that one include alternative analysis from Al Qaeda to insure "balance"? Peace educators should not bludgeon students with critical facts, but a fetish for balance is not always the solution. Some degree of contrasting views is important in classroom analysis and for promoting critical thinking among students, but we should not jettison accuracy altogether in the search for balance. More importantly, educators should facilitate bonds of trust and a safe classroom environment so that alternative views can be expressed without hesitation or fear.

Ironically, those who manage the war system have little regard for balance. Take, for instance, a news story that featured an Iraqi-American saying, "Thank you, Bush. Thank you, U.S.A." It turns out it was produced by the U.S. State Department, a sample of pre-packaged news disseminated by the Bush administration to media outlets, sometimes with reporters working "under false names." According to the *New York Times*, the Bush administration spent $254 million on public relations contracts during its first term. Following the 9/11 tragedy, the Bush administration formed the "Office of Broadcasting Services," a State Department agency that released favorable news stories. The unit fed the media news stories that were "widely distributed" and picked up by major news agencies such as the *Associated Press* and *Reuters* and then sent out for local broadcasting. These reports, among other things, sought to promote "American achievements in Afghanistan and Iraq and reinforcing the administration's rationale for the invasions." The Government Accounting Office found that in certain instances the government "news" stories were created "to be indistinguishable from news stories produced by the private sector television news organizations." Another agency, the Army and Air Force Hometown News Service, disseminated "news" that reached 41 million American households. In these stories, reporters are not identified by their military titles. "If we put a rank on there," the unit's deputy director admits, "they're not going to put it on the air." The administration distributed a variety of stories to support its programs. One feature of these reports was that they frequently portrayed "interviews" with administration officials, but "questions are scripted and answers rehearsed." The U.S. Government Accountability Office suggests that government disseminated news segments appear to constitute "covert propaganda."[8]

The so-called liberal media ran these stories repeatedly, reports that excluded critics and alternative views. At least part of this effort has "been judged to have been illegal" in the words of the Government Accountability Office. Such behavior has led to a Senate Resolution 266, "to stop taxpayer funded government propaganda."⁹ The case of conservative commentator Armstrong Williams drew attention to the administration's propensity to influence the media. Apparently, Williams was paid $240,000 by the administration to promote its No Child Left Behind education policy. Williams, described by the *Washington Post* as "one of the most recognizable conservative voices in America," appeared on CNN, CNBC, and "as a regular guest" on National Public Radio, but did not disclose that he was being paid by the Bush administration. His biography on the "Right Side" Web site explained that William's offered "an independent view."¹⁰

Part of the problem that is relevant to this study is that the Bush administration compromised the integrity and independence of a highly visible commentator to promote a major education initiative, No Child Left Behind. Many critics questioned some of the provisions, such as Section 9528, "Armed Forces Recruiter Access to Students and Student Recruiting Information." Under this clause, school districts must allow military recruiters "access to secondary school students names, addresses, and telephone listings." The military once again gains access to our children. According to a U.S. Department of Education publication, the purpose of No Child Left Behind is to "improve student achievement and close achievement gaps."¹¹ Mandating school districts to provide the military with student records has little bearing on improving educational achievement. Equally disconcerting is that the National Education Association actively criticized the No Child Left Behind act and the group was derided by former education secretary Rod Paige as a "terrorist organization."¹² These attacks coupled with paid commentators such as Williams surely limit the possibility of an honest and open exchange about No Child Left Behind and its link to militarism.

Williams apologized for an apparent conflict of interest, adding that he believed in such policies long before he had been paid. One wonders what the reaction would be toward an op-ed writer promoting socialism, who received payments from Castro, noting that s/he believed in Marxism long before Castro wrote him/her checks for such favorable coverage. Armstrong is hardly an isolated case as the Government Accounting Office report indisputably reveals a massive effort on the part of the Bush administration to flood the media with biased, favorable stories. All of this propaganda contributes to what Michael Apple, professor of Educational Policy Studies at the University of Wisconsin, calls a "hidden curriculum of compulsory patriotism," which works to silence dissent.¹³

There is a long history of American schools being used as a conduit for social control. One manifestation of this social control is when schools are employed in times of crisis to induce patriotism and service to the industrial order. Joel Spring's *Education and the Corporate State* and David Nasaw's *Schooled to Order: A Social History of Public Schooling in the United States* stand out among the many works that have demonstrated the link between industrial capitalism and education as a means to promote the "American way of life." In the early twentieth century, sociologist Thorstein Veblen worried that the modern university was not free from "vainglorious patriotism," and the community was "divided — between patriotism in the service of the captains of war, and commerce in the service of the captains of finance." According to his biographer, John Dewey similarly believed that American schools tilted heavily in the direction of indoctrination, particularly troubling was a "narrow nationalism under the name of patriotism, and with reference to economic needs."[14] Both historically, and more recently, the American public sphere has been assaulted with a hidden curriculum to induce support for the state. There are, of course, critiques of the state that help to maintain democracy in the public sphere.

Critical peace educators must work diligently to uncover this hidden curriculum as well as many other abuses so that we can have an honest public dialogue regarding the war on terrorism that was launched in October 2001 with the bombing of Afghanistan.

Liberating Afghanistan? Uncovering the Hidden Curriculum of Patriotism

The Bush administration's war on terrorism first targeted Afghanistan's Taliban leadership, Islamic extremists known for their suppression of women and basic human rights. Recall, however, that U.S. leaders aided the Taliban during the Cold War to fight the Soviet Union. A State Department Report admits that the mujahideen were "Poorly armed at first," but "began receiving substantial assistance from the U.S."[15] This aid contributed to Afghanistan becoming a "training ground for international terror," the *Toronto Globe and Mail* reports.[16]

After the end of the Cold War, the United States continued to support reactionary elements inside Afghanistan. This support was, in part, connected to a proposed pipeline project in the region during the late 1990s. Elsewhere I have written:

> The *Economist* reports that the doctrine of jihad was fading in the Muslim world when the U.S. funded the mujahideen militants, including money for Osama bin Laden's training camps. It turns out that bin Laden was "central to the recruitment of the mujahideen" for America's campaign against Moscow.... Equally striking are the United States' actions after the end of the Cold War. When the former holy warrior Mullah Omar began solidifying power in 1995, border nations worried. Ultra-conservative, intolerant regimes tend to raise eye-

brows. Fearing the Taliban's threat to stability in South Asia, Russian president Boris Yelstin requested a summit of the Commonwealth Independent States (CIS). Surprisingly the U.S. did not see the Taliban as a danger. The "Taliban movement," noted Robin Raphel, assistant secretary of state for South Asian affairs, "expressed support for a peaceful settlement" among "factional leaders." Acting State Department spokesperson, Glyn Davies, reinforced this ill-fated position, saying that the U.S. found "nothing objectionable" in the Taliban's Islamic rule. Here was the U.S.'s chance to clean up the debacle that it created with the mujahideen; instead it declared the Taliban a potential arbiter of peace.

Unocal, an American oil corporation, also considered the Taliban a "positive development" in 1996. While Unocal later changed its position, their initial response provided legitimacy to an illegitimate power. A stable Taliban was part of a broader plan by the U.S. and multinational petroleum companies to run pipelines through South Asia. Respected journalist Ahmed Rashid reports that U.S. support for the Taliban up to 1997 intensified because of its willingness to back the Unocal project. When the Taliban was unable to deliver the expected stability for the pipeline project, the U.S. reversed its position toward the Afghan regime. Feminists, led by Mavis Leno, comedian Jay Leno's wife, simultaneously pressured the Clinton administration to denounce the Taliban's grossly sexist practices. By 1997, Unocal retreated due to public pressure, but privately maintained ties with Afghanistan. From 1997–99 Unocal awarded $1.8 million to the Center for Afghanistan Studies at the University of Nebraska. The center established a school in Afghanistan, where it taught its students how to build pipelines. A Taliban delegation also visited the Texas home of Unocal's vice president, Marty Miller, who spoke before a Senate committee on the benefits of a South Asia pipeline.[17]

Scores of journalists have uncovered these petroleum deals. It is now widely reported that Hamid Karzai, selected as Afghanistan's "interim" president in 2001, once had ties to a consulting firm that engaged in business with the firm of Unocal. Zalmay Khalilzad, a U.S. ambassador to Afghanistan in 2001 and later Iraq, also reportedly had a connection to Unocal and published an article in the *Washington Post* that encouraged U.S. cooperation with the Taliban. On the eve of the Afghan pipeline negotiations, Khalilzad wrote that:

> The war has been ... an obstacle to building pipelines to bring Central Asian oil and gas to ... world markets.... It is time for the United States to reengage.... The Taliban does not practice the anti–U.S. style of fundamentalism practiced by Iran.... We should use as a positive incentive the benefits that will accrue to Afghanistan from the construction of oil and gas pipelines.... These projects will only go forward if Afghanistan has a single authoritative government.[18]

Khalilzad, like many U.S. officials in the 1990s, supported engagement with the Taliban. It is not unreasonable to conclude that U.S. strategists paid greater attention to petroleum rights than national security in this instance. Khalilzad went so far as to say that the Taliban did not practice "anti–U.S. style fundamentalism," yet the second Bush administration still awarded Khalilzad an important diplomatic post in its war against terror. The

United States continues to misjudge its alliance partners in Afghanistan, a gross miscalculation that requires careful scrutiny and consideration of alternatives.

Specific information about the Northern Alliance can help peace educators to illustrate the problems of military solutions. In the war against Afghanistan, the United States turned to a group that the Western media routinely calls the Northern Alliance, but which is more properly known as the United Islamic Front for the Salvation of Afghanistan. The United Front was established by former mujahideen fighters, such as Burhanuddin Rabbani. The International Committee of the Red Cross, Human Rights Watch and other respected agencies have documented the United Front's penchant for recruiting child soldiers, rape and summary executions. The United States offered covert support, ammunition and logistical support and appointed an ambassador to the renegade group.[19] Ismail Khan, who was affiliated with the United Front, was considered "an appealing person ... thoughtful and self-confident," by former defense secretary Donald Rumsfeld. The U.S.–led coalition forces backed Khan's group in their successful defeat of the Taliban. Khan assumed control of Herat, where this "appealing" and "thoughtful" person ruled as a warlord. According to human rights groups, Khan ruled Herat in ways similar to the Taliban insofar as there were prohibitions against government criticism, restrictions on the press as well as reports of political arrests and torture. "Physical assault with thorny branches ... to more elaborate and severe torture techniques, such as hanging upside down, whipping and shocking with electric wires," occurred throughout Herat. Ismail Khan had ordered some of the beatings, in one instance he "struck a prisoner and ordered him to be tortured," writes Human Rights Watch.[20] Just as Khalilzad misread the Taliban as a group that did not practice anti–U.S. terror, Rumsfeld seemed to misread Khan's political style.

Administration supporters would have us believe that these unhealthy alliances were worth the price of freedom. The United States delivered successful elections to Afghanistan in 2004, the nation drafted a new constitution, and President Karzai discarded Khan from a government post that same year. On the surface, it appeared as if the U.S.–led coalition accomplished its mission following news reports regarding this "Afghan miracle." Mehmooda Shekiba of the Revolutionary Association of the Women of Afghanistan challenges this mainstream account. She bemoaned the systematic fraud in the elections, claiming that the number of voters was far lower than reported. Moreover, "Most of the Afghan Ambassadors, governors and secretaries," she wrote, "are affiliated with the [Northern Alliance] mafia."[21] Human rights groups confirmed at least some of Shekiba's charges, noting that several candidates were linked to war crimes and human rights violations and that there was fear of local warlords throughout the country.[22]

Iraq, Bush and Chosenness

The worsening situation in Afghanistan was overshadowed in the West by the U.S. invasion of Iraq. The justifications for the war were related in part to the chosenness syndrome. Dubbing the mission Operation Iraqi Freedom and with battle plans under the name Operation Plymouth Rock, the Bush team pledged to liberate Iraq. Redemptive, even apocalyptic, discourse permeated the early stages of Operation Iraqi Freedom. The administration presented itself as a global crusader that would "liberate" oppressed Iraqis, who were terrorized by the demonic Saddam Hussein. In the confrontation with Iraq, the president behaved more like an all-powerful and all-knowing deity than a leader of a nation among nations. Bush's rhetoric resurrected apocalyptic scenarios, biblical distinctions of good versus evil and integrated them with the United States' duty to spread God-given liberties.

Bush initially cast the growing confrontation with Iraq as a doomsday scenario. On the eve of war, Bush's televised speech in March 2003 warned that terrorists with mass destruction weapons threatened the world. "The danger is clear," Bush argued, "the terrorists could fulfill their stated ambitions and kill thousands or hundreds of thousands of innocent people in our country." "Before this day of horror can come," Bush promised, "this danger will be removed." If the United States does not "tear down the apparatus of terror," and "evil men," we will witness "destruction of a kind never before seen on this earth." Bush concluded with his familiar refrain: "may God *continue* to bless America" (italics mine).[23]

The crisis in Iraq seemed to embody biblical proportions for Bush, or at least the administration wished to make it appear that it did. Bush piously warned the U.S. public of imminent doom. Bush not only promised a preemptive strike against Iraq to halt this potential nuclear nightmare, but he also avowed to regenerate the misguided country. Just as God in the Book of Revelation split apart Babylon to renew it, Bush sought to "tear down the apparatus of terror" and "build a new Iraq."[24] Putting aside that ancient Babylon was located in current-day Iraq, Bush equated U.S. military prowess to a religious redemption after he sensed a victory was on the horizon. In sermonic fashion, Bush declared an end to major combat operations from the USS *Abraham Lincoln* in May 2003. Quoting the prophet Isaiah, Bush thundered, "To the captives come out — and to those in darkness be free."[25] More U.S. soldiers have died since Bush supposedly set the captives free and the war rages on, yet Bush appears to be blinded by his missionary vision.

Remember that the United Nation's weapons inspectors and skeptical allies challenged Bush's initial doomsday picture. Many felt that Iraq's weapons program was a remote threat. Bush confronted these nonbelievers at the UN headquarters in a fatherly, perhaps godly tone, insisting that, "the purposes of the United States should not be doubted."[26] A nation anointed by God cannot be hampered by the UN as U.S. morals are infallible and not subject to international adjudication, according to the chosenness motif. Bush does not place is faith in the United Nations, but rather "in a loving God behind all of life and all of history," as stated in his January 2003 State of the Union address.

Complicating matters, General William Boykin presented slide shows of Saddam Hussein with announcements that, "Satan wants to destroy this nation ... and he wants to destroy us as a Christian army." While Bush distanced himself from the general's zealotry, Rumsfeld reminded curious reporters that Boykin was entitled to free speech. Boykin should indeed exercise his First Amendment rights, but we should also question the appropriate line between church and state. The general was assigned to bring the interrogation techniques from Guantánamo Bay to the infamous Abu Ghraib prison, allegedly on Rumsfeld's order. It is both reckless and frightening that Boykin, who described the U.S. Army as "warriors in this spiritual war," was assigned to the godforsaken torture chambers at Abu Ghraib. "America's God" at Abu Ghraib fits better with the axis of evil than any war for liberation. Curiously, Bush supporters do not reject all of Boykin's theological assumptions; there seems to be some agreement that the president was chosen by God to lead America. "George Bush was not elected by a majority of the voters in the U.S. He was appointed by God," Boykin startlingly proclaimed. Recall that Bush's personal minister Marc Craig believes that Bush was elected by God and the president has repeatedly told close advisers that God wanted him to lead the United States.[27]

Boykin's rhetoric is extreme, yet it is consistent with some popular currents regarding U.S. patriotism. Consider that several entertainers who performed for overseas troops with the United Service Organization (USO) also articulated a messianic nationalism. During the summer of 2004, the congressionally chartered organization sponsored a tour by rock star Ted Nugent and the country singer Toby Keith. The tour included trips to U.S. military installations in Kosovo, Italy, Germany, Afghanistan and Iraq. Like Boykin, Nugent characterized U.S. troops as "warriors," insisting that we should "pray for the warriors." Boykin and Nugent seem to articulate a version of the divine warrior archetype expressed in America's civil religion. For Nugent, the sight of American fighter planes "cleanse the soul," and a ride on Blackhawk helicopters supplied him with "spiritual invigoration." The rock-and-roll performer claimed that he was "on a mission from God," and even chastised the United Nations, as a "corrupt, soulless gang," who evidently hindered the United States' global mandate to spread freedom. Fellow performer Toby Keith offered the obligatory "God Bless" our troops, and reportedly sang a song titled, "Courtesy of the Red, White and Blue (The Angry American)," which celebrates the flag and pledges revenge against those who attacked the United States. Nugent and Keith are not alone in blending God and country. Singer Johnny Ramone felt compelled to say "God Bless George W. Bush, and God Bless America" when his band was inducted into the Rock and Roll Hall of Fame in 2002.[28]

The City on a Hill on the Home Front

Journalist and radio talk show host Dennis Prager also believes that the United States holds a providential mission. The nationally syndicated broadcaster unapologetically declares that the United States "has a divine mandate to be a shining light to mankind." In fact, "no other country approaches America as a force for good on the planet," Prager goes on, and the "Old Testament–oriented" United States believes in "destroying evil."[29]

The influence of religion in U.S. culture is incontestable and it received special attention during the 2004 presidential elections. The *New York Times* reported that among the four out of ten voters who regularly attended church, over 60 percent voted for Bush in the previous election. In Allentown, Pennsylvania, a Bush supporter rented a billboard with the message "One nation under God."[30] Stories also surfaced that the Republican Party in two states sent mass mailings with the message that "liberals" planned to ban the Bible.

Civil religion was also alive and well at the Republican National Convention in New York City in late August 2004. It should come as no surprise that the Republican National Convention was saturated in religious imagery. It was a rally cry for the president of good and evil. Former New York City mayor Rudy Giuliani declared on the opening night of the convention that, "an important part of the Bush Doctrine" entails having "faith in the power of freedom," which always "prevails." It is the "story of the Old Testament," Giuliani insisted.[31] Reverend Max Lucado buttressed the former mayor's observation that same day: "God of our fathers, you direct the affairs of all nations.... Thank you for this nation."[32] Later in the convention, the Democrat turned Republican senator Zell Miller (R–Ga.), encouraged the delegates to appreciate the president's moral embrace of this divine destiny. "I am moved," the senator said, by the fact that Bush "is unashamed of his belief that God is not indifferent to America." Bush is "a God-fearing man," with a "spine of tempered steel," qualities that inspired Miller to demand that we, "God Bless George W. Bush."[33] Miller's extravagant rhetoric locates God's presence among U.S. citizens and politicians.

California governor Arnold Schwarzenegger also placed a divine stamp on U.S. global power as well as all things American. The former action hero and bodybuilder first pledged that the Republicans will "terminate terrorism," adding a dose of comic book masculinity to Bush's righteous proclamations. Schwarzenegger's litmus test for determining whether or not one is Republican relies on all the trappings of civil religion. "If you have *faith* in free enterprise, *faith* in the resourcefulness of the American people, and *faith* in the U.S. economy," (italics mine) then you are a Republican.[34] Freedom is reduced to free markets and free enterprise. Polls at the time suggested that U.S. citizens were losing faith in the economy, with Gallup reporting that two-thirds of respondents felt the economy was declining.[35] Schwarzenegger nonetheless joined the priests of the dominant culture in performing the ritual of the nation's religion.

Cardinal Egan of the archdiocese of New York enhanced Schwarzenegger's more secular version of civil religion. Egan reminded the convention that the United States was God's shining city on a hill, the New Israel that leads the world:

> Lord of all, we are Your children, "one nation under God," a people called to be a light of righteousness in a troubled world, a city set on a mountain-top from which all humankind might draw strength, inspiration, and hope.[36]

George W. Bush capped off the ceremonies in a similarly homiletic tone, "Freedom ... is the Almighty God's gift to every man and women in the world ... we have a calling from beyond the stars to stand for freedom. This is the everlasting dream of America — and tonight, in this place, that dream is renewed."[37] Here again Bush's redemptive language conflates God's will with U.S. values, conjuring up a civil religion, or the sense that the United States is on a divine mission to liberate the world. While the Republicans congratulated themselves for upholding "godly" freedoms, Iraq was spinning out of control.

It should be said that the good and evil paradigm so characteristic of a narrow civil religion fits neatly with the secular neo-conservatives associated with the Bush administration. Neo-conservatism is an ideology that embraces U.S. interventionism to spread democracy and liberty. It gained widespread attention under the second Bush administration when so-called neo-conservatives such as Paul Wolfowitz, Douglas Feith, and I. Lewis Libby and others held significant policy posts. Before gaining office, these policymakers were associated with a group calling itself the Project for a New American Century (PNAC). The project's statement of principles argued that "we need to accept responsibility for America's unique role in preserving and extending an international order friendly to our security, our prosperity and our principles." History demands that we "embrace the cause of American leadership," and pursue a "policy of military strength and moral clarity" that "may not be fashionable today," the PNAC asserted. In 2000, the group issued a report that identified Iraq, Iran and North Korea as key opponents that cannot be permitted to "undermine American leadership."[38] These three nations, of course, would be identified by Bush as the "axis of evil." And, during the Clinton years, the neo-conservative PNAC aggressively called for the removal of Saddam Hussein from power. Where Bush might speak of good and evil, the secular neo-conservatives articulate a dichotomy of "democracy against dictatorship." Their global vision of spreading democracy by way of toppling dictators like Saddam Hussein constitutes a "secular version of fundamentalism," as Bacevich and Prodromou explain. The secular neo-conservative embraces "American righteousness" and is a "crusader of sorts, if not on God's behalf at least on behalf of democratic ideals."[39]

Iraq and Historical Accuracy: A Task for Peace Educators

The neo-conservative "secular crusade" to spread free markets abroad and Bush's messianic compact to save Iraq now look painfully like a broken covenant. Strategic failures in the Middle East have led to global dissent against the war, and the Bush administration has responded to this dissent by trying to rewrite the history of how the war began. Responsible peace educators are now forced to revise Bush's rewritten version so that it is closer to the facts. In June 2003, President Bush told a group of business leaders that "This nation acted to a threat from the dictator of Iraq," but "now there are some who would like to rewrite history — revisionist historians is what I like to call them."[40] Following Bush's Veterans' Day speech in November 2005, the BBC featured a story, "Bush Slams Iraq War Revisionism." Historian Staughton Lynd reminds us that one hundred years ago three officers of the Western Federation of Miners were indicted for murder. President Theodore Roosevelt declared that they were "undesirable citizens." Working people and radicals all over the country responded with insignia stating, "I am an undesirable citizen."[41] Something similar is now required of peace educators in the United States. Bush's sanctimonious posturing compels the responsible educator to declare: I am a revisionist. The president's critique of revisionism needs to be rejected both as a specific comment on the origins of the Iraq War and as a general proposition.

In Bush's Veterans' Day speech in 2005, he declared that, "Some Democrats and anti-war critics are now claiming we manipulated the intelligence and misled the American people about why we went to war. These critics are fully aware that a bipartisan Senate investigation found no evidence of political pressure to change the intelligence community's judgments related to Iraq's weapons programs."[42] The panel that Bush is likely referring to is the Commission on the Intelligence Capabilities of the United States Regarding Weapons of Mass Destruction. On the one hand, it reported that analysts working on the WMD issue were not subject to pressure. On the other, the report noted, "It is hard to deny that the intelligence analysts worked in an environment that did not encourage skepticism about the conventional wisdom."[43] It is difficult to explain this discrepancy; perhaps the commission was, well, under pressure. Elsewhere, former Chief United Nations weapons inspector Hans Blix bemoaned that "the [Bush] administration leaned on us."[44]

Bush believes that "it is deeply irresponsible to rewrite the history of how [the Iraq] war began."[45] Four well-known examples should suffice to show that the Bush administration deceived the U.S. public, and that "revisionists" are those who simply want to keep the record accurate for future historians of the Iraq War.

1. Bush (in a March 2003 speech on the eve of invasion): There is "no doubt that the Iraq regime continues to possess and conceal some of the most lethal weapons ever devised."[46]

Revisionist correction: The International Atomic Energy (IAEA) update for the Security Council pursuant to Iraq Resolution 1441 stated that: "In the first eight weeks of the IAEA inspections, the IAEA has visited all sites identified by it or States as significant. No evidence of ongoing prohibited nuclear or nuclear-related activities at those locations has been detected."[47] In early March 2003, Mohamed ElBaradei, head of the IAEA, reported that "there was no evidence Iraq had a nuclear development program," according to the *Sydney Morning Herald*.[48] In February 2001, Colin Powell acknowledged that Iraq "has not developed any significant capability with respect to weapons of mass destruction."[49] Demonstrators and "revisionists" across the globe also challenged the administration on what is now a fully discredited claim.

2. Bush (State of the Union 2003): "Iraq recently sought significant quantities of uranium from Africa."[50]

Revisionist correction: UN inspectors almost immediately disputed the allegation. One letter used to prove the purchase was signed by someone who last served in the Nigerian government in 1989.[51] Bush shifted the blame to George Tenet, then head of the CIA, who allegedly allowed the statement to enter the State of the Union address. However, according to the *Wall Street Journal*, the CIA sent a memo to Condoleezza Rice that "challenged the African uranium sale" before the speech. Rice accepted responsibility for the "error," the article notes.[52]

3. Bush in October 2002: "I have not ordered the use of force. I hope the use of force will not become necessary."[53]

Revisionist correction: In July 2002, Sir Richard Dearlove, head of Britain's M16, reported that, "Military action was now seen as inevitable. Bush wanted to remove Saddam, through military action, justified by the conjunction of terrorism and WMD."[54]

4. Dick Cheney: Iraq constitutes "the geographic base of the terrorists who have had us under assault for many years, but most especially on 9/11."[55]

Revisionist Correction: Iraq had nothing to do with 9/11, which even Bush and Rumsfeld admitted. Al Qaeda operatives in custody spoke of the conflict between Hussein and the organization.[56]

This last piece of propaganda is especially disconcerting. A Zogby poll has found that 85 percent of U.S. soldiers serving in Iraq stated that the U.S. mission is "to retaliate for Saddam's role in the 9-11 attacks." Cheney's misinformation has infiltrated the minds of our long-suffering troops. Despite the administration's attempts to mislead its own troops, they are not simply vassals of administration propaganda. The same Zogby poll has found that 72 percent of U.S. troops in Iraq believe that the United States should withdraw from the country within a year. In fact, 29 percent of these soldiers felt that the United States should leave immediately.[57]

The Iraqi people also feel that the U.S. forces should leave. A poll by the British Ministry of Defence revealed that 82 percent of Iraqis are "strongly opposed" to the U.S. led occupation and 45 percent of Iraqis felt that the attacks on U.S./U.K. troops were justified.[58] In 2003, a Gallup poll, once cited by the Bush administration to illustrate that Iraqis welcomed the U.S. forces, showed instead that 94 percent of Iraqis felt Baghdad was more dangerous since the U.S. "liberation."[59] Even if we allow for a wide margin of error, these polls reveal that U.S. soldiers and the Iraqi people oppose the occupation.

In addition to the Iraqi people and U.S. soldiers, the conservative Cato Institute offers a compelling case for withdrawal. Its director, former Navy officer Christopher Preble convened a task force that calls for U.S. withdrawal "at the earliest possible date." The study, *Exiting Iraq*, acknowledges that a departure will cause a short-term loss of honor, but holds a long-term gain against Al Qaeda, which uses the U.S. invasion as a primary recruiting tool for new members. U.S. forces are "a lightning rod" for dissent and rebellion. According to Preble, 57 percent of Iraqis also want the United States out immediately. An orderly exit should take "no more than six months," Preble says. Although the Cato study dismantles the administration's plan to stay in Iraq, it speaks in strictly strategic and not moral terms. Nonetheless, this important book makes a cogent argument for an "expeditious withdrawal." Although Preble hints at the economic dimension of the war, he stops far short of contemplating the consequences of imperialism. Muslims see the war as motivated by the United States' "desire to control Iraq's oil resources," Preble writes, but such arguments "seem absurd at face value."[60] A Center for Public Integrity report regarding Executive Order 13303 helps illuminate why these "absurd" charges hold currency. Bush's order states that "judicial process is prohibited" against the Iraq Development Fund and "petroleum and petroleum products." Consider that the 1992 Defense Planning Guidance fantasized about controlling Iraqi resources. The United States should "establish and protect a new world order," the document attributed to Paul

Wolfowitz reads, including "access to vital raw materials, primarily Persian Gulf oil."[61] Even the *American Conservative* has questioned U.S. economic behavior in Iraq. "We have imposed policies," the conservative journal explained, "that worked against the recovery of Iraq's industry and commerce." It reported in 2005 that seven out of ten Iraqis were unemployed, a situation exacerbated by the invasion.[62]

While the invasion is not simply about petroleum, these measures only confirm the arguments of those opposed to the U.S. invasion. As William Appleman Williams noted regarding the Cold War, it is "in reality only the more recent phase of a more general conflict between the established system of Western capitalism and its internal and external opponents."[63] The Iraq invasion seems to fit the pattern. Consider that the United States quickly ratified Paul Bremer's infamous Article 39, which privatized much of Iraq's infrastructure, turning it over to foreign corporations along with other measures that ensure a favorable tax scheme on all profits rendered.[64] At the same time, the United States has refused for decades to ratify the UN International Covenant on Economic, Social and Cultural Rights, which calls for people to control their own resources. *Harper's Magazine* interviewed Iraqis on the street in 2004, plagued by astronomical unemployment, who complained about factories shut down due to lack of electricity. Some even moaned about "privatization."[65] The United States argues that it wants to bring democracy to Iraq. If so, it should not have issued Article 39 and related provisions that prohibit full control by Iraq of its industries and resources. Holding Iraqi banks, factories and businesses hostage is simply incompatible with democracy. Halliburton and Bechtel contracts certainly do not help the U.S. cause.

By 2004, former military strategists considered the war a failure and insisted that it must be terminated. William Odom, director of the National Security Agency in the 1980s, described Iraq as a "strategic disaster," the "sooner we leave, the better." Former chairman of the Joint Chiefs of Staff William Crowe put it even more bluntly: "we screwed up ... we have got to get out."[66] The invasion of Iraq is a monumental crisis that begs for an evaluation of the U.S. Empire.

Part of this evaluation concerns the U.S. track record with the battling parties in Iraq. Recent U.S. actions in Iraq and the region appear to be incompatible with a peaceful, orderly solution. U.S. foreign policy behavior is structurally incompatible with stability and democracy in the region. During the 1980s, we now know that the United States supported the Ba'athists, providing logistics and support to the murderous Hussein, even during the Halabja massacre in 1988. As for the Kurds, the United States double crossed them twice, in 1975 and 1991. In 1972, Iraq nationalized its petroleum industry and the Nixon administration drafted a covert plan to disrupt the Iraqi move. It entailed a Kurdish uprising, aided by the Iranian shah Pahlavi. But, the shah was able to cut a deal in 1975 turning a strategic waterway over to Iran at the last moment, and the covert program was aborted. Kurds desperately fled into Iran, with almost no assistance. Kurds also seek statehood, a complicated matter, but one that is opposed by U.S. ally Turkey.

Historically, the United States also hindered democracy in the Middle East. We examined how Shah Pahlavi was installed in Iran in 1953, replacing the democratically elected Mossadegh. In 1949, the United States encouraged a military chief, Hunsai Zaim, to overthrow the existing government of Syria, setting the stage for a military dictatorship. According to historian Douglas Little, Zaim immediately authorized a Western pipeline project. Of course, the reasons for these interventions are complicated, but they illustrate that the United States is most successful in subverting democracy in the region rather than building it. Such observations are not lost on those living in the region, nor were they lost on Eisenhower who admitted that U.S. actions in the Middle East fomented hate.[67]

Bush bordered on offering a similar confession regarding the U.S. occupation of Iraq: "I wouldn't be happy if I were occupied," Bush said.[68] The Cato Institute adds that the ongoing occupation incites resentment. It seems that the deaths of Iraqi civilians are a primary source of this hostility. A study in 2004 in the British journal *Lancet* estimated that 100,000 Iraqi civilians were killed as a result of U.S. actions. Disputes over the number of Iraqi citizens killed during the war persist. The United Nations Assistance Mission estimated that 34,000 Iraqis were killed in a single year in 2006. The exact number of Iraqi civilians killed in the war will likely be disputed for some time, but by any humane measure the number is excessive. That 50 U.S. air strikes against Iraqi leaders missed their targets in 2003 certainly suggests that significant numbers of Iraqi civilians were killed. Abu Ghraib, Camp Cropper, what the Red Cross calls "serious violations of International Humanitarian Law," add to the toll of suffering.[69] Despite these gruesome realities, Bush supporters say it is unrealistic to ask for immediate withdrawal. It is far more unrealistic to expect the very nation that snubbed world opinion and went to war anyway, then destroyed and tortured a nation, to bring democracy to Iraq.

Informed observers note that an orderly withdrawal is more sensible than prolonging an unsuccessful intervention. This withdrawal should include the removal of economic orders that privatize Iraq. It would illustrate to the world that the United States is serious about democracy. Even terrorists kill for a reason; this is one reason that they attack American targets. Second, a massive international coalition, comprised of both Arab and UN forces, should enter Iraq. It might be well to consider a referendum whereby the Iraqi people vote on what form of outside intervention the country requires. Whatever force is ultimately decided upon, it should be trained as a police force without any economic control over Iraq's resources. UN consultant Johan Galtung rightly suggests a Conference on Security and Cooperation in the Middle East, led by Jordan or a nation in the region. Related issues such as Israel/Palestine, Kurdish independence, and a Middle East common market with Israel's participation should be part of the discussion to avoid isolating issues that matter to the conflict parties, Galtung concludes.[70] Third, the international community should invite significant participation of the Red Crescent in Iraq. Fourth, a U.S. aid package without any restrictive clauses should be employed to help rebuild the Iraqi infrastructure. The presence of U.S. soldiers is hardly necessary to begin this healing; a multinational force and massive aid is far more desirable than a U.S. force that has encountered what appear to be insurmountable obstacles in Iraq. This scheme is only a starting point and is hardly perfect, but it is far better than a U.S. occupation that researchers tell us is only encouraging resistance and violence. Some critics are tempted to describe this analysis as "revisionist," even anti–American. Within the United States it sounds radical, yet outside the country it comports with mainstream world citizen's perspective on Iraq, to borrow Galtung's phrase. Remember, too, that most of the world's citizens and governments as well as the UN opposed the invasion in the first place. The Bush administration opted instead for "unilateral" action, while Condoleezza Rice warned of "mushroom clouds." It turns out there were no WMDs; no mushroom clouds; no "yellow cake;" no Saddam link to 9/11; and no Atta meeting in Prague. In fact, just about everything the administration claimed about Iraq's weapons program was wrong. Their argument that United States cannot simply withdraw from Iraq is equally incorrect; it is as misguided as barking, "Bring 'em on."

Lastly, President Bush expressed regret over his "Bring 'em on" comment. Maybe it symbolizes a rare moment of introspection. If so, the president may wish to consult his autobiography for further reflection. "I also learned the lesson of Vietnam," Bush wrote, "Our nation should be slow to engage troops." Not only did we have "no exit strategy" the president complained, but interventions must "respect and nurture our traditional alliances."[71] The United States rushed to war in Iraq with no exit strategy while simultaneously straining traditional alliances.

An Almost Chosen People: The Republic Challenges Bush's Empire

Citizens across the United States and the world grew impatient with the administration's deceptions and errors. Since its inception U.S. civil religion or chosenness rhetoric has faced challenges, and the Iraq conflict is no exception. Consider that a group of some two hundred theologians sent Bush a letter that cautioned against the "danger of being co-opted by a theology of nationalism and militarism."[72] Even the pope has questioned the legitimacy of the Iraq war.

Bush's second inaugural address attempted to weaken this assault. The president accented the United States' unique role to deliver the gift of freedom to other nations. During the inauguration, Bush drew directly from Leviticus 25:10, which states that, "you shall make sacred by proclaiming liberty in the land for all its inhabitants." In the Book of Leviticus, God delivers liberty, but in "this young century," it is America who "proclaims liberty throughout the world, and to all inhabitants thereof." According to newspaper reports, Bush mentioned freedom forty-four times in the speech so as to remind an uncertain nation of its special mission.[73] Despite the president's efforts, many skeptics remained. Bush's goal to rally the nation behind his mission to spread divinely inspired freedom abroad requires some restraint. During national crisis, civil religion walks a delicate tightrope, and Bush has difficulty maintaining his balance.

To overuse these sacred constructs is to risk cheapening them, and making oneself appear insincere. To avoid appearing inauthentic, Bush harkened back to Lincoln's eloquent 1865 second inaugural address. Lincoln spoke about God having his own purposes and avoided any references to the United States as God's chosen nation. When Bush was on the 2000 campaign trail, he boldly asserted that the United States was chosen by God and commissioned by history, but Bush was more careful in his second inaugural as antiwar opposition spread:

> We will go forward with complete confidence in the eventual triumph of freedom.... Not because we consider ourselves a chosen nation; God moves and chooses as He wills. We have confidence because freedom is the permanent hope of mankind, the hunger in dark places, the longing of the soul. When our Founders declared a new order for the ages; when soldiers died in wave upon wave for a union based on liberty; when citizens marched in peaceful outrage under the banner "Freedom Now"—they were acting on an ancient hope that is meant to be fulfilled. History has an ebb and flow of justice, but history also has a visible direction, set by liberty and the Author of liberty.[74]

Although Bush avoided explicit references to chosenness in the speech, he indirectly articulated it. According to Bush, God is the author of liberty, while the United States is the exemplar of freedom. Hence, the United States is either chosen by God to spread freedom or it is the earthly example of a nation that follows God's script to spread liberty. Bush tempered his chosenness rhetoric, but the president's religious discourse still unsettled critics. This criticism came from some surprising sources. Les Csorba, a former adviser to George H.W. Bush, astutely noted that, "Bush's America has become more divided, pessimistic about exporting democracy," so his inaugural speech sought to heal the scars of the Iraq War.[75] We might add that this healing is inextricably linked to uniting the nation behind its celebratory civil religion. For Bush, this meant reminding U.S. citizens that they are connected by the gift of freedom, rather than directly evoking the more contentious claim that America is God's New Israel. Bush attempted to satisfy both critics and supporters by focusing on the abstract concept of freedom.

However, Bush's speech failed to accomplish this task. Even the president's supporters chastised his theological language. Peggy Noonan, a former Reagan speechwriter, reported that Bush's address left her with "a bad feeling." It was a "God-drenched speech" that was somewhere between "dreamy and disturbing," expressive of a president inflicted with "mission inebriation."[76] The very fact that Peggy Noonan has criticized Bush's religious language points to a crisis in U.S. civil religion. In moments of turmoil, countervailing traditions openly challenge the national religion and establishment writers tend to modify their understanding of the proper use of a triumphalist theology under such circumstances. Thomas Cronin, the president of Whitman College, was so unimpressed by Bush's speech that he called it "messianic ... a proclamation of almost a crusade."[77] It is worth noting that Bush tempered his divine mandate by adding that it was "not because we consider ourselves a chosen nation," but he nonetheless appeared overzealous. Such criticism reflects the nation's general dissatisfaction over the Iraq war and subsequent discomfort with any claim that Bush was spreading the gift of liberty to the devastated country.

Bush's nationalist civil religion had failed because it is rooted in mythology. His civil religion depends on a consensus view of U.S. citizens that is more imagined than real. When the framework is tested in times of crisis such as the Iraq War, the "invisible" voices indeed rise to the surface to remind the nation of its hypocrisy. All the talk of liberating Iraq was contradicted by the record. U.S. citizens who have long been denied freedom and equality challenged Bush's view of the nation's destiny. Consider that in August 2005, when hurricane Katrina devastated the Gulf Coast, the entire nation was shaken from complacency. It was at once obvious that Bush's discussion of the U.S. as God's arbiter of freedom was an empty slogan. As Cornel West has observed, "Bush talks about God, but he has forgotten the point of prophetic Christianity is compassion and justice for those who have least.... It takes something as big as Hurricane Katrina and the misery we saw among the poor black people of New Orleans to get America to focus on race and poverty."[78] The "invisible" Americans who have been denied the American Dream were no longer hidden from view. Simplistic metaphors about the United States defeating evil and protecting timeless values of liberty appear rather hollow in light of the Iraq War and Katrina disaster.

Another potent example of Bush's spiritual platform inciting discontent occurred on the anniversary of Dr. King's birthday in January 2004. It serves as a useful example of civil religion in conflict. King's legacy embodies the "prophetic civil-religion tradition" (the republic) in collision with Bush's messianic nationalism (the Empire). During the King dedications in Atlanta that week, Bush placed a wreath at the civil rights leader's tomb in an uninvited visit. One disturbed participant, Reverend Timothy McDonald, explained, "There's a reason why African American voters overwhelmingly turn out for Democrats. King's philosophies could not be more different from Bush's. King, a man of peace, was one of the first to publicly oppose the Vietnam War. Bush, by contrast, has unilaterally and preemptively declared war on another country." Some 800 people gathered in protest, carrying signs that asked, "What would King say ... about our affairs in Guantanamo Bay?" Several protestors called Bush's visit a photo opportunity, complaining that the president stopped by on his way to a $2,000 a plate fundraiser.[79]

Elsewhere, the Associated Press reported that "Protests mark King Day." Throughout the nation, people openly challenged the Bush administration on what would have been King's 75th birthday. In Boston, the first woman bishop of the A.M.E. Church questioned Bush's integrity. In a service at the Ebenezer Baptist Church, King's son, Martin Luther King III, exclaimed that "you can not end terrorism by terrorizing others." Atlanta mayor Shirley Franklin received a standing ovation after she criticized Bush's tomb visit.[80] Legendary civil rights preacher and Dr. King's steadfast comrade, Reverend Fred Shuttlesworth, chastised Bush for opposing affirmative action and engaging in a "media ploy" at the tomb. "I hope the American people understand and see this wreath laying ceremony for what it is," the reverend bemoaned. The Southern Christian Leadership Conference, the organization that King himself once led, commented that the Bush administration "consistently contradicted" King's philosophy.[81] Bush's visit, simply to participate in a spiritual celebration, ignited a firestorm of protest. Far from uniting the nation, Bush's theology and policies elicit criticism from the United States' leading civil rights figures. While Bush's application of civil religion seeks to bind, those who are marginalized or generally excluded from the "American dream" highlight the hypocrisy behind the national creed. The Bush administration's reckless adventures abroad coupled with its insensitivity toward African Americans at home, as evidenced in the Katrina hurricane debacle, has revitalized the debate concerning the contrast between the nation's professed values and its actual behavior. George W. Bush heralds the chosenness idiom, but marginalized groups offer a potent challenge to the contradictions of empire.

Bush's political career always seemed to navigate the difficult fault line between church and state, but after September 11 Bush's messianic proclamations seemed to sooth a wounded nation. This unity, however, crumbled as quickly as the twin towers as Bush has become increasingly rigid and inflexible, seemingly trapped in a Manichean framework indicative of the chosenness complex. This inflexibility has made a solution to the war on terrorism and the Iraq intervention more difficult.

There are alternatives to this paralyzing paradigm. United Nation's consultant and peace researcher Johan Galtung writes that there are several alternatives. These options are supported by most global public opinion and most U.S. citizens, according to Gallup polls. Even after the watershed even of September 11 there existed global support for nonmilitary solutions to terrorism. Roughly 80 percent of those polled throughout the world following the September 11 massacre preferred a police action to a military campaign.[82] A UN police force could arrest, detain and convict those responsible for crimes against humanity. Only about 50 percent of U.S. citizens polled immediately after September 11 responded that they favored military action as against this option. This action requires bringing the suspects before the International Criminal Court; a similar tribunal has condemned the United States for its role in the massacre of Latin Americans in the 1980s. Washington, D.C., policymakers would prefer to conceal this type of unlawful behavior from the American public, so they eliminate an action that most of the world supports. U.S. leaders ignore this viable option, while simultaneously manipulating the public's understandable anger and fear by suggesting that war is the only means by which terrorism can be halted. Operation Enduring Freedom and Operation Iraqi Freedom follow the U.S. foreign policy pattern of joining forces with dangerous groups, including segments of Pakistan's ISI and the Northern Alliance. In respect to eradicating terrorism, a United Nations tribunal could bring Al Qaeda to justice without U.S. involvement, which might help to reduce the hostility toward the United States while at the same time offering genuine security to Americans. As for the Iraq War, a multinational force and greater participation of the Arab League instead of U.S. domination over the country would also reduce the tension between the United States and the Middle East while satisfying the expressed desires of the Iraqi people.

6

The International Criminal Court
as a Peace Educator: A Challenge
for the United States

We will take the actions necessary to ensure that our efforts to meet
our global security commitments and protect Americans are not impaired
by the potential for investigations, inquiry, or prosecution by the International Criminal Court (ICC), whose jurisdiction does not extend to
Americans and which we do not accept. We will work together with
other nations to avoid complications in our military operations and
cooperation, through such mechanisms as multilateral and bilateral
agreements that will protect U.S. nationals from the ICC.
— *National Security Strategy of the United States
of America*, September 20, 2002.[1]

Some 160 countries met in Rome, Italy, during July 1998 to put in place
an International Criminal Court (ICC) that would hold individuals who committed genocide, war crimes and crimes against humanity accountable. We
discussed in chapter two that international law forbids these violations; however, before the formation of the ICC, there was no permanent, institutional
vehicle to convict such perpetrators. As the ICC home page explains, it is
"the first ever permanent international institution, with jurisdiction to prosecute individuals responsible for the most serious crimes of international concern: genocide, crimes against humanity and war crimes."[2] Supporters of the
court have explained that Cold War tensions precluded the formation of an
international tribunal. Both the Soviet Union and the United States worried
that such a court would be used by the other side as a cold war weapon to
inhibit action in the international arena. In the post–Cold War world, shocking crimes and "ethnic cleansing" in places such as the former Yugoslavia and
Rwanda reinforced the need for an International Criminal Court. Hence, the

ICC was ratified in July 2002. Some seventy-nine nations ratified what is commonly called the Rome Statute, bringing the court to fruition. The entire European Union backed the court and Canada expressed "strong support" for its formation. As much of the world celebrated the inauguration of the court, the United States remained in lonely opposition.[3] U.S. officials maintain that the court is at odds with the U.S. Constitution. A close inspection of the United States' complaints about the court reveals that they are a bit overblown. In addition to exaggerating the court's problems, the United States aggressively challenges those countries that ratified the Rome Statute. This chapter shall analyze the U.S. opposition to the court while illustrating how this resistance erodes global peacemaking efforts and the war on terrorism.

Several supporters of the ICC have noted the incongruity between the United States' celebration of human rights and its resistance to a court that protects these very rights. President George W. Bush's National Security Strategy, released in 2002, vows to defend human rights, but insists that "we do not accept" the ICC. This contradictory stance is made more troubling by Bush's decision to nullify President Clinton's signature to the 1998 ICC treaty. According to the European delegation at the court, these aggressive measures against the court are "unacceptable," and they risk "eroding support for the global coalition against terrorism."[4] Regardless of these grave dangers, the United States resists the ICC.

The general complaint regarding the court is that its legal frameworks are unclear. It is worth repeating that the court addresses only the most nefarious crimes, such as genocide, crimes against humanity and war crimes. The statute clearly outlines each of these crimes, having based its own definitions on existing international law. Genocide is explicitly understood as "acts committed with the intent to destroy, in whole or part, a national ethnic, racial or religious group." This definition is derived from the UN General Assembly's Genocide Convention, a document that the United States has already accepted. Crimes against humanity are described as "systematic attack directed against any civilian population," including rape, sexual slavery and murder. The ICC definition here is based on the Nuremberg Charter and the statues of the International Criminal Tribunal for the former Yugoslavia (ICTY), both of which the United States supports. As for war crimes, it deals with serious violations of the Geneva Conventions of 1949.[5] It should be clear that the ICC covers only the most atrocious crimes, ones that are hardly unclear.

More serious objections involve the ICC's alleged violation of national sovereignty in general and the U.S. Constitution in particular. "We believe that the United States, not international institutions, are primarily responsible for assuring justice," the State Department reports, and that the "International Criminal Court undermines the democratic rights of our people."[6] Contrary to U.S. claims, Article I of the ICC statute specifically empowers national judicial systems to handle cases. Known as "the principle of complementarity," it states that the ICC "shall be complementary to national" courts. What this means is that the ICC is a court of "last resort," intervening only when there is a "substantial collapse" in national judicial institutions. Countries from across the globe have made clear that they understand that the court's provisions do not undermine national governments.

Another concern is that the ICC prosecutor constitutes an unchecked power who threatens the constitutional principle of checks and balances. Henry Kissinger writes that the court risks "substituting the tyranny of judges for that of governments." U.S. undersecretary of state for political affairs Marc Grossman agrees that the ICC establishes a "prosecutorial system that is an unchecked power." Here too the court's statute belies U.S. claims. Article 15 places several limits on the prosecutor, such as a pretrial chamber that screens all cases. The chamber must find "reasonable grounds" to proceed. Individual nations also have the right to challenge these charges. The ICC is not an unchecked power; rather, it is one with procedures similar to the U.S. system of checks and balances. Given the safeguards against the "tyranny" of judges, the American Bar Association concludes that the ICC contains "extensive rights and protections for defendants ... which are functionally equivalent to the protections provided by our own Bill of Rights."[7]

Not only does the United States reject a court that resembles its own judicial system, it also threatens those who support the ICC. "Should the ICC seek to detain any American," former U.S. ambassador to the United Nations John Negroponte warns, "it would have serious consequences." The ambassador's threats are buttressed by the American Servicemembers' Protection Act (ASPA), signed into law by President Bush in August 2002. The act's various provisions are designed to protect the United States from the court. This legislation, and similar attempts to dilute the court's power, led a Canadian ambassador to bemoan that the U.S. machinations represented "a sad day for the United Nations." Famed Holocaust survivor Elie Wiesel adds that the ASPA represents an "acceptance of impunity for the world's worst atrocities ... ensuring that the U.S. will never again join the community of nations against perpetrators of genocide."[8]

Wiesel's harsh indictment of U.S. belligerence toward the ICC is underscored by Section 8 of the American Servicemembers' Protection Act. It appears to authorize the United States to attack The Hague, Netherlands, home of the ICC headquarters. The provision, which informed observes have sarcastically labeled as the "Hague Invasion Act," led to a resolution against it in the Netherlands parliament. Even David Schaffer, U.S. ambassador, calls it an "alarmist provision" insofar as it "contemplates" an armed invasion of a NATO ally.[9] The attacks of September 11 are a crime against humanity. It is unfortunate that America's military agenda is preoccupied with undermining a court designed to detain such heinous criminals, rather than investigating the potential of this peace-building device. This bellicose attitude is "a damaging blow" to the global coalition against terrorism, the European Parliament warns.

Threatening to withdraw aid to nations that join the ICC is yet another way that the United States undermines the war on terrorism. Section 7 of the ASPA prohibits aid to any nation that joins the ICC, except for NATO allies and those willing to sign "Article 98," or bilateral agreements. Article 98 is part of the ICC's Rome Statute and is designed to respect existing status of force agreements (SOFAs). These agreements address the means by which a nation prosecutes visitors from other nations who commit war crimes. The aim of these contracts is to guarantee prosecution while protecting state rights. The United States manipulates the purpose of SOFA contracts by using them as a way to gain immunity from the ICC. Although the ICC recognizes these "status of force" agreements, Article 98 is based on the right to intervene in cases in which individual countries refuse to prosecute. For this reason, the European Parliament considers U.S.–led bilateral agreements "incompatible" with membership in the European Union. Nonetheless, President Bush brazenly announces that "we will fully implement the American Servicemembers' Protection Act" and "bilateral agreements that will protect U.S. nationals from the ICC."[10]

What the United States should be asking is not whether U.S. nationals will be tried for offenses covered by the ICC, but if they are guilty of such crimes, to closely paraphrase Mike Kitzman. Recall that the ICC deals with war crimes, genocide and crimes against humanity. Former UN Secretary-General Kofi Annan perhaps idealistically believed that the magnitude of such crimes "could not be anywhere near" anything that Americans might commit.[11] The previous chapters document the United States' role in a series of outrageous offenses, including My Lai and the unlawful destruction of Nicaragua. While the ICC cannot convict for past crimes, the U.S. track record presents a problem. Because the United States repeatedly seeks violent solutions to conflict, it finds itself committing human rights abuses. Hearings by Senator Frank Church (D–Ida.) in 1975 brought such abuses to the public's attention. Since that time, the Pentagon has sought ways to prevent accountability. Two major initiatives that permit the United States to escape scrutiny involve the U.S. Joint Combined Exchange Training Program (JCET) and the privatization of the armed forces. These measures provide a level of secrecy that appears to permit soldiers and hired mercenaries to commit crimes with near impunity. Perhaps part of the reason why U.S. planners abhor the ICC is that it poses a threat to these two new approaches to American secrecy.

In the early 1990s, Section 2011 of the U.S. Code helped to establish the Joint Combined Exchange Training Program. The program deployed U.S. Special Forces in 110 countries, "unencumbered by public debate" and with almost no oversight, reports the *Washington Post*. U.S. military officials dispute this charge, but a brief overview of the JCET's maneuvers support the newspaper's findings. Despite a congressional ban on assistance to Colombia's military because of their human rights record, JCET trains these soldiers. Worse yet, U.S. Special Forces are also exempt from documenting and recording the Colombian military's human rights behavior, a group well known for its brutality. Similar problems surround the JCET program in Indonesia, where U.S. forces assist the notorious Kopassus troops, who are designated by the United States as "torturers." One final example, among many others, is JCET's role training the Turkish military in combat exercises, an army known for its mistreatment of the Kurdish population. Former secretary of defense William Cohen maintains that the program promotes "democratic values," an observation contradicted by the examples above.[12] A court, such as the ICC, might uncover the truth behind such rhetoric. If the United States undermines the court's power, the JCET will continue to aid pernicious military commandos across the globe with little accountability.

Washington policymakers also evade responsibility with what the *New York Times* calls "America's for Profit Secret Army." The Pentagon and State Department issue contracts to private companies to train armies abroad. These firms are not subject to freedom of information act requests, providing a formidable layer of secrecy. The *New York Times* explains that private firms are under no obligation to divulge their operations to Congress or the U.S. public, who largely subsidize these companies. The extent of this private and largely secret industry is not entirely clear, but evidence suggests that it is very broad indeed. Military Professional Services (M.P.R.I) alone received over $100 million in taxpayer-based government contracts.[13]

Nonetheless, they provide little information to the public regarding their overseas engagements. M.P.R.I. does acknowledge that they trained the Bosnian Muslims, a group that was connected to Islamic extremists. In Croatia, M.P.R.I. trained soldiers who later carried out well-coordinated crimes against humanity. They are accused of destroying entire villages and leaving some 100,000 people homeless. Employees of another firm, Dyncorp, allegedly operated a sex slave ring in Bosnia. These employees forced women into prostitution and have not been brought to justice, indicating that the privatized forces escape accountability.[14] This scandal did not dissuade the United States from awarding Dyncorp a security contract in Iraq. Its offices in Baghdad "directs and manages our many faceted operations in the region," the firm explains on a U.S. State Department Web page. A nation that claims to prioritize human rights probably would not award a contract to a business embroiled in a sex-ring scandal. Consider that it was reported that over two dozen of the interrogators at the infamous Abu Ghraib prison were private military contractors.[15] U.S. personnel sexually abused and tortured Iraqi detainees, and they sadistically photographed these dehumanizing acts. If the United States persuades nations to sign bilateral agreements, it further decreases the likelihood that such violators will be taken to task.

Another case of private firms supporting human rights violators involves the work of Vinnell. According to *The Nation*, Vinnell is managed by the Carlyle Group and it trains the Saudi Arabian National Guard, who are known to commit torture while protecting the extremist royal family.[16] If the United States continues to diminish the ICC's power, it is precisely these types of corporate mercenaries outlined in this chapter who escape criminal prosecution.

In light of the private contractor's activities, it is startling that the State Department described one firm as helping foreign troops to avoid "excess or atrocities," and offers "advice" about the "role of the army in a democratic society." This inaccurate assessment is part and parcel of U.S. leader's self-deceptions regarding U.S. military operations, whether it concerns the conventional army or secretive programs. It seems that U.S. planners see their actions as noble and uplifting, helping foreigners to obtain freedom and democracy. The reality, of course, is that U.S. policy often undermines liberty and democracy.

7

Toward a Critical Peace
Pedagogy of Nonviolent Tension

My times in Colombia helped me comprehend the distinction between
the old American republic and the new global empire. The republic
offered hope to the world. Its foundation was moral and philosophical
rather than materialistic. It was based on concepts of equality and justice
for all.... The global empire, on the other hand, is the republic's nemesis.
It is self-centered, self-serving, greedy, and materialistic.... Like empires
before, its arms only open to accumulate resources, to grab everything in
sight.

— John Perkins, *Confessions of an Economic Hit Man*[1]

The notion of American exceptionalism — that the United States alone
has the right, whether by divine sanction or moral obligation, to bring
civilization ... to the rest of the world, by violence if necessary — is not
new ... but George W. Bush has made a specialty of it.... Divine ordina-
tion is a very dangerous idea, especially when combined with military
power.... What is the answer to ... American exceptionalism...? That the
ethical norms concerning peace and human rights should be observed....
I think of William Lloyd Garrison ... [who wrote] "My country is the
world. My countrymen are mankind."

— Howard Zinn[2]

Strike against war, for without you no battles can be fought. Strike
against manufacturing shrapnel and gas bombs and all other tools of
murder. Strike against preparedness that means death and misery to millions of human beings. Be not dumb, obedient slaves in an army of
destruction. Be heroes in an army of construction.

— Helen Keller[3]

Perhaps the most ominous symptom of cultural decay, however, is in
the realm of international affairs, where diplomacy, negotiation, mutual
cooperation, and the building of strong cultural and political relationships threaten to be overshadowed by an exclusive dependence on military strategy and military technology. For a people who begin to think of
national security as resting primarily in military might and supremacy,

136

and based on weapons of a kind whose use would incinerate millions and probably poison the earth irreparably, rather than primarily in the creation of a society committed to justice, to the enhancement of its cultural and natural riches and beauty, and to the dignity and freedom of the human being — for such a people there has been an educational failure of the first order.

— Douglas Sloan[4]

From Chosen People to Global Citizens

The previous chapters chronicled how U.S. civil religion offers a vague set of quasi-religious signals that attempt to unify a nation. All too often these metaphors are manipulated to justify war and conceal one's misdeeds. Although these symbols carry religious undertones, they are essentially cultural forms that serve as carriers of solidarity and community. This community should extend beyond the geographic borders of the United States and reach toward Thomas Paine's declaration that "my country is the world." In fact, the Declaration of Human Rights examined in chapter two and the International Criminal Court explored in chapter six are rooted in ethical norms that transcend any single nation and emanate from the heart of humanity.[5] The following chapter is an invitation to discover the language and discourse needed to transform parochial notions of the United States as the chosen nation to a country that belongs to what Martin Luther King, Jr. and civil rights workers called a blessed community. To avoid misunderstanding, this chapter in no way calls for a religious revival. It does, however, suggest that rebuilding community requires metaphors that tap into the deeper well springs of human connection as expressed in universal norms that insist on the sanctity and dignity of all members of the human family. My understanding of these ethical norms overlaps with the Teachers College Center for Peace Education's spiritual and ethical foundations of peace education. This foundation draws on the values rooted in human rights conventions as well as the basic premise of justice located in the major world religions.[6]

Universal norms are often expressed in religious discourse, but they are not reducible to any spiritual tradition. Notions of freedom and human dignity, expressed since ancient times, are what Helen Merrell Lynd calls "transcultural values."[7] Consider that voices as diverse as the Russian anarchist Mikhail Bakunin, who characterized this sentiment as the human "instinct for freedom," and George W. Bush, who declares that "freedom is the permanent hope of mankind," embrace these values.[8] The versatility of these ethical norms and how they are transmitted by way of spiritual metaphors is captured by Staughton Lynd, director of the Mississippi Freedom Schools during the Civil Rights movement:

It was the dimension that the church contributed to the southern civil rights movement. One just took it for granted that freedom meetings were in churches, and there was an entire rhetoric — not just We Shall Overcome but Solidarity Forever, and how many others that were originally hymns — because people shared a common religious background. Somehow, after they had all become atheists, that still continued in the cultural forms that they found to express themselves.[9]

The challenge for educators is to facilitate a conception of freedom and reverence for ethical norms that transcend a narrow nationalism, parochial religion or general self-righteousness. Recall that the dominant paradigm for U.S. power is that of God's chosen people. As Johan Galtung observes, a perverted theology drives U.S. foreign policy behavior. If a distorted theology guides American supremacy, it follows that a new "cosmology" is required to halt it. The towering figure of American educational philosophy, John Dewey, also bemoaned what he called the "religious aureole" that protected the dominate U.S. institutions. "The religious character of nationalism," Dewey wrote in *The Public and Its Problems* has led to the "actuality of religious taboos" that have "more and more gathered about secular institutions, especially those connected to the nationalist state." Consistent with Galtung's depiction of chosenness as a syndrome, Dewey continued that the "riotous glorification" of the status quo was a "social pathology," which precludes "effective inquiry into social institutions."[10] Hence, this chapter suggests that a holistic cosmology of humility and empathy can refashion the United States' role in the world. Instead of embracing the "social pathology" of a crusader theology, U.S. educators might promote a more humble national narrative to open the channels of "effective inquiry."

The difficulty here is that this process entails the sharpening of one's awareness about discrepancies in U.S. society. While this book encourages a realization of the inconsistency of U.S. values and actions, such "sudden awareness" of shame can be demoralizing and destructive. "Ways of life that one has accepted without question may appear in this new light to be cruel," Helen Lynd cautions. "If this is my society, my country, then the world is not good," which leads to the cynical conclusion that "I do not belong here. I want none of it." When cultural identifications are destroyed, the feeling of shame can be overwhelming. For this reason, we owe it to children and students to provide opportunities for "identifications with a wider than national group that provide a sustaining equivalent" of cultural identities, to borrow Helen Lynd's phrase.[11] These broader identifications are what the widely studied Kohlberg's stages aim for, namely universal values. And they are not difficult to find in our immediate surroundings. Everyone from Thomas Paine to William Lloyd Garrison to Mohandas Gandhi to Martin Luther King, Jr. articulated a vision of my country is the world.

Effective education should not simply denounce the dark side of U.S.

history; it should explore both the positive and the negative elements in U.S. civilization. Critics of U.S. history likely have conflicted thoughts about the nation's past. There is the "shame" of slavery, extermination of Native Americans and aggressive adventures abroad. But there is also an honorable tradition of "inalienable rights" and a "natural higher law" that upholds the sanctity of the entire human family.[12] Historian Staughton Lynd locates an American radical tradition that continually resists the advantaged classes while attempting to build an egalitarian society:

> The intellectual origins of the American radical tradition were rooted in men's effort to make a way of life at once free and communal. What held together these dissenters from the capitalist consensus was more than ideology: it was also the daily practice of libertarian and fraternal attitudes in institutions of their own making. The clubs, the unorthodox congregations, the fledging trade unions were the tangible means, in theological language the "works," by which revolutionaries kept alive their faith that men could live together in a radically different way. In times of crisis resistance turned into revolution; the underground congregation burst forth as a model for the kingdom of God on earth.... Parallel to Leviathan, the Kingdom is dreamed, discussed, in miniscule form established.[13]

This vision of local community (and its attendant wider global citizenship) requires humility and the ability to shed parochial attitudes about the supremacy of one's own nation or culture. A mature study of U.S. history can facilitate the ability to criticize the U.S. Empire while celebrating the U.S. Republic. We can chastise the U.S. role in foreign affairs and simultaneously celebrate the ordinary American citizens who fought to preserve universal values of equality and liberty. Often these universal values find expression in religion, but secular educators can discuss these sentiments as historical examples, not necessarily spiritual truths. This exploration into how U.S. citizens have utilized spiritual metaphors is not a promotion of religion, but rather a study into how spiritual metaphors galvanized people at certain points in history. Sometimes human norms such as dignity and rights energized groups more so than religion and the point is to illustrate that upholding the dignity and sanctity of the human being is a central theme in history.

Another most powerful example of this allegiance to ethical norms that yield a sense of purpose and self-confidence is found in the civil rights movement. During the 1960s, the Student Non-Violent Coordinating Committee (SNCC), a group of activists who operated in the hostile and dangerous milieu of the segregationist South, declared that:

> We affirm the philosophical and religious ideal of nonviolence as the foundation of our purpose, the presupposition of our faith, and the manner of our action. Nonviolence as it grows from Judaic-Christian traditions seeks a social order of justice permeated by love.... Through nonviolence, courage displaces

fear; love transforms hate. Acceptance dissipates prejudice; hope ends despair. Peace dominates war; faith reconciles doubt. Mutual regard cancels enmity. Justice for all overthrows injustice. The redemptive community supercedes systems of gross immorality.... By appealing to conscience and standing on the moral nature of human existence; nonviolence nurtures the atmosphere in which reconciliation and justice become actual possibilities.[14]

Although many peace studies initiatives are dismissed as idealistic, it would be a gross distortion to apply such charges to SNCC and the civil rights movement. Surely the movement left a permanent, positive mark on U.S. society. It would be equally misleading to reduce such visions to the African-American quest for desegregation alone. These same SNCC students, living under the daily threat of physical harm, linked their moral ideals to the broader question of U.S. warfare. In July 1965, SNCC issued a call for draft resistance; while one of its members announced that, "We have to convince the country that civil rights workers get killed in the South because the government has a certain attitude toward killing in Vietnam. The concept that it is all right to kill an 'enemy' affects the morality of the country so that people can be killed here."[15] In an important sense, SNCC workers *lived* a critical pedagogy, both in the formation of "Freedom Schools" and in their critical stance toward U.S. power. While far from perfect, they built that critical stance on the foundation of universal values of love and community, values that inform the contemporary holistic education movement.

In this way, critical pedagogy and holistic education can help us to deconstruct U.S. power while fostering what Reardon calls a planetary consciousness necessary to build a more humane world. Holistic educator Dale Snauwaert's conception of a "shared humanity" and his cosmopolitan theory of democratic education advance a similar theme. He understands cosmopolitan as "an ethic that transcends national, communal and civilization values;" it means that we are "citizens of the world."[16] Holistic education can enable students to grasp these long-standing values of human dignity and connection, allowing for a serious and mature consideration of history. Critical pedagogy prevents this project from slipping into a narrow-minded nationalism by way of analyzing negative aspects in U.S. history, while holistic education enables us to preserve universal values of care, love, empathy and freedom without succumbing to cynicism. Critical pedagogy and holistic education are invaluable and complimentary tools for addressing U.S. international behavior.

Holistic Education and Empathy

While this framework calls for both critical engagement and holistic awareness, a full-fledged philosophy of peace education that synthesizes critical reason with a deeper understanding of human connectedness is needed. Such a premise demands a paradigm shift in our thinking, one that redefines both American power and what it means to be human. Holistic education's focus on human connection and empathy serves as the foundation for this new cosmology. Experiencing the interrelationship of all life requires empathy, the feeling of a common bond that stimulates moral responsibility. The intersection among holism, empathy and moral engagement is captured in Martin Luther King, Jr.'s *Letter from Birmingham Jail.* He wrote that, "Injustice anywhere is a threat to justice everywhere. We are caught in an inescapable network of mutuality, tied together in a single garment of destiny."[17] Not only is empathy a holistic value, but it is also the exact opposite of the psychological projections that underpin U.S. foreign policy behavior. Projection entails denying one's feelings and displacing them onto others. Empathy subsumes other people's emotions and suffering as one's own. It is only by way of genuine empathy for the victims of U.S. foreign policy that we can begin the process of reformulating American hegemony.

Throughout this book, the urgency of discovering a new way of thinking about U.S. power has been stressed. One way to reconceptualize U.S. dominance is to critically analyze U.S. policy, which is the content of critical pedagogy. Yet, the more pressing task is to "deal imaginatively" with this content.[18] To accomplish this task, we must probe the deeper sources of our thinking that contribute to the sense of alienation that so readily permits us to project our misdeeds onto adversaries. The philosophical and political dualisms that animate U.S. foreign policy are in part a product of centuries-old modern thinking. U.S. leader's distortion of ideals of good and evil into categories of standing either for or against us is the political expression of the philosophical tendency to divide reality into sharp distinctions of man and nature, knowledge and values. Holistic education aims to transcend these modern dualisms and highlight human connection that fosters creative conflict resolution. It takes seriously Einstein's belief that the "most important function of [critical reason]" is to "awaken the religious feeling" and "experience the universe as a whole."[19] This awakening is not to be confused with a religious revival, but a sense of connecting with others and can be experienced in secular and spiritual ways.

Modern skeptics frequently dismiss such visions as utopian and idealistic, as qualities that are unrealistic. Holistic education is crucial insofar as it transforms these seemingly immature dreams into living realities. Therefore, this section outlines two distinctive features of holistic education and thinking: (1) the quality of human connection and the empathy it engenders; and (2) the threefold process that cultivates the resources for a new way of thinking about ourselves and U.S. supremacy. After firmly establishing the resources for a new way of knowing, we discuss how critical pedagogy proceeds from this holistic awareness, which provides a foundation for critiques of U.S. policy without generating shame and an excessive degree of tension.

Before we discuss the elements of holistic education, it is necessary to understand the sources of this modern skepticism that shuns so-called idealistic images. The modern mind-set, which is our dominant way of knowing, began roughly in the seventeenth century with Descartes's famous demarcation of mind and body. Equally significant was his separation of all substances into primary and secondary qualities, borrowed from Galileo, which divides mind and matter as well as the material and spiritual. This Cartesian dualism signifies a turning point in human history. The demarcation of mind and body symbolizes the assumption that humankind no longer participates in nature, but is instead an "onlooker." As a spectator set apart from nature, humankind has developed a scientific consciousness that seeks to divide, measure, count and classify the physical world. This scientific onlooker consciousness — known variously as mechanism, materialism, reductionism or scientism — is both a blessing and a curse. It is a blessing insofar as it yields clear thinking, individuality and freedom. Mechanism is a curse in its obsessive drive to carve up, calculate and categorize the entire spectrum of reality, and insert itself as the dominant way of knowing. It is this attempt to quantify human existence that is most problematic as it renders the realm of feeling, community and empathy insignificant to the degree to which they are immeasurable. Under this paradigm, Martin Luther King, Jr. and Einstein's observation that we are interrelated appear idealistic. Yet, an error-prone missile defense system known as "Star Wars" is considered a realistic solution to international crisis.

The basic idea here is that modernity is an evolutionary process marked by the rise of reason, science and competitive nation-states, as Richard Falk puts it.[20] This process appeared in the Western world from the Middle Ages to the industrial revolution, climaxing in the nuclear age. As the philosopher David Ray Griffin aptly notes, "the modern mechanical framework by itself would not, of course, have led to a global crisis, it did this only as it became expressed through modern economics and the accompanying industrial revolution."[21] And, "not only is America more responsible than any other nation for the present condition of the planet," Falk and Griffin collectively conclude, "it is also the main symbol and embodiment of modernity" in the twenty-first century.[22] Indeed, the modern assumption that humans (the subject) stand above nature (the object) is channeled into the dominant structures of modernity, spawning divisions of class and nation, with the United States as the supreme nation or superpower.

Holistic educator Douglas Sloan has shown that, despite its vast achievements, this modern framework cannot deal with the ultimate facets of human existence. The realm of meaning, hope, empathy, love and human connection clearly fall outside the parameters of modern rational explanation. Along these lines, it is gradually becoming clear that the authority of modern thinking cannot address the complexity of the world's crises, from global warming to war. Consider the widespread interest in environmental recycling, organic gardening and a peace movement that mobilized millions of demonstrators across the globe in February 2003. All of these developments suggest that people crave a new way of thinking. In these attempts to imagine a better world, people seem to be asking if there is "some deep connection between our attitude toward the earth and the kind of thinking and knowing that have also produced things like nuclear bombs?"[23]

Sloan also reminds us that education at all levels has a responsibility to address such questions. It must nurture the imagination to move beyond technical solutions to the world's problems. The realism that propels U.S. foreign policy lacks imagination, offering only the most technical solutions to international dilemmas. American planners promise sophisticated weapons — "smart bombs" and "missile defense" — as the only realistic approach to international crises. It is clear that these modern technological solutions alone cannot produce a lasting security. Although critical reason can reveal the failures of these military options, we must encourage a new way of thinking that moves beyond the technical and rational. Educators can join this effort by cultivating holistic values such as empathy.

Empathy should be understood as a way of knowing and not simply a sentimental treat; it is knowledge about another's suffering. In fact, the very concept of human rights that critical pedagogy utilizes to unmask U.S. misdeeds arises from empathy. Recall that the Universal Declaration of Human Rights insists that all human beings should be free from unmerited harm. According to this historic document, individuals and nations must empathize with the pain of others. In effect, empathy entails a moral responsibility to care about others because we comprehend our connection to them; it captures the essence of King's sentiment that we are all tied together by a single garment of destiny.

What empathy also permits is the acknowledgment of our role in causing other people to suffer, paving the way for moral, corrective action. For one thing, the celebrated psychologist Carl Rogers reminds us that empathy is central to caring, altruistic behavior. The role of care and empathy is important here as they provide the moral foundation for accepting guilt, which paves the way for reparative action. Most importantly, psychologists Tangney and Dearing conclude that "guilt and empathy work together in a mutually enhancing fashion," while Baumeister finds that accepting guilt originates in empathy. Indeed, the acknowledgment of guilt is rooted in what psychologists call "other-oriented empathy."[24] Empathy, then, is a holistic value that requires an understanding of human interrelatedness. To care about how one's actions impact the well-being of others ultimately requires an intimate comprehension of the feelings and emotions of others. It is exactly this penetrating consciousness or deeper awareness of others that is the purpose of holistic education.

It is worth noting that Scheff directly links this sense of empathy to foreign policy. He illustrates that war is rooted in alienated, broken relationships that lack empathy. Staub similarly found a marked inability among violent combatants to empathize with their victims as they remained alienated from them. A fragmented, alienated mind-set clearly accompanies violent behavior. Scheff argues that the solution to such attitudes is to "develop a new language, one that does not deny interdependence or emotion."[25] A language of connection encourages the expression of emotions, moving us from denial toward the acceptance of guilt.

Holistic education is one model for changing the language of alienation to one of connection. It permits students to see beyond simplistic, dualistic frameworks. Essentially, holistic thinking demands a transformation of our consciousness, creating mature human beings capable of the empathy and self-awareness to build a new language about ourselves and U.S. foreign policy. But how can we develop the capacities to obtain this transformation?

Holistic educators, principally those associated with Waldorf education, suggest what they call "threefold imagination"—thinking, feeling and willing—is what is needed to steer us off a cycle of detachment and denial.[26] We do not need to agree with all the tenets of holism and "threefold thinking" to appreciate its role in facilitating empathy. This threefold process transcends subject/object dualisms that sustain alienation. The subject and the object, the knower and the known, interpenetrate. The participatory nature of the threefold imagination yields a sense of belonging—a meaning, value and purpose—an identity. That is, "threefold thinking" helps us to see that our individual identity and creative impulses are part of the whole nature of being. When these impulses become an active, participating part within the whole matrix of meaning, the identity of the part is confirmed by the whole and vice versa. Our individual "part" belongs to the whole. As David Steindl-Rast says, this belonging is precisely what love is; it is the "yes to belonging." Such a realization amounts to the rediscovery of meaning insofar as it says "yes" to our interdependence. A similar observation can be seen in Erich Fromm's concept of erotic love as being exclusive among two individuals, but it loves in the other person all of humankind.[27] The threefold imagination facilitates the experience of identifying with the world by way of the creative interaction with our environment. On the surface, the threefold process appears obscure, yet it speaks to the love, which is perhaps the most elemental of human experiences. The specific components (thinking, feeling and willing) of the threefold imagination help us to grasp how a participatory thinking develops love and empathy rather than projection and violence.

Douglas Sloan's *Insight-Imagination: The Emancipation of Thought and the Modern World* offers a succinct and readable overview of this threefold process. Thinking signifies our detached, alienated modern thinking. The past three hundred years of Cartesian experience push thinking away from nature into a detached, onlooker mode of consciousness. Thinking is simply our conscious separation from the world, a vital part of the imagination as it provides our rational self and individuality. On the other end of the spectrum is willing. Willing is our direct, immediate unconscious participation in the world. What is absent in willing is the conscious awareness of participation. For example, this brand of participation is expressed by athletes who "lose themselves in the zone." When you are in the "zone," you must avoid thinking as it disrupts the rhythm of unconscious activity. Feeling is our conscious participation that mediates thinking and willing. In other words, feeling brings together the isolation associated with thinking and the "sleeping" participation of willing to inspire a wakeful, mindful participation in the whole of existence.[28]

Eugene Schwartz provides a practical example of how educators might activate this threefold imagination.[29] In a geometry lesson, students first walk the shape of the geometrical figure. They would later draw that figure, not as a didactic form, but with colors chosen by the students to demonstrate the geometric principles involved. This example shows how children can learn to think with their whole being. After walking the figure, when it comes time to draw it, the image comes from the child's entire being rather than from a teacher's command. In this way, geometry is not only memorized in the brain but also experienced with the body, as Schwartz explains. The child permits the form to penetrate her being, while at the same time developing her inner capacity to comprehend and re-create the outside world. Gradually, the student learns to trust her own image-making capacities and is more likely to think in morally creative ways. Such a systematic imagination encourages one to refashion the prevailing images of the world.

In brief, holistic education may contribute to a new way of knowing through thinking, feeling and willing. This qualitative change of thinking and relating instills human connection and empathy, which are inextricably linked to moral engagement. Borrowing strategies from holistic pedagogy aids the development of creative changes in our thinking that is necessary to construct a new national narrative.

Critical Pedagogy and Transforming Images

While the two schools of thought choose different entry points, critical pedagogy and holistic education both seek to foster human freedom and agency. Critical pedagogy's entry point is more politically explicit, focusing on economic and social injustice. We should first note that there is no uniform definition of critical pedagogy. One of its leading U.S. proponents, Peter McLaren, describes critical pedagogy as "struggling at the level of social relations of production for economic justice for all working people. It is also about re-creating culture and agency through the practice of criticism." Another American critical educator, Henry Giroux, explains that pedagogy "refers to the production of and complex relations among knowledge, texts, desire and identity, it signals how questions of voice, power and evaluation work to construct particular relations among teachers and students, institutions and society and classrooms and communities." Critical pedagogy illuminates the relationship among "knowledge, authority and power," and highlights concerns over "who has control over the conditions for the pedagogical production of knowledge."[30] Simply put, critical pedagogy stimulates critical consciousness about oppressive structures, particularly the educational system.

Critical pedagogy, properly understood, flows naturally from holistic education's participatory consciousness. Consider Paulo Freire's insistence that students discover what constitutes injustice on their own. Freire was a Brazilian educator whose *Pedagogy of the Oppressed* (1970) popularized the concept of critical education. Much like holistic education, Freire (and critical pedagogy) rejects the "banking system" of education whereby the teacher deposits facts into the student's brain to be memorized and recited. Instead, teachers should promote a "dialogue" that stimulates the student's "creative power." This dialogic encounter is not a technique; it is a space where human beings "meet to reflect on their reality as the make and remake it." Freire adds that "dialogue cannot exist ... in the absence of a profound love for the world ... love is commitment to others."[31] Here we notice that critical pedagogy's success rests on the human connection that holistic education facilitates. That is, both approaches demand a participatory knowledge rooted in love. Whereas critical pedagogy sees participation largely as political action, it depends on holistic concepts of human connection and cooperation for its success. Critical pedagogy's political awareness and demand for action coupled with holistic education's emphasis on human connection provides a solid foundation for rethinking U.S. imperial power.

This observation is most obvious when we trace the historical roots of critical pedagogy. The theory is inseparable from Latin American religious revolts, and it achieved its greatest success in this arena. Freire himself was a devout Catholic and his method gained notoriety as a result of what it accomplished in Christian Base Communities in the 1960s. Liberation theology (the idea that the church should embrace a "preferential option" for the poor) swept across Latin America at the time. Freire's method was used by priests and catechists to teach literacy to landless peasants, and the results were extraordinary. For example, Freire's method was put to use to resist a U.S.–sponsored dictatorship in Brazil, where the Basic Education Movement rallied against the "national security state."[32] It is crucial to note that the historical foundation for critical pedagogy is inextricably bound to a communal revolution against government repression.

However, there is a tendency among North American educators to overlook the link between liberation theology and critical pedagogy. This omission might help to explain critical pedagogy's lack of success in North America. Freire openly acknowledged this failure, stating that, "In the U.S. there is a habit to think ... in a positivist way."[33] Whatever the reason for critical pedagogy's limits in the United States, it is important to understand its deep debt to liberation theology. The liberationists employed an image of a humble God who sides with the poor, which accounts for the early success of critical pedagogy. As Freire writes, "a revolution cannot manage without a prophetic vision," and "this prophetic attitude emerges in the praxis of numerous Christians challenging the historical situation in Latin America ... inviting them to a new exodus."[34] It is the image of a downtrodden Jesus, crucified by Roman imperialists that inspired the poor throughout Latin America.

Again, this chapter is not a call for inserting religion into U.S. schools, which are not nearly as homogenous as the communities where the Basic Education Movement achieved success. But humble, quasi-spiritual, perhaps even existential images can be utilized to refashion America's narrative of chosenness. Critical educators can work to counter what John Dewey described as the "religious idealization of, and reverence for, established institutions." For instance, "in our own politics, the Constitution, the Supreme Court, private property ... the words 'sacred' and 'sanctity' come readily to our lips when such things come under discussion," Dewey cautioned.[35] Teaching about the role of religion in empire/nation-building is not to teach theology; nor is the presentation of counter-hegemonic uses of spirituality in history a religious exercise. The important church/state separation can not be eroded simply by studying the historical uses of religious metaphors. Critical pedagogy can enter the foreign policy critique by way of analyzing the U.S. dominant metaphor and contrasting it with heroic figures who adopted the image of a humble creator. For example, educators might examine the critical-holistic vision that sustained Harriet Tubman, the "Moses of her people." Consider also the spiritual resources that Oscar Romero and Martin Luther King, Jr. utilized to directly challenge U.S. militarism. A cosmology of domination indeed drives U.S. power and it will likely take fresh, new images of humility and empathy to unseat it. In rediscovering its historical connection to liberation theology, critical pedagogy can go a long way in rethinking U.S. power. However, on the U.S. terrain, more inclusive secular substitutes must supplement its use and can play the same role as the religious language that galvanized the Latin American masses.

Something similar is presented in Maxine Greene's essay "In Search of a Critical Pedagogy" in the *Harvard Educational Review*. She praises the work of Freire while understanding that "a critical pedagogy relevant to the United States today must go beyond" the prevailing image of Latin American critical education and call on "different memories." While U.S. educators certainly should not discard Freire and the global roots of liberation pedagogy, it might be well to locate a parallel experience in the American tradition. Greene instructs critical educators to "make audible" the U.S. tradition of "rebellious figures" who demanded justice and equality. "Rebellious figures" like Henry David Thoreau, Frederick Douglass, Sarah Grimke, and Elizabeth Cady Stanton employed the "language of those who carried on the original demand for independence." Indeed, ordinary freedom fighters inherit a critical pedagogy that upholds their right to resistance. Public school teachers and university academics "seldom speak the language of resistance," owing principally to their allegiance to "educational bureaucracies."[36] There is a long history of challenging the dominant ideology on the American terrain.

The present book maintains that perhaps the most powerful example of this countervailing tradition that North American peace educators should turn to is the Mississippi Freedom Schools in 1964, which is a uniquely North American critical pedagogy. Like Freire, the Freedom Schools promoted "problem-solving through case studies dealing with relevant political, economic and social issues." A Teacher's Manual from Freedom Summer instructs teachers to use materials that are directly relevant to the student's life and experience. The overall approach was "open-ended," and reached for "real dialogue among students and between students and teachers, which more than anything else, constitutes a learning situation."[37] Teaching materials were designed to empower disenfranchised African Americans, but they were not limited to civil rights issues alone. Students examined James Joyce, the philosophy of Sartre and they were engaged in a variety of theater activities.

Of special significance to this study is that the freedom schools also tackled American foreign policy. The students drafted the "1964 Platform of the Mississippi Freedom School Convention" at the end of the summer. It highlighted the importance of addressing foreign affairs, noting that "The United States should stop supporting dictatorships in other countries." The platform went on to describe the importance of academic freedom, direct action and civil disobedience, which the students strongly suggested were educational matters that must be subsumed by the schools. One youngster maintained that this platform should be sent to the Mississippi legislature, the president of the United States and the Secretary-General of the United Nations. The student was asking that the Mississippi Freedom School Convention "be taken seriously."[38] Critical pedagogy should indeed take seriously the freedom summer campaign in developing curriculum and teaching philosophies for the twenty-first century. In short, it provides a viable model of student-centered, critical education that frequently dealt with spiritual metaphors, while retaining its secular independence. As much as Freire deserves our admiration and continued attention, critical peace educators should turn to the Mississippi Freedom Schools as both an example to shape their own pedagogy and a model to students as a glimpse of what is possible.

Diplomatic historian William Appleman Williams also enables us to understand how educators can dismantle the religious language of empire without succumbing to teaching theology. Instead of "a theology of the City on A Hill," that is "inherently destructive," the United States needs to think of religion as "another word for community."[39] U.S. citizens, Williams continued, must examine the "psychopathology of empire," particularly the belief that the City on the Hill "has the right to expect to control the world."[40] In the United States, people tend to "confus[e] metaphor with reality," but they fail to comprehend that the metaphor is like a "cookie, held too long in a hot fist it will crumble." We need a "different hierarchy of values," Williams insisted, which understand that "love comes before power." U.S. power constitutes a "benevolent despotism," or control by the few and submission by the many. Such a relationship breeds contempt and undermines genuine community inasmuch as it "fails to satisfy the demands for love and participation." Indeed, true community understands that "Love is a I-Thou relationship," based on the empathy and human connection that this chapter articulates. Creating these "new visions, virtues and procedures" requires creative energy, which is one reason why Williams invited conservatives and radicals to collectively build an "American community," with an identity that moves beyond national pride, power and empire.[41] Hence, Williams asked if the U.S. Republic has the "imagination or the courage to say 'no' to empire."[42]

More practically, critical educator Peter McLaren is well known for his attempt to say no to empire within school settings. In an article with Ramin Farahmandpur, he argues that "critical media literacy" can help to transcend the all-consuming images of empire. Teachers can empower students to gain a "language of critique." The authors "believe that educators have a moral and ethical obligation" to provide the space for students to "question and critique the right-wing's efforts to rally people around ... foreign U.S. policy initiatives." Chapter 5 in this text that mentions some examples of the administration's manipulation of the media might serve as case studies. Judith Miller's reporting for the *New York Times* that uncritically repeated the administration's claim that Iraq possessed weapons of mass destruction can be utilized to examine charges of "liberal" media bias while promoting critical media literacy. Similarly, journalists and government officials collaborated to "out" CIA employee Valerie Plame, who was the wife of Joseph Wilson, a government operative who refuted the administration's allegations that Iraq purchased uranium from an African nation. Moreover, "critical media literacy" can help students to discover how patriotism is frequently conflated with capitalism and consumerism in American culture.[43] This process can be readily applied to U.S. metaphors, such as the City on a Hill.

Peace educators can say no to empire by way of refashioning cultural metaphors and analyzing specific instances of U.S. international aggression. On the one hand, this stance requires a critical pedagogy that uncovers the perils of empire. On the other hand, this creative, imaginative stance requires a deeper grasp of human connection that holistic thinking provides. Holistic education and critical pedagogy offer the ideal tools for rebuilding the United States' dominant narrative of chosenness, moving us away from moral superiority and toward a more humble vision.

Nonviolence Works

Part of this vision entails teachers modeling empathy and pointing to practical examples of nonviolent struggles that grow out of these peace values. For one thing, as Birgit Brock-Utne has argued, peace educators must do far more than simply critique structures of dominance. We must facilitate alternative visions. One seemingly simple and obvious way that educators can develop alternative visions is to cultivate a sense of security, confidence and self-esteem in our students. A sense of security and genuine self-worth are the building blocks for the capacities of empathy and peace. Too often school structures tend to "rank" students in a competitive struggle over grades and individual achievement, an environment that lends itself to anxiety and insecurity. The teacher's daily routine must consciously break through these institutional constraints that militate against cooperation and harmony. A basic starting point begins with the question, "Do I as a teacher do whatever I can to help my pupils gain a feeling of self-security and self-esteem?"[44] Affirmation of the student is critical, not for professional success, but for modeling compassion and what it means to empathize with others.

Equally important is that we do not slide into the trap of critiquing structures of dominance without a corresponding emphasis on the traditions of successful peace activism. In the social studies classroom, for instance, the curriculum is often presented in thematic form. Perhaps educators should consider the inclusion of nonviolence as a theme; it has been practiced across the globe in a variety of settings and offers constructive visions for students. History abounds with examples of nonviolent action, such as the antislavery movement, women's suffrage, labor strikes and sit-ins, student demonstrations, civil rights activism, and anti-imperialist struggles. While success is not gained in every case of direct action, there are countless examples of nonviolent movements that made considerable gains.

Texts such as Fredrik Heffermehl's *Peace Is Possible*, Peter Akerman's *A Force More Powerful: A Century of Non-Violent Conflicts*, Gene Sharp's *The Politics of Non-Violent Action*, Staughton and Alice Lynd's *Nonviolence in America: A Documentary History* and Charles Debenedetti's *Peace Heroes in Twentieth Century America* are exemplary in promoting awareness about peace movements. We owe it to our students and future generations to affirm all that is good in the world just as we owe it to them to open the door to what is wrong in the world. We do our students and ourselves a disservice if we debunk U.S. foreign policy without highlighting the grand achievements of ordinary Americans, both north and south of the equator, who keep alive human democracy and human community through nonviolent struggle. Here we can turn to the U.S. Republic to appraise the U.S. Empire. As one historian observes, "the United States has more often been teacher than student in the history of the nonviolent idea."[45] In fact, that African Americans in U.S. history often responded to white terrorism with nonviolent, direct action serves as one of the world's most potent examples of peace activism. Peace educators Berlowitz, Long and Jackson have pointed out how black freedom movements are often linked to broader issues of peace and war. Consider A. Phillip Randolph's call for draft resistance, W.E. B. DuBois's Peace Information Center, Bayard Rustin's conscientious objection to war, Diane Nash Bevel's trip to Vietnam and Martin Luther King, Jr.'s opposition to U.S. imperialism.[46] These movements grow out of the U.S. Republic but are rooted in the concepts of global citizenship and human dignity for all. The African American freedom struggle was hardly a single-issue organization, and it deserves greater attention as an example of how to envision positive peace as we critique structures of dominance. "In measuring the full implications of the civil rights revolution," Martin Luther King, Jr. notes, "the greatest contribution may be in the area of world peace."[47] Indeed, peace educators should emphasize this critical contribution to a nonviolent philosophy.

The civil rights movement also helps us to understand that nonviolence is not simply pacifism. Gene Sharp points out that nonviolence is a political strategy that includes mass action, noncooperation, civil disobedience, including the "occupation of offices, sit-downs on the street, hunger strikes, establishment of new economic institutions, nonviolent invasions, overloading of administrative facilities, seeking imprisonment and parallel government." These strategies have been implemented throughout the world, sometimes with remarkable success. Many are familiar with Mohandas Gandhi's nonviolent campaigns against the British Empire. Dictatorships in El Salvador and Guatemala in 1944 were removed in large part as a consequence of nonviolent demonstrations. At a time when some scholars deemed the notion of revolution as outdated, the world watched as nonviolent movements ousted Communist regimes in Estonia, East Germany and Lithuania in the early 1990s. The attempted hard-line coup in Russia at the same time was halted by nonviolent action. One can include struggles against apartheid in South Africa and Marcos in the Philippines during the 1980s and our list would remain incomplete.[48] It is worth noting that nonviolent movements have achieved success across time and place. Although we must never romanticize such movements, they have worked in both democracies and dictatorships. Students and citizens deserve a balanced curriculum that treats nonviolence as a viable theme. Too often students are treated with examples on how non-violence only encourages tyrants or is a melodramatic fantasy reserved for hippies and dreamers. While this depiction is a bit of an exaggeration, text-books and curriculum frequently devote considerable space to war, and fail to illustrate how nonviolence surfaces in some unexpected events. Paying closer attention to these nonviolent movements offers greater "balance" and permits students to decide for themselves where such action is appropriate. To be sure, peace educators should never impose a particular view, but merely present constructive visions for our students. One dramatic case entails non-violent resistance to Nazism that is often overshadowed by the glorification of the "good war" in U.S. schools.

During the Second World War, we witnessed the ghastly extermination of some six millions Jews, but some states defied Nazi extermination orders. In Bulgaria 90 percent of its Jewish population was saved from the Holocaust as a result of courageous action.[49] King Boris III, Dimitar Peshev and members of the Bulgarian National Assembly opposed the deportation of the Jew-ish community. Public protests against anti–Semitic laws were carried out by "trade associations, the Central Jewish Consistory and the Holy Synod, ordi-nary citizens and politicians," observes one study of the resistance.[50] Church leaders and regular office workers spoke out against deportation and opposed Hitler, providing a striking example of the power of nonviolence. In 1993, Michael Bar-Zohar, a Bulgarian survivor, visited Emory University in the southern United States; he was surprised to learn that the Second World War's "largest" rescue of Jews "was almost completely unknown." After learning about the Bulgarian success, some incredulous listeners said, "If it were true, we would have known about it."[51]

The frequent dismissal of nonviolent alternatives, often obfuscated by the Munich analogy in the case of the Second World War, renders them unbe-lievable. Munich refers to the 1938 conference in the Germany city, where Britain and France ceded parts of Czechoslovakia to Hitler in exchange for his pledge to take no more territory. British prime minister Neville Cham-berlain declared that the conference constituted "peace in our time," and ever since proponents of war evoke Munich to suggest that nonviolence aids and abets despotism. In truth, Munich was as much about power politics as it was about maintaining *negative* peace. We should keep in mind that British and U.S. companies continued to trade valuable war materials to the Nazis at this time.[52] The U.S. State Department found that "fascism was compatible with free trade," and even classified Hitler as a "moderate" Nazi.[53] Franklin Delano Roosevelt also turned to Mussolini, whom he earlier called an "admirable Italian gentleman," to work toward a favorable settlement at Munich. The Czechs and Russians were largely excluded from the negotiations, leading Stalin to accuse the Western powers of pushing Germany toward the Soviet Union. This controversial accusation is not easily dismissed as Breckenridge Long, an ambassador to Italy and U.S. undersecretary of state in the Second World War, wrote that "if Germany should be dominant throughout the greater part of Europe, she would act as a bulwark against the Western progress of Russia."[54]

Many complicated factors led to the Munich agreement, which cannot be properly reduced solely to economic interests and the desire to frustrate the Soviets. Yet to simply characterize Munich as a failure of peace is to distort history. The point here is that the Munich analogy improperly obscures the power of nonviolence as illustrated in the Bulgarian example. The Munich analogy has been employed to diminish peace efforts and its role in distorting history requires attention.

History is replete with cases of everyday people overcoming seemingly insurmountable power. As noted, U.S. educators can turn to the civil rights movement and its wider connections to the Vietnam War as a lived example of a "critical-peace pedagogy." Nonviolent boycotts in Montgomery, Alabama, led to a Supreme Court decision that declared that city's segregated buses illegal in 1956. Mass action culminated in the Civil Rights Act (1964) and Voting Rights bill (1965); the black freedom struggle represents the hope that the U.S. Republic offers and allows us to say with confidence that nonviolence works.

Practical nonviolence skills can be practiced in the schools alongside a more balanced curriculum that studies peace as carefully as it studies war. It is important to illustrate to students that nonviolence can be successful both in history and in their immediate surroundings, but it requires commitment and hard work. For instance, *Waging Peace in Our Schools* by Linda Lantieri and Janet Patti is an indispensable resource for helping educators to create a more peaceful classroom environment. They offer practical strategies to foster conflict resolution skills. Such skills, the others argue, paves the way to creating peaceful schools. The book serves as a practical manual, owing principally to the author's experience working in the New York City public schools. In fact, Lantieri is cofounder of the Resolving Conflict Creatively Program (RCCP), which has enjoyed nationwide success.

Lantieri and Patti seek "the creation of a non-violent, pluralist society." This peaceful society is characterized by safe schools and revitalized communities built by individuals who understand how to resolve conflicts nonviolently. It entails a new vision of education, one predicated upon the social and emotional life of the child, the authors argue. When schools create "caring, safe communities," they facilitate the broader social concept of a peaceful society.[55]

While Lantieri and Patti do not address broader structural violence headon, they remind us that the "content-based" curriculum of traditional schooling lends itself to "elitism, competition [and] isolation."[56] Because U.S. schooling is frequently preoccupied with educating the "mind and not the heart," it serves as a stumbling block to peace insofar as it does not provide the adequate resources for children to resist a culture of violence. Lantieri and Patti offer practical strategies that accent an education of the heart that serves as a countervailing force to militarism. Indeed, they supply a concrete strategy to obtain their pedagogical goal of creating "peaceable schools." Three major aims inform their pedagogical approach: the ability to resolve conflicts creatively, the valuing of diversity and the enhancement of social and emotional learning. With an emphasis on conflict resolution, children are empowered to discuss their feelings, hear other people's point of view and develop an awareness of the multiple solutions available to resolve conflicts. The notion that students work together to generate multiple solutions to a conflict sits at the heart of resolving conflicts creatively. Through cooperative learning and "I-messages," students develop the capacity to express feelings, listen to each other and validate their peers.

As the authors explain it, the role of "I-messages" in conflict resolution pedagogy is essential to building peaceable schools. "I-messages" are an effective method for students to discuss their feelings. It enables them to locate their anger or frustration, what they are *feeling*, and then state it in a clear manner. Instead of focusing on blaming and casting one's adversaries as "trouble-makers" or even "ignorant," "I-messages" empower students to be assertive without attacking others. This assertiveness is gained by way of mastering the four parts of an "I-message." Lantieri and Patti write that the first part is stating, '*I feel*' (saying the emotion), the second part, '*when you,*' locates the other person's behavior. The next part '*because*' explains the impact of the behavior, while the last component is a constructive proposal, '*and I would like.*' As Lanteiri and Patti note, it may be difficult to incorporate this tool into one's teaching practice. The students "may feel foolish, phony or insincere because this is not the way they are used to acting."[57] Teachers must be patient and allow for the gradual development of this skill through repeated practice. "I-messages" are a practical vehicle for students and teachers to discuss difficult issues, including U.S. foreign policy behavior.

Conclusion

The critical analysis in this book targets the U.S. Empire, not the U.S. Republic. Simply put, we must say no to the U.S. Empire, a declaration that begins with a broader conception of the Republic, one that is bold and confident enough to say: "my country is the world." If peace education begins a systematic critique of U.S. imperial behavior, it is likely to be charged with bias, with imbalance or with suffocating the precious human freedom it intends to facilitate. As noted throughout the present book, peace educators should not promote a standard dogma or force students to agree with their analysis. Educators have the right and responsibility to offer alternatives to war, and peace educators must disclose this basic aim to their audience. This disclosure does not mean that such alternatives are infallible; it simply demands that alternative strategies must be part of any democratic dialogue. Students must still be offered a variety of perspectives and problems to solve, rather than the "right" answer to repeat. The problem, as conservative scholar Bacevich observes, is that "a consensus has been formed in mainstream politics ... that force works.... They all think that there are no plausible alternatives." Whether or not these alternatives are defective, mainstream analysts "never really looked for them," complains Bacevich.[58] To effectively examine these alternative methods we must compare and contrast them to the military option, which is why the present author wishes to encourage peace educators to explore U.S. interventionism. In fact, this book can be considered an attempt to "look for" the options that Bacevich believes are missing themes in U.S. political discourse. Such an approach is neither unbalanced nor biased; rather, it expands the discussion to include views that are frequently overlooked and avoided.

U.S. foreign policy presents a significant impediment to peace education. The Bush II administration's preference for war assaults international standards and has contributed to the militarization of our culture, as spelled out in Bacevich's recent study. Peace education can slow this dangerous trend insofar as it systematically tackles the difficult realities behind American military prowess.

Peace education is perhaps the most appropriate educational field for tackling U.S. interventionism, while offering alternatives to war. The fundamental concepts of peace education promote vital skills for comprehending the U.S. role in the world. For instance, Reardon identifies planetary stewardship, global citizenship and humane relationships as the central tasks of peace education. Ian Harris builds on Reardon's key factors, citing peace education's distinctive features as addressing fear; understanding violent behavior; developing intercultural understanding; obtaining information about security systems; acquiring a respect for life; teaching peace as a process; fostering a future orientation; working to end violence and promoting social justice. All of these factors seek to teach students to think as global citizens, which fosters a human connection that moves beyond the nationalist identity promoted by U.S. themes of chosenness outlined in this work.

Moreover, peace education has developed extensive pedagogical tools that can be used to assess the U.S. role in international situations. Consider UNESCO's Integrated Framework of Action and Education for Peace, Human Rights and Democracy (1995) and the Hague Appeal for Peace, "Global Plan for Peace Education," which offer curriculum materials on the causes of war, weapons of mass destruction, interstate violence and cultural conflict. Under these circumstances, peace educators can go a long way in helping us to understand the United States' global role, using already existing resources and materials on global citizenship and the United Nations. Indeed, this book argues that we should measure U.S. behavior against the Universal Declaration of Human Rights, a document that already informs many peace education agendas.

We have witnessed how U.S. foreign policy often protects economic interests over human interests. A viable peace education that is firmly rooted in constructive, nonviolent tension must directly confront the U.S. Empire. As David Dellinger once wrote, "Nonviolence simply cannot defend property rights over human rights."[59] Or we might return to Galtung's foreword and affirm our distaste for the U.S. Empire and insist on a U.S. Republic that sees itself as part of the global community rather than above it.

Appendix: Using Primary Documents to Teach Contemporary U.S. Foreign Policy

The following documents are designed for use with this text and are most suitable to undergraduate courses in peace education, peace studies and international relations. Many of the documents can be easily adapted for use in a high school classroom. Document-Based Questions (DBQ) have become a major component of high school classrooms and they are part of standardized examinations in places such as New York State. While we can debate the legitimacy of these standardized examinations, the concept of a DBQ is educationally sound and can enhance college teaching as well. A document-based question requires that students analyze and interpret a "document," usually a primary source. This interpretation fosters critical thinking and the application of a student's prior knowledge. Some documents might ask a student to take a stand, which entails backing up their stance with evidence and logical arguments.

Political cartoons, opposing viewpoints and related material can be used to generate document-based questions as well. Peace educators can employ these documents in a classroom to inspire critical thinking, while at the same time offering students skills that can be applied elsewhere. It is important to include open-ended questions that permit students to explore alternative and opposing conclusions. This does not mean that a teacher must shy away from provocative questions. In fact, the National Council for Social Studies in its guide *Expectations for Excellence* rightly argues that "teaching and learning are powerful when they are value-based." That organization encourages teachers to introduce ethical dilemmas into instruction, especially those that are controversial. This approach affords students the opportunity to reflect seriously on their decisions while they consider the moral and social implications of their positions. Examining controversial issues facilitates the civic values that educators across the political spectrum tend to agree is important.

In the exercises that follow, significant documents related to U.S. foreign policy were selected as a companion to the content chapters. Questions follow each document that are deliberately provocative and designed to facilitate the critical thinking and analysis described above. Most of the questions follow Bloom's now famous and well known taxonomy of questioning. They proceed from the simple to the complex, where students are first asked "knowledge" questions to identify the date, place and context of the document. From here, the questions quickly work toward synthesis and especially Bloom's level of "evaluation." Questions that require evaluation center on students selecting a position that is supported by logical thinking, detecting bias and/or evaluating the worthiness of evidence.

Examining the Military-Industrial Complex

INTRODUCTION

This document would work well if students are assigned to read chapter 2 as homework. They can then determine the degree to which the chapter offers sufficient evidence for the presence of the military-industrial complex. If not, further research should be encouraged!

Due to time constraints in a high school classroom, it might be necessary to trim this passage. Paragraph 7, beginning with "This conjunction..." and paragraph 8 are essential to understanding the military-industrial complex and should be included in any modification.

* * *

President Dwight D. Eisenhower, "Farewell Address," January 17, 1961

This evening I come to you with a message of leave-taking and farewell, and to share a few final thoughts with you, my countrymen.... We now stand ten years past the midpoint of a century that has witnessed four major wars among great nations. Three of these involved our own country. Despite these holocausts America is today the strongest, the most influential and most productive nation in the world. Understandably proud of this pre-eminence, we yet realize that America's leadership and prestige depend, not merely upon our unmatched material progress, riches and military strength, but on how we use our power in the interests of world peace and human betterment.

Throughout America's adventure in free government, our basic purposes have been to keep the peace; to foster progress in human achievement, and to enhance liberty, dignity and integrity among people and among nations. To strive for less would be unworthy of a free and religious people.... Progress toward these noble goals is persistently threatened by the conflict now engulfing the world. It commands our whole attention, absorbs our very beings. We face a hostile ideology — global in scope, atheistic in character, ruthless in purpose, and insidious in method. Unhappily the danger it poses promises to be of indefinite duration. To meet it successfully, there is called for, not so much the emotional and transitory sacrifices of crisis, but rather those which enable us to carry forward steadily, surely, and without complaint the burdens of a prolonged and complex struggle — with liberty at stake. Only thus shall we remain, despite every provocation, on our charted course toward permanent peace and human betterment. Crises there will continue to be. In meeting them, whether foreign or domestic, great or small, there is a recurring temptation to feel that some spectacular and costly action could become the miraculous solution to all current difficulties. A huge increase in newer elements of our defense; development of unrealistic programs to cure every ill in agriculture; a dramatic expansion in basic and applied research — these and many other possibilities, each possibly promising in itself, may be suggested as the only way to the road we wish to travel.

But each proposal must be weighed in the light of a broader consideration: the need to maintain balance in and among national programs — balance between the private and the public economy, balance between cost and hoped for advantage — balance between the clearly necessary and the comfortably desirable; balance between our essential requirements as a nation and the duties imposed by the nation upon the individual; balance between action of the moment and the national welfare of the future. Good judgment seeks balance and progress; lack of it eventually finds imbalance and frustration.

The record of many decades stands as proof that our people and their government have, in the main, understood these truths and have responded to them well, in the face of stress and threat. But threats, new in kind or degree, constantly arise. I mention two only.

A vital element in keeping the peace is our military establishment. Our arms must be mighty, ready for instant action, so that no potential aggressor may be tempted to risk his own destruction.

Our military organization today bears little relation to that known by any of my predecessors in peace time, or indeed by the fighting men of World War II or Korea.

Until the latest of our world conflicts, the United States had no armaments industry. American makers of plowshares could, with time and as required, make swords as well. But now we can no longer risk emergency improvisation of national defense; we have been compelled to create a permanent armaments industry of vast proportions. Added to this, three and a half million men and women are directly engaged in the defense establishment. We annually spend on military security more than the net income of all United States corporations.

This conjunction of an immense military establishment and a large arms industry is new in the American experience. The total influence — economic, political, even spiritual — is felt in every city, every state house, every office of the Federal government. We recognize the imperative need for this development. Yet we must not fail to comprehend its grave implications. Our toil, resources and livelihood are all involved; so is the very structure of our society.

In the councils of government, we must guard against the acquisition of unwarranted influence, whether sought or unsought, by the military-industrial complex. The potential for the disastrous rise of misplaced power exists and will persist.

We must never let the weight of this combination endanger our liberties or democratic processes. We should take nothing for granted only an alert and knowledgeable citizenry can compel the proper meshing of huge industrial and military machinery of defense with our peaceful methods and goals, so that security and liberty may prosper together.

Akin to, and largely responsible for the sweeping changes in our industrial-military posture, has been the technological revolution during recent decades.

In this revolution, research has become central; it also becomes more formalized, complex, and costly. A steadily increasing share is conducted for, by, or at the direction of, the Federal government.

Today, the solitary inventor, tinkering in his shop, has been over shadowed by task forces of scientists in laboratories and testing fields. In the same fashion, the free university, historically the fountainhead of free ideas and scientific discovery, has experienced a revolution in the conduct of research. Partly because of the huge costs involved, a government contract becomes virtually a substitute for intellectual curiosity. For every old blackboard there are now hundreds of new electronic computers.

The prospect of domination of the nation's scholars by Federal employment, project allocations, and the power of money is ever present and is gravely to be regarded.

Yet, in holding scientific research and discovery in respect, as we should, we must also be alert to the equal and opposite danger that public policy could itself become the captive of a scientific-technological elite.

It is the task of statesmanship to mold, to balance, and to integrate these and other forces, new and old, within the principles of our democratic system — ever aiming toward the supreme goals of our free society.

Another factor in maintaining balance involves the element of time. As we peer into society's future, we — you and I, and our government — must avoid the impulse to live only for today, plundering, for our own ease and convenience, the precious resources of tomorrow. We cannot mortgage the material assets of our grandchildren without risking the loss also of their political and spiritual heritage. We want democracy to survive for all generations to come, not to become the insolvent phantom of tomorrow.

Down the long lane of the history yet to be written America knows that this world of ours, ever growing smaller, must avoid becoming a community of dreadful fear and hate, and be, instead, a proud confederation of mutual trust and respect. Such a confederation must be one of equals. The weakest must come to the conference table with the same confidence as do we, protected as we are by our moral, economic, and military strength. That table, though scarred by many past frustrations, cannot be abandoned for the certain agony of the battlefield.

Disarmament, with mutual honor and confidence, is a continuing imperative. Together we must learn how to compose difference, not with arms, but with intellect and decent purpose. Because this need is so sharp and apparent I confess that I lay down my official responsibilities in this field with a definite sense of disappointment. As one who has witnessed the horror and the lingering sadness of war — as one who knows that another war could utterly destroy this civilization which has been so slowly and painfully built over thousands of years — I wish I could say tonight that a lasting peace is in sight. Happily, I can say that war has been avoided. Steady progress toward our ultimate goal has been made. But, so much remains to be done. As a private citizen, I shall never cease to do what little I can to help the world advance along that road.

So — in this my last good night to you as your President — I thank you for the many opportunities you have given me for public service in war and peace.

Reflection Questions (these questions can be incorporated into a lesson, where only select queries are used or they can serve as the basis of a cooperative learning activity)

1. When did Eisenhower deliver this speech?
2. Eisenhower said that "Progress toward [America's] noble goals is persistently threatened by the conflict now engulfing the world." What conflict was engulfing the world?
3. According to Eisenhower, what exactly is the military-industrial complex?
4. In Eisenhower's speech is the military-industrial complex necessary or even useful?

5. Does Eisenhower think that the military-industrial complex is dangerous? If so, what does he say that makes it sound dangerous? What, if any, are the dangers of the military-industrial complex?

6. Consult chapter 2: Read the quotation from George Kennan and the sections on Iran and Guatemala. It is suggested that these interventions show the dangers of the military-industrial complex. To what degree are these interventions as presented solid evidence of the dangers of the military-industrial complex?

7. General Smedley Butler described the military as musclemen for big business. Some historians say that Butler's captures the essence of the military-industrial complex; others say that his comment is an exaggeration. Which position is more accurate and why?

8. Chapter 2 discusses U.S. interventions from roughly 1947 to the 1980s. Rate the following reasons for U.S. interventions in order of importance:

    ___spread democracy and freedom

    ___corporate pressures/profits for "big business"

    ___prevent dictators from seizing power

    ___oil

    ___contain communism.

Analyzing the Manipulation of Information

INTRODUCTION

Reprinted below are portions of the Central Intelligence Agency's (CIA) "Iraq's Weapons of Mass Destruction Program" and the International Atomic Energy Agency's (IAEA) overview of Iraq's weapons program. Both documents were drafted in the months immediately preceding the U.S. invasion of Iraq. Students should be asked to read each document and answer the questions that follow. The purpose of this exercise is to determine the degree to which the United States' exaggerated Iraq's threat based on reliable information that was available at the time and to critically analyze any discrepancies that may appear among the documents.

As for the IAEA report, it was drafted to address the concerns of UN Resolution 1441. In November 2002, the United Nation's Security Council Resolution passed UN Resolution 1441. It strongly admonished Iraq, yet it also established a new set of weapons inspections for the regime. Supporters of the war have argued that UN 1441 permitted the United States to invade Iraq; however, the document does not appear to endorse any such action on the part of the United States. The UN charter allows for the use of force for self-defense and in cases where the Security Council specifically endorses the necessity of force. The relevant passages of UN 1441 do not seem to authorize the use of force by the United States. Sections 4, 11 and 12 of UN 1441 address the issue of how to proceed if Iraq failed to comply with inspections:

4. *Decides* that false statements or omissions in the declarations submitted by Iraq pursuant to this resolution and failure by Iraq at any time to comply with, and cooperate fully in the implementation of, this resolution shall constitute a further material breach of Iraq's obligations and will be reported to the Council for assessment in accordance with paragraphs 11 and 12 below....

11. *Directs* the Executive Chairman of UNMOVIC [United Nations Monitoring, Verification and Inspection Commission] and the Director-General of the IAEA to report immediately to the Council any interference by Iraq with inspection activities, as well as any failure by Iraq to comply with its disarmament obligations, including its obligations regarding inspections under this resolution;

12. *Decides* to convene immediately upon receipt of a report in accordance with paragraphs 4 or 11 above, in order to consider the situation and the need for full compliance with all of the relevant Council resolutions in order to secure international peace and security.

Once again, these passages do not call for the use of force. The IAEA document printed below was prepared following UN 1441 and it describes Iraq's weapons program in such a way that contradicts the Bush administration's portrait as well as portions of the Central Intelligence Agency's report on Iraq's weapons of mass destruction.

In October 2002, the Central Intelligence Agency drafted what is known as the National Intelligence Estimate (NIE), which appears here under the title, "Iraq's Weapons of Mass Destruction Programs." Since its release, mainstream politicians and journalists have noted that it contains several inaccurate judgments about Iraq's weapons program. It has been suggested that the Bush administration pressured the CIA to exaggerate the threat that Iraq's program posed. Government insiders report that Vice President Dick Cheney visited the CIA an "unprecedented" number of times in the buildup to war.

* * *

Instructions:

Read the CIA's Key Judgments in respect to Iraq's Weapons of Mass Destruction Programs and the IAEA report related to UN 1441. Answer the questions that follow.

CIA Key Judgments
"Iraq's Weapons of Mass Destruction Programs" (October 2002)

Iraq has continued its weapons of mass destruction (WMD) programs in defiance of UN resolutions and restrictions. Baghdad has chemical and biological weapons as well as missiles with ranges in excess of UN restrictions; if left unchecked, it probably will have a nuclear weapon during this decade.

Baghdad hides large portions of Iraq's WMD efforts. Revelations after the Gulf War starkly demonstrate the extensive efforts undertaken by Iraq to deny information.

Since inspections ended in 1998, Iraq has maintained its chemical weapons effort, energized its missile program, and invested more heavily in biological weapons; most analysts assess Iraq is reconstituting its nuclear weapons program.

— Iraq's growing ability to sell oil illicitly increases Baghdad's capabilities to finance WMD programs; annual earnings in cash and goods have more than quadrupled.

— Iraq largely has rebuilt missile and biological weapons facilities damaged during Operation Desert Fox and has expanded its chemical and biological infrastructure under the cover of civilian production.

— Baghdad has exceeded UN range limits of 150 km with its ballistic missiles and is working with unmanned aerial vehicles (UAVs), which allow for a more lethal means to deliver biological and, less likely, chemical warfare agents.

— Although Saddam probably does not yet have nuclear weapons or sufficient material to make any, he remains intent on acquiring them.

IAEA Update Report for the Security Council
Pursuant to Resolution 1441 (2002)

[The IAEA is an inter–governmental body with over 2,000 members. It works to "promote safe, secure and peaceful nuclear technologies." The IAEA reports regularly to the United Nation's Security Council, and is the "world's nuclear inspectorate," having worked for over forty years on the nuclear verification process across the globe.]

1. This report is submitted by the International Atomic Energy Agency (IAEA) to the Security Council in accordance with resolution 1441 (2002), adopted on 8 November 2002, in paragraph 5 of which the Council requested the IAEA and the United Nations Monitoring, Verification and Inspection Commission (UNMOVIC) to resume inspections in Iraq no later than 45 days following adoption of that resolution, and to update the Council 60 days thereafter. Inspections in Iraq pursuant to resolu-

tion 1441 (2002) were resumed by the IAEA and UNMOVIC on 27 November 2002....

60. In support of the IAEA inspections, the Iraqi authorities have provided access to all facilities visited — including presidential compounds and private residences — without conditions and without delay, despite some complaints about the inconvenience or intrusive nature of the inspection activities....

65. In the first eight weeks of inspections, the IAEA has visited all sites identified by it or by States as significant. No evidence of ongoing prohibited nuclear or nuclear-related activities at those locations has been detected to date during these inspections, although not all of the laboratory results of sample analysis are yet available. Nor have the inspections thus far revealed signs of new nuclear facilities or direct support to any nuclear activity. However, further verification activities will be necessary before the IAEA will be able to provide credible assurance that Iraq has no nuclear weapons....

66. The IAEA has started to work at resolving the key issue of whether Iraqi nuclear activities or nuclear-related capabilities have changed since December 1998. Marked progress has already been made in areas about which major concerns had been expressed prior to the resumption of inspections: concerns raised over the construction or reconstruction of buildings at known facilities have been defused; and it appears, prima facie, that the high strength aluminum tubes were to be for the production of rockets and not for use in centrifuges for uranium enrichment, although assessment of the possibility that Iraq may have intended to modify the tubes in question later for use in centrifuges remains to be completed.... The disposition of the 32 tons of the previously monitored HMX [High Melting Point Explosives] that Iraq declared to have been used for civilian purposes, however, will be difficult to confirm....

71. The IAEA expects to be able, within the next few months, barring exceptional circumstances and provided there is sustained proactive cooperation by Iraq, to provide credible assurance that Iraq has no nuclear weapons programme. In the meantime, the presence in Iraq of inspectors with broad investigative and monitoring authority serves as a deterrent to, and insurance against, the resumption by Iraq of proscribed nuclear activities.

Reflection Questions

1. According to the Central Intelligence Agency, did Iraq possess nuclear weapons in the fall of 2002?

2. According to the International Atomic Energy Agency (IAEA), was it likely that Iraq had nuclear weapons during the fall of 2002?

3. The Central Intelligence Agency reported that Iraq engaged in "extensive efforts" to "deny information." The IAEA inspectors wrote that "Iraqi authorities have provided access to all facilities visited."

   What might account for the two agencies holding different opinions on Iraq's compliance? In your view, which agency is more reliable? Explain your answer.

4. In December 2002, President Bush said that "We don't know whether or not [Iraq] has a nuclear weapon." The IAEA document reported that inspections have not "revealed signs of new nuclear facilities or direct support to any nuclear activity." Some say Bush's remark was designed to deceive the American people; others say it was a reasonable assessment of the available information. Which position is more accurate and why?

5. President Bush announced in March 2003 that, "Intelligence gathered by this and other governments leaves no doubt that the Iraq regime continues to possess and conceal some of the most lethal weapons ever devised.... Before that day of horror can come, before it is too late to act, this danger will be removed." To what degree does the IAEA report raise some doubt about Iraq having the "most lethal weapons ever devised"? Does Bush's use of the words "no doubt" suggest that he was exaggerating or manipulating the facts? Why or why not?

Changing the Terminology from "War" to "Peace"

INTRODUCTION

In 1947, the National Defense Act centralized and expanded the national security state. Out of this legislation the War Department's name was changed to the Department of Defense. The previous chapters on U.S. interventionism indicate that the Department of Defense has frequently undertaken actions that are sometimes more aggressive than defensive. Congressman Dennis Kucinich (D–Ohio) has offered the nation a department that might serve as a balance to the War/Defense Department. In September 2005, he introduced a bill to form a cabinet-level Department of Peace and Nonviolence. The bill was reintroduced as House Resolution 808 in February 2007.

The notion of a peace department has deep roots in U.S. history. In 1792, African American scientists Benjamin Banneker and Benjamin Rush advocated for the formation of a peace department. During the 1930s, advocates of a peace department proposed various bills and again under the Carter administration in the late 1970s a U.S. Academy of Peace gained attention. While such efforts have been largely unsuccessful, the concept warrants debate and discussion.

Readers notice that the bill promotes a refashioning of America's understanding of the "City on a Hill," and appears to complement the arguments throughout this book. The bill also advocates the development of a peace education curriculum that points to the civil rights movement for guidance and inspiration.

Below is the full text of the Department of Peace and Nonviolence bill, followed by questions for reflection.

* * *

H.R. 808: Department of Peace and Nonviolence Act

110th CONGRESS
1st Session
H. R. 808
February 2007

A BILL
To establish a Department of Peace and Nonviolence.

Be it enacted by the Senate and House of Representatives of the United States of America in Congress assembled,

SECTION 1. SHORT TITLE; TABLE OF CONTENTS.

(a) Short Title — This Act may be cited as the 'Department of Peace and Nonviolence Act.'
(b) Table of Contents — The table of contents for this Act is as follows:
Sec. 1. Short title; table of contents.
Sec. 2. Findings.

TITLE I — ESTABLISHMENT OF DEPARTMENT OF PEACE AND NONVIOLENCE

Sec. 101. Establishment of Department of Peace and Nonviolence.
Sec. 102. Responsibilities and powers.
Sec. 103. Principal officers.
Sec. 104. Office of Peace Education and Training.
Sec. 105. Office of Domestic Peace Activities.
Sec. 106. Office of International Peace Activities.
Sec. 107. Office of Technology for Peace.
Sec. 108. Office of Arms Control and Disarmament.

Sec. 109. Office of Peaceful Coexistence and Nonviolent Conflict
Resolution.
Sec. 110. Office of Human Rights and Economic Rights.
Sec. 111. Intergovernmental Advisory Council on Peace and Nonviolence.
Sec. 112. Consultation required.
Sec. 113. Authorization of appropriations.

**TITLE II — ADMINISTRATIVE PROVISIONS AND
TRANSFERS OF AGENCY FUNCTIONS**

Sec. 201. Staff.
Sec. 202. Transfers.
Sec. 203. Conforming amendments.

**TITLE III — FEDERAL INTERAGENCY COMMITTEE
ON PEACE AND NONVIOLENCE**

Sec. 301. Federal Interagency Committee on Peace and Nonviolence.

TITLE IV — ESTABLISHMENT OF PEACE DAY

Sec. 401. Peace Day.

SEC. 2. FINDINGS.

Congress finds the following:

(1) On July 4, 1776, the Second Continental Congress unanimously declared
the independence of the 13 colonies, and the achievement of peace was
recognized as one of the highest duties of the new organization of free
and independent States.

(2) In declaring, "We hold these truths to be self–evident, that all Men are
created equal, that they are endowed by their Creator with certain unalien-
able rights, that among these are Life, Liberty and the Pursuit of Hap-
piness," the drafters of the Declaration of Independence, appealing to the
Supreme Judge of the World, derived the creative cause of nationhood
from "the Laws of Nature" and the entitlements of "Nature's God," such
literal referrals in the Declaration of Independence thereby serving to celebrate the unity of human thought, natural law, and spiritual causation.

(3) The architects of the Declaration of Independence "with a firm reliance
on the protection of divine providence" spoke to the connection between
the original work infusing principle into the structure of a democratic government seeking to elevate the condition of humanity, and the activity of
a higher power which moves to guide the Nation's fortune.

(4) The Constitution of the United States of America, in its Preamble, further

sets forth the insurance of the cause of peace in stating: "We the People of the United States, in Order to Form a more perfect Union, establish Justice, insure domestic Tranquility, provide for the common defense, promote the general welfare, and secure the Blessings of Liberty to ourselves and our Posterity."

(5) The Founders of this country gave America a vision of freedom for the ages and provided people with a document which gave this Nation the ability to adapt to an undreamed of future.

(6) It is the sacred duty of the people of the United States to receive the living truths of our founding documents and to think anew to develop institutions that permit the unfolding of the highest moral principles in this Nation and around the world.

(7) During the course of the 20th century, more than 100,000,000 people perished in wars, and now, at the dawn of the 21st century, violence seems to be an overarching theme in the world, encompassing personal, group, national, and international conflict, extending to the production of nuclear, biological, and chemical weapons of mass destruction which have been developed for use on land, air, sea, and in space.

(8) Such conflict is often taken as a reflection of the human condition without questioning whether the structures of thought, word, and deed which the people of the United States have inherited are any longer sufficient for the maintenance, growth, and survival of the United States and the world.

(9) Promoting a culture of peace has been recognized by the United Nations Educational, Scientific and Cultural Organization (UNESCO) through passage of a resolution declaring an International Decade for a Culture of Peace and Non-Violence for the Children 2001–2010. The objective is to further strengthen the global movement for a culture of peace following the observance of the International Year for the Culture of Peace in 2000.

(10) We are in a new millennium, and the time has come to review age-old challenges with new thinking wherein we can conceive of peace as not simply being the absence of violence, but the active presence of the capacity for a higher evolution of the human awareness, of respect, trust, and integrity; wherein we all may tap the infinite capabilities of humanity to transform consciousness and conditions which impel or compel violence at a personal, group, or national level toward developing a new understanding of, and a commitment to, compassion and love, in order to create a "shining city on a hill," the light of which is the light of nations.

TITLE I — ESTABLISHMENT OF DEPARTMENT OF PEACE AND NONVIOLENCE

SEC. 101. ESTABLISHMENT OF DEPARTMENT OF PEACE AND NONVIOLENCE.

(a) Establishment — There is hereby established a Department of Peace and Nonviolence (hereinafter in this Act referred to as the 'Department'), which shall —

(1) be a cabinet-level department in the executive branch of the Federal Government; and

(2) be dedicated to peacemaking and the study of conditions that are conducive to both domestic and international peace.

(b) Secretary of Peace and Nonviolence — There shall be at the head of the Department a Secretary of Peace and Nonviolence (hereinafter in this Act referred to as the 'Secretary'), who shall be appointed by the President, with the advice and consent of the Senate.

(c) Mission — The Department shall —

(1) hold peace as an organizing principle, coordinating service to every level of American society;

(2) endeavor to promote justice and democratic principles to expand human rights;

(3) strengthen nonmilitary means of peacemaking;

(4) promote the development of human potential;

(5) work to create peace, prevent violence, divert from armed conflict, use field-tested programs, and develop new structures in nonviolent dispute resolution;

(6) take a proactive, strategic approach in the development of policies that promote national and international conflict prevention, nonviolent intervention, mediation, peaceful resolution of conflict, and structured mediation of conflict;

(7) address matters both domestic and international in scope; and

(8) encourage the development of initiatives from local communities, religious groups, and nongovernmental organizations.

SEC. 102. RESPONSIBILITIES AND POWERS.

(a) In General — The Secretary shall —

(1) work proactively and interactively with each branch of the Federal Government on all policy matters relating to conditions of peace;

(2) serve as a delegate to the National Security Council;

(3) call on the intellectual and spiritual wealth of the people of the United States and seek participation in its administration and in its development of policy from private, public, and nongovernmental organizations; and

(4) monitor and analyze causative principles of conflict and make policy recommendations for developing and maintaining peaceful conduct.

(b) Domestic Responsibilities — The Secretary shall —

(1) develop policies that address domestic violence, including spousal abuse, child abuse, and mistreatment of the elderly;

(2) create new policies and incorporate existing programs that reduce drug and alcohol abuse;

(3) develop new policies and incorporate existing policies regarding crime, punishment, and rehabilitation;

(4) develop policies to address violence against animals;

(5) analyze existing policies, employ successful, field-tested programs, and develop new approaches for dealing with the implements of violence, including gun-related violence and the overwhelming presence of handguns;

(6) develop new programs that relate to the societal challenges of school violence, gangs, racial or ethnic violence, violence against gays and lesbians, and police-community relations disputes;

(7) make policy recommendations to the Attorney General regarding civil rights and labor law;

(8) assist in the establishment and funding of community-based violence prevention programs, including violence prevention counseling and peer mediation in schools;

(9) counsel and advocate on behalf of women victimized by violence;

(10) provide for public education programs and counseling strategies concerning hate crimes;

(11) promote racial, religious, and ethnic tolerance;

(12) finance local community initiatives that can draw on neighborhood resources to create peace projects that facilitate the development of conflict resolution at a national level and thereby inform and inspire national policy; and

(13) provide ethical-based and value-based analyses to the Department of Defense.

(c) International Responsibilities — The Secretary shall —

(1) advise the Secretary of Defense and the Secretary of State on all matters relating to national security, including the protection of human rights and the prevention of, amelioration of, and de-escalation of unarmed and armed international conflict;

(2) provide for the training of all United States personnel who administer postconflict reconstruction and demobilization in war-torn societies;

(3) sponsor country and regional conflict prevention and dispute resolution initiatives, create special task forces, and draw on local, regional, and national expertise to develop plans and programs for addressing the root sources of conflict in troubled areas;

(4) provide for exchanges between the United States and other nations of individuals who endeavor to develop domestic and international peace-based initiatives;

(5) encourage the development of international sister city programs, pairing United States cities with cities around the globe for artistic, cultural, economic, educational, and faith-based exchanges;

(6) administer the training of civilian peacekeepers who participate in multinational nonviolent police forces and support civilian police who participate in peacekeeping;

(7) jointly with the Secretary of the Treasury, strengthen peace enforcement through hiring and training monitors and investigators to help with the enforcement of international arms embargoes;

(8) facilitate the development of peace summits at which parties to a conflict may gather under carefully prepared conditions to promote nonviolent communication and mutually beneficial solutions;

(9) submit to the President recommendations for reductions in weapons of mass destruction, and make annual reports to the President on the sale of arms from the United States to other nations, with analysis of the impact of such sales on the defense of the United States and how such sales affect peace;

(10) in consultation with the Secretary of State, develop strategies for sustainability and management of the distribution of international funds; and

(11) advise the United States Ambassador to the United Nations on matters pertaining to the United Nations Security Council.

(d) Human Security Responsibilities — The Secretary shall address and offer nonviolent conflict resolution strategies to all relevant parties on issues of human security if such security is threatened by conflict, whether such conflict is geographic, religious, ethnic, racial, or class-based in its origin, derives from economic concerns (including trade or maldistribution of wealth), or is initiated through disputes concerning scarcity of natural resources (such as water and energy resources), food, trade, or environmental concerns.

(e) Media-Related Responsibilities — Respecting the first amendment of the Constitution of the United States and the requirement for free and independent media, the Secretary shall —

(1) seek assistance in the design and implementation of nonviolent policies from media professionals;

(2) study the role of the media in the escalation and de-escalation of conflict at domestic and international levels and make findings public; and

(3) make recommendations to professional media organizations in order to provide opportunities to increase media awareness of peace-building initiatives.

(f) Educational Responsibilities — The Secretary shall —

(1) develop a peace education curriculum, which shall include studies of—

(A) the civil rights movement in the United States and throughout the world, with special emphasis on how individual endeavor and involvement have contributed to advancements in peace and justice; and

(B) peace agreements and circumstances in which peaceful intervention has worked to stop conflict;

(2) in cooperation with the Secretary of Education —

(A) commission the development of such curricula and make such curricula available to local school districts to enable the utilization of peace education objectives at all elementary and secondary schools in the United States; and

(B) offer incentives in the form of grants and training to encourage the development of State peace curricula and assist schools in applying for such curricula;

(3) work with educators to equip students to become skilled in achieving peace through reflection, and facilitate instruction in the ways of peaceful conflict resolution;

(4) maintain a site on the Internet for the purposes of soliciting and receiving ideas for the development of peace from the wealth of political, social and cultural diversity;

(5) proactively engage the critical thinking capabilities of grade school, high school, and college students and teachers through the Internet and other media and issue periodic reports concerning submissions;

(6) create and establish a Peace Academy, which shall —

(A) be modeled after the military service academies;

(B) provide a 4-year course of instruction in peace education, after which graduates will be required to serve 5 years in public service in programs dedicated to domestic or international nonviolent conflict resolution; and

(7) provide grants for peace studies departments in colleges and universities throughout the United States.

SEC. 103. PRINCIPAL OFFICERS.

(a) Under Secretary of Peace and Nonviolence — There shall be in the Department an Under Secretary of Peace and Nonviolence, who shall be appointed by the President, by and with the advice and consent of the Senate. During the absence or disability of the Secretary, or in the event of a vacancy in the office of the Secretary, the Under Secretary shall act as Secretary. The Secretary shall designate the order in which other officials of the Department shall act for and perform the functions of the Secretary during the absence or disability of both the Secretary and Under Secretary or in the event of vacancies in both of those offices.

(b) Additional Positions — (1) There shall be in the Department —

    (A) an Assistant Secretary for Peace Education and Training;

    (B) an Assistant Secretary for Domestic Peace Activities;

    (C) an Assistant Secretary for International Peace Activities;

    (D) an Assistant Secretary for Technology for Peace;

    (E) an Assistant Secretary for Arms Control and Disarmament;

    (F) an Assistant Secretary for Peaceful Coexistence and Nonviolent Conflict Resolution;

    (G) an Assistant Secretary for Human and Economic Rights; and

    (H) a General Counsel.

(2) Each of the Assistant Secretaries and the General Counsel shall be appointed by the President, by and with the advice and consent of the Senate.

(3) There shall be in the Department an Inspector General, who shall be appointed in accordance with the provisions in the Inspector General Act of 1978 (5 U.S.C. App.).

(4) There shall be in the Department four additional officers who shall be appointed by the President, by and with the advice and consent of the Senate. The officers appointed under this paragraph shall perform such functions as the Secretary shall prescribe, including —

    (A) congressional relations functions;

    (B) public information functions, including providing, through the use of the latest technologies, useful information about peace and the work of the Department;

(C) management and budget functions; and

(D) planning, evaluation, and policy development functions, including development of policies to promote the efficient and coordinated administration of the Department and its programs and encourage improvements in conflict resolution and violence prevention.

(5) In any case in which the President submits the name of an individual to the Senate for confirmation as an officer of the Department under this subsection, the President shall state the particular functions of the Department such individual will exercise upon taking office.

(c) Authority of Secretary — Each officer described in this section shall report directly to the Secretary and shall, in addition to any functions vested in or required to be delegated to such officer, perform such additional functions as the Secretary may prescribe.

SEC. 104. OFFICE OF PEACE EDUCATION AND TRAINING.

(a) In General — There shall be in the Department an Office of Peace Education and Training, the head of which shall be the Assistant Secretary for Peace Education and Training. The Assistant Secretary for Peace Education and Training shall carry out those functions of the Department relating to the creation, encouragement, and impact of peace education and training at the elementary, secondary, university, and postgraduate levels, including the development of a Peace Academy.

(b) Peace Curriculum — The Assistant Secretary of Peace Education and Training, in cooperation with the Secretary of Education, shall develop a peace curriculum and supporting materials for distribution to departments of education in each State and territory of the United States. The peace curriculum shall include the building of communicative peace skills, nonviolent conflict resolution skills, and other objectives to increase the knowledge of peace processes.

(c) Grants — The Assistant Secretary of Peace Education and Training shall —

(1) provide peace education grants to colleges and universities for the creation and expansion of peace studies departments; and

(2) create a Community Peace Block Grant program under which grants shall be provided to not-for-profit community and nongovernmental organizations for the purposes of developing creative, innovative neighborhood programs for nonviolent conflict resolution and local peacebuilding initiatives.

SEC. 105. OFFICE OF DOMESTIC PEACE ACTIVITIES.

(a) In General — There shall be in the Department an Office of Domestic Peace Activities, the head of which shall be the Assistant Secretary for

Domestic Peace Activities. The Assistant Secretary for Domestic Peace Activities shall carry out those functions in the Department affecting domestic peace activities, including the development of policies that increase awareness about intervention and counseling on domestic violence and conflict.

(b) Responsibilities — The Assistant Secretary for Domestic Peace Activities shall —

(1) develop policy alternatives for the treatment of drug and alcohol abuse;

(2) develop new policies and build on existing programs responsive to the prevention of crime, including the development of community policing strategies and peaceful settlement skills among police and other public safety officers; and

(3) develop community-based strategies for celebrating diversity and promoting tolerance.

SEC. 106. OFFICE OF INTERNATIONAL PEACE ACTIVITIES.

(a) In General — There shall be in the Department an Office of International Peace Activities, the head of which shall be the Assistant Secretary for International Peace Activities. The Assistant Secretary for International Peace Activities shall carry out those functions in the Department affecting international peace activities and shall be a member of the National Security Council.

(b) Responsibilities — The Assistant Secretary for International Peace Activities shall —

(1) provide for the training and deployment of all Peace Academy graduates and other nonmilitary conflict prevention and peacemaking personnel;

(2) sponsor country and regional conflict prevention and dispute resolution initiatives in countries experiencing social, political, or economic strife;

(3) advocate the creation of a multinational nonviolent peace force;

(4) provide training for the administration of postconflict reconstruction and demobilization in war-torn societies; and

(5) provide for the exchanges between individuals of the United States and other nations who are endeavoring to develop domestic and international peace-based initiatives.

SEC. 107. OFFICE OF TECHNOLOGY FOR PEACE.

(a) In General — There shall be in the Department an Office of Technology for Peace, the head of which shall be the Assistant Secretary of Technology for Peace. The Assistant Secretary of Technology for Peace shall carry out those functions in the Department affecting the awareness, study, and impact of developing new technologies on the creation and maintenance of domestic and international peace.

(b) Grants — The Assistant Secretary of Technology for Peace shall provide grants for the research and development of technologies in transportation, communications, and energy that —

(1) are nonviolent in their application; and

(2) encourage the conservation and sustainability of natural resources in order to prevent future conflicts regarding scarce resources.

SEC. 108. OFFICE OF ARMS CONTROL AND DISARMAMENT.

(a) In General — There shall be in the Department an Office of Arms Control and Disarmament, the head of which shall be the Assistant Secretary of Arms Control and Disarmament. The Assistant Secretary of Arms Control and Disarmament shall carry out those functions in the Department affecting arms control programs and arms limitation agreements.

(b) Responsibilities — The Assistant Secretary of Arms Control and Disarmament shall —

(1) advise the Secretary on all interagency discussions and all international negotiations regarding the reduction and elimination of weapons of mass destruction throughout the world, including the dismantling of such weapons and the safe and secure storage of materials related thereto;

(2) assist nations, international agencies and nongovernmental organizations in assessing the locations of the buildup of nuclear arms;

(3) develop nonviolent strategies to deter the testing or use of offensive or defensive nuclear weapons, whether based on land, air, sea, or in outer space;

(4) serve as a depository for copies of all contracts, agreements, and treaties that deal with the reduction and elimination of nuclear weapons or the protection of outer space from militarization; and

(5) provide technical support and legal assistance for the implementation of such agreements.

SEC. 109. OFFICE OF PEACEFUL COEXISTENCE AND NONVIOLENT CONFLICT RESOLUTION.

(a) In General — There shall be in the Department an Office of Peaceful Coexistence and Nonviolent Conflict Resolution, the head of which shall be the Assistant Secretary for Peaceful Coexistence and Nonviolent Conflict Resolution. The Assistant Secretary for Peaceful Coexistence and Nonviolent Conflict Resolution shall carry out those functions in the Department affecting research and analysis relating to creating, initiating, and modeling approaches to peaceful coexistence and nonviolent conflict resolution.

(b) Responsibilities — The Assistant Secretary for Peaceful Coexistence and Nonviolent Conflict Resolution shall —

(1) study the impact of war, especially on the physical and mental condition of children (using the ten-point agenda in the United Nations Childrens Fund report, State of the World's Children 1996, as a guide), which shall include the study of the effect of war on the environment and public health;

(2) publish a monthly journal of the activities of the Department and encourage scholarly participation;

(3) gather information on effective community peacebuilding activities and disseminate such information to local governments and nongovernmental organizations in the United States and abroad;

(4) research the effect of violence in the media and make such reports available to the Congress annually; and

(5) sponsor conferences throughout the United States to create awareness of the work of the Department.

SEC. 110. OFFICE OF HUMAN RIGHTS AND ECONOMIC RIGHTS.

(a) In General — There shall be in the Department an Office of Human Rights and Economic Rights, the head of which shall be the Assistant Secretary for Human Rights and Economic Rights. The Assistant Secretary for Human Rights and Economic Rights shall carry out those functions in the Department supporting the principles of the Universal Declaration of Human Rights passed by the General Assembly of the United Nations on December 10, 1948.

(b) Responsibilities — The Assistant Secretary for Human Rights and Economic Rights shall —

(1) assist the Secretary, in cooperation with the Secretary of State, in furthering the incorporation of principles of human rights, as enunciated in the United Nations General Assembly Resolution 217A (III) of December 10, 1948, into all agreements between the United States and other nations to help reduce the causes of violence;

(2) gather information on and document human rights abuses, both domestically and internationally, and recommend to the Secretary nonviolent responses to correct abuses;

(3) make such findings available to other agencies in order to facilitate nonviolent conflict resolution;

(4) provide trained observers to work with nongovernmental organizations for purposes of creating a climate that is conducive to the respect for human rights;

(5) conduct economic analyses of the scarcity of human and natural resources as a source of conflict and make recommendations to the Secretary for nonviolent prevention of such scarcity, nonviolent intervention in case of such scarcity, and the development of programs of assistance for people experiencing such scarcity, whether due to armed conflict, maldistribution of resources, or natural causes;

(6) assist the Secretary, in cooperation with the Secretary of State and the Secretary of the Treasury, in developing strategies regarding the sustainability and the management of the distribution of funds from international agencies, the conditions regarding the receipt of such funds, and the impact of those conditions on the peace and stability of the recipient nations; and

(7) assist the Secretary, in cooperation with the Secretary of State and the Secretary of Labor, in developing strategies to promote full compliance with domestic and international labor rights law.

SEC. 111. INTERGOVERNMENTAL ADVISORY COUNCIL ON PEACE AND NONVIOLENCE.

(a) In General — There shall be in the Department an advisory committee to be known as the Intergovernmental Advisory Council on Peace and Nonviolence (hereinafter in this Act referred to as the 'Council'). The Council shall provide assistance and make recommendations to the Secretary and the President concerning intergovernmental policies relating to peace and nonviolent conflict resolution.

(b) Responsibilities — The Council shall —

(1) provide a forum for representatives of Federal, State, and local governments to discuss peace issues;

(2) promote better intergovernmental relations; and

(3) submit, biennially or more frequently if determined necessary by the Council, a report to the Secretary, the President, and the Congress reviewing the impact of Federal peace activities on State and local governments.

SEC. 111. CONSULTATION REQUIRED.

(a) Consultation in Cases of Conflict —

(1) In any case in which a conflict between the United States and any other government or entity is imminent or occurring, the Secretary of Defense

and the Secretary of State shall consult with the Secretary concerning nonviolent means of conflict resolution.

(2) In any case in which such a conflict is ongoing or recently concluded, the Secretary shall conduct independent studies of diplomatic initiatives undertaken by the United States and other parties to the conflict.

(3) In any case in which such a conflict has recently concluded, the Secretary shall assess the effectiveness of those initiatives in ending the conflict.

(4) The Secretary shall establish a formal process of consultation in a timely manner with the Secretary of the Department of State and the Secretary of the Department of Defense:

(A) prior to the initiation of any armed conflict between the United States and any other nation; and

(B) for any matter involving the use of Department of Defense personnel within the United States.

(b) Consultation in Drafting Treaties and Agreements — The executive branch shall consult with the Secretary in drafting treaties and peace agreements.

SEC. 113. AUTHORIZATION OF APPROPRIATIONS.

There is authorized to be appropriated to carry out this Act for a fiscal year beginning after the date of the enactment of this Act an amount equal to at least 2 percent of the total amount appropriated for that fiscal year for the Department of Defense.

TITLE II — ADMINISTRATIVE PROVISIONS AND TRANSFERS OF AGENCY FUNCTIONS

SEC. 201. STAFF.

The Secretary may appoint and fix the compensation of such employees as may be necessary to carry out the functions of the Secretary and the Department. Except as otherwise provided by law, such employees shall be appointed in accordance with the civil service laws and their compensation fixed in accordance with title 5 of the United States Code.

SEC. 202. TRANSFERS.

There are hereby transferred to the Department the functions, assets, and personnel of—

(1) the Peace Corps;

(2) the United States Institute of Peace;

(3) the Office of the Under Secretary for Arms Control and International Security Affairs of the Department of State;

(4) the Gang Resistance Education and Training Program of the Bureau of Alcohol, Tobacco and Firearms; and

(5) the SafeFutures program of the Office of Juvenile Justice and Delinquency Prevention of the Department of Justice.

SEC. 203. CONFORMING AMENDMENTS.

Not later than 90 days after the date of the enactment of this Act, the Secretary shall prepare and submit to Congress proposed legislation containing any necessary and appropriate technical and conforming amendments to the laws of the United States to reflect and carry out the provisions of this Act.

TITLE III — FEDERAL INTERAGENCY COMMITTEE ON PEACE AND NONVIOLENCE

SEC. 301. FEDERAL INTERAGENCY COMMITTEE ON PEACE AND NONVIOLENCE.

There is established a Federal Interagency Committee on Peace and Nonviolence (hereinafter in this Act referred to as the 'Committee'). The Committee shall —

(1) assist the Secretary in providing a mechanism to assure that the procedures and actions of the Department and other Federal agencies are fully coordinated; and

(2) study and make recommendations for assuring effective coordination of Federal programs, policies, and administrative practices affecting peace.

TITLE IV — ESTABLISHMENT OF PEACE DAY

SEC. 401. PEACE DAY.

All citizens should be encouraged to observe and celebrate the blessings of peace and endeavor to create peace on a Peace Day. Such day shall include discussions of the professional activities and the achievements in the lives of peacemakers. There are several models for such a Peace Day that have been endorsed by Congress and the United Nations.

Reflection Questions

1. Describe how Section 2 "Findings" affirm the positive elements of America's civil religion discussed throughout this book.

2. The bill calls for a "new understanding" of the "shining City on a Hill." Explain what this new understand should include. In your view, are the legislators promoting the same vision as that noted in chapter 7, where arguments are made for more humble, holistic national metaphors?

3. The Department of Peace and Nonviolence would include a peace education curriculum for use in the public schools. Should the government be involved in developing peace curricula? Why or Why not? To what degree should a critique of U.S. foreign policy be included in this proposed curriculum?

4. The bill envisions "grants for peace studies departments in colleges and universities throughout the United States." Some people have argued that the government should not spend badly needed funds on peace studies programs; others have suggested that such funding will help bring about a more peaceful and equal society and is money well spent. Which position is more accurate? Explain your answer.

5. Section 103 describes various officers of the peace department. Some activists have said that a "people's congress" comprised of concerned citizens should make up the bulk of any peace department. Do you agree or disagree? Why?

6. Which aspects of the plan do you think are most useful? Which aspects are least useful?
Explain your answer.

7. One scholar said that a department of peace is too unrealistic; peace educators argue that it is a necessary balance against the Department of Defense. Which position makes better sense and why?

8. Would you vote for or against a department of peace? Why or why not?

Notes

The Foreword by Staughton Lynd

1. Gordon S. Wood, "Never Forget: They Kept Lots of Slaves," *New York Times Book Review*, 14 December 2003, p. 10.

2. Henry Wiencek, *An Imperfect God: George Washington, His Slaves, and the Creation of America* (New York: Farrar, Straus and Giroux, 2003), pp. 313–334.

3. Edmund S. Morgan, "The Big American Crime," in *The Genuine Article: A Historian Looks at Early America* (New York and London: W.W. Norton, 2004), p. 99.

4. Quoted in W.E.B. DuBois, *John Brown* (New York: International Publishers, 1962), p. 96.

5. DuBois, *John Brown*, p. 348.

6. A classmate of John Brown, Jr. said that the father made sure to guide discussions with his family and employees in such a way as to "enforce conformity with his ideas." Another son commented in old age that his father approached his children thinking that "what he cared for they must of necessity be made to care for." Marvin Kent, a business associate, concluded that Brown "simply had to do things his way, and in so doing ran his business affairs aground, sometimes stranding others with him." Brown's greatest business failure, in seeking to organize Midwestern wool growers in their dealings with manufacturers, is thought to have occurred not merely because he lacked a business head but because "he was obstinate and invariably refused counsel from any direction." Louis A. DeCaro, Jr., *"Fire from the Midst of You": A Religious Life of John Brown* (New York: New York University Press, 2002), pp. 86, 96, 137, 141.

7. On Lippman, Carr and Kennan see my "How the Cold War Began," *Commentary* (November 1960), pp. 383, 387–388.

8. Arthur Schlesinger, Jr., "Eyeless in Iraq," *The New York Review of Books*, 23 October 2003.

9. Ralph Stavins, Richard Barnet, and Marcus Raskin, *Washington Plans an Aggressive War* (New York: Random House, 1971), pp. 34, 39, 194, 252.

10. Tony Judt, "A Story Still to Be Told," *The New York Review of Books*, 23 March 2006.

11. John Dominic Crossan, *The Historical Jesus: The Life of a Mediterranean Jewish Peasant* (San Francisco: HarperSanFrancisco, 1991).

12. See, to begin with, John Dominic Crossan and Jonathan L. Reed, *Excavating Jesus: Beneath the Stones, Behind the Texts* (San Francisco: HarperSanFrancisco 2001), pp. 274–275: "[T]wo popular movements, the Baptism movement of John and the Kingdom movement of Jesus, started in the territories of Herod Antipas in the 20s C.E. The power of the Kingdom of Rome ... was confronted by the Kingdom of God, which asked quite simply this: how would this world be run if our God sat on Caesar's throne or if our God lived in Antipas's palace? It was not a military confrontation.... It was, instead, a programmatically nonviolent resistance but, emphatically, it confronted present economic, social and political realities." The Lord's Prayer, the authors continue, is a request "for enough food for today and no debt for tomorrow." In a book about the early church after the death of Jesus, Crossan con-

cludes that the most important text in the Bible is Psalm 82 in which God says, "How long will you judge unjustly and show partiality to the wicked? Give justice to the weak and the orphan; maintain the right of the lowly and the destitute. Rescue the weak and the needy; deliver them from the hand of the wicked." John Dominic Crossan, *The Birth of Christianity: Discovering What Happened in the Years Immediately after the Death of Jesus* (San Francisco: HarperSanFrancisco, 1998), p. 575.

13. John 8:3–11, Matthew 25:31–46.

14. Barrie Stavis, *John Brown: The Sword and the Word* (South Brunswick and New York: A.S. Barnes and Co., 1970), p. 49.

15. Paine, "Rights of Man, Part II," in *Complete Writings*, ed. Philip Foner (New York: 1945), v. 1, p. 414 ("my country is the world, and my religion is to do good"); Garrison, quoted in Staughton Lynd, *Intellectual Origins of American Radicalism* (Cambridge, MA: Harvard University Press, 1982), p. 134. Parsons, addressing the court after he was sentenced to death, quoted in James Green, *Death in Haymarket* (New York: Pantheon Books, 2006), p. 237 ("Opening his arms wide, he declared: 'The world is my country, all mankind my countrymen'").

16. Likewise, a labor movement built merely on protection of its own members is unlikely ever to espouse genuine international solidarity. Almost all the European Social Democratic parties supported their respective national governments in World War I. So I have found it to be in the United States. During the 1960s, the first impulse of trade unions in the United States was to support Democratic Party politicians who could protect the short-run economic interests of union members. Since Presidents Kennedy and Johnson were promoting war in Vietnam, trade unions lined up behind them. Again in the first manifestation of the "anti-globalization" movement — the events in Seattle in 1999 — it was painfully clear that the Steelworkers union was in Seattle to keep steel made in other countries out of the United States, and the Teamsters union was there to keep Mexican truck drivers from crossing the Rio Grande. Both in the 1960s and 1990s opposition to war and an imperialist foreign policy, solidarity with the similarly oppressed in other countries, might come later — or not come at all.

17. *Somersett v. Stewart*, 20 How. St. Tr. 1, 79–82 (K.B. 1772), cited in *Rasul et al. v. Bush et al.*, No. 03-334 (28 June 2004), Slip Opinion at 13 n. 11.

18. *Sosa v. Alvarez-Nachain et al.*, No. 03-339 (29 June 2004), Slip Opinion at 17, 19, 30.

19. *Hamden v. Rumsfeld et al.*, No. 05-184 (29 June 2006), at 62–68.

20. Henry David Thoreau, "Civil Disobedience," in *Nonviolence in America: A Documentary History*, ed., Staughton and Alice Lynd (revised edition; Maryknoll, NY: Orbis Books, 1995), p. 25.

21. Henry David Thoreau, "Slavery in Massachusetts," in *Anti-Slavery and Reform Papers* (Montreal: Harvest House, 1963), p. 35.

The Introduction

1. Johan Galtung, "September 11, 2001: Diagnosis, Prognosis, Therapy," http://www.transcend.org and Richard F. Grimmet, *Instances of Use of United States Armed Forces Abroad, 1798–1999* (Washington D.C.: Congressional Research Service) 96-119F, 19 May 1999.

2. It is problematic to refer to the United States as "America," which geographically encompasses Canada and all of Latin America. One might charge that the author, too, is trapped in imperial language when referring to the United States simply as America, but recall that using English can subject one to this charge. Throughout this text, we should remember that a criticism of the architects of the U.S. Empire is not a criticism of the citizens who inhabit and helped to create the U.S. republic.

3. Ervin Staub, *The Roots of Evil: The Origins of Genocide and Other Group Violence* (Cambridge: Cambridge University Press, 1989), p. 273.

4. Johan Galtung, "Global Projections of Deep-Rooted U.S. Pathologies," Institute for Conflict Analysis and Resolution: Occasional Paper 11 (October 1996); Bertrand Russell, *Why Men Fight* (New York: The Century Company, 1916); Thomas Scheff, *Bloody Revenge: Emotions, Nationalism and War* (1994, reprint, Lincoln, NE: iUniverse, 2000).

5. U.S. Department of State, "Human Rights Week 2001," http://www.stategov./g/drl/hr/index.cfm?id=5042; For Bush quote, see William Blum, *Rogue State: A Guide to the World's Only Superpower* (Monroe, ME: Common Courage, 2000), p. 227. For a general philosophical discussion concerning U.S. national identity consult Cornel West, *Prophecy Deliverance! An Afro-American Revolutionary Christianity* (Philadelphia: Westminster Press, 1982), pp. 27–44.

6. Ian Harris, "Peace Education Theory," *Journal of Peace Education*, v. 1, n. 1 (March 2004), pp. 10–11.

7. Noam Chomsky, *American Power and the New Mandarins* (New York: Vintage Books, 1969), pp. 17–18. Chomsky also warns that confessions of guilt can be misused to block action and prevent change. The goal of this study is to open a dialogue that permits the acknowledgment of guilt alongside positive action, a delicate and challenging endeavor.

8. Central Intelligence Agency, "Report of the Special Study Group on the Covert Activities of the Central Intelligence Agency" (30 September 1954). Reprinted in *The Central Intelligence Agency: History and Documents*, ed. William Leary (Alabama: University of Alabama Press, 1984), pp. 143–145.

9. Riita Wahlstrom, "Peace Education Meets the Challenge of the Cultures of Militarism," *Peace Education Miniprints, No. 11*. Lund University (Sweden), Malmö School of Education (March 1991), p. 17. I wish to thank Monisha Bajaj for providing this essay.

Chapter 1

1. Betty Reardon, "Peace Education: A Review and Projection," Lund University (Sweden), Malmö School of Education, *Peace Education Reports*, no. 17 (August 1999), pp. 31–32.

2. Edward Said, *Culture and Imperialism* (New York: Vintage Books, 1993), pp. 54–57.

3. Birgit Brock-Utne, "Peace Education in an Era of Globalization," *Peace Review* 12, no.1 (March 2000); Betty Reardon, *Comprehensive Peace Education: Educating for Global Responsibility* (New York: Teachers College Press, 1988), pp.11–25. Quotation in Reardon, "Peace Education: A Review and Projection," Malmö (Sweden) School of Education, *Peace Education Reports*, no. 17 (August 1999), p. 6.

4. The vast and disparate civic groups that promote peace education are probably more likely to include critiques of U.S. foreign affairs. Noam Chomsky argues that, "the entire school curriculum, from kindergarten through graduate school, will be tolerated only so long as it continues to perform its institutional role.... [Universities are] dependent on wealthy alumni, on corporations, and on the government ... as long as the universities serve those interests, they'll be funded." See Chomsky, "The Function of Schools," in *Education and Enforcement: The Militarization and Corporatization of Schools* eds. Kenneth Saltman and David Gabbard (New York: Routledge Falmer, 2003), p. 25. Their book provides an excellent evaluation of military and corporate influences in the U.S. school system. While there are counterhegemonic forces within the U.S. university system, those that challenge the core narrative of "democratic" capitalism confront serious obstacles. Part of my aim is to illustrate that challenging this narrative, which presents U.S. foreign policy as largely benevolent, is necessary for the betterment of both "elites" and citizens alike.

5. Reardon, *Comprehensive Peace Education: Educating for Global Responsibility*, pp. 34–35.

6. Reardon, *Comprehensive Peace Education: Educating for Global Responsibility*, p. 34.

7. Betty Reardon, "Peace Education needs Human Rights Education," in *Human Rights Education for the Twenty-first Century*, eds. George J. Andrepoulous and Richard Pierre Claude (Philadelphia: University of Pennsylvania Press, 1997); Aline Stomfay-Stitz and Edyth Wheeler, "Human Rights Education can be Integrated throughout the School Day," *Childhood Education* 81, no. 3 (Spring 2005): 158. Preliminary studies by Monisha Bajaj suggest that human rights education might have a positive effect on student self-concepts, see Bajaj, "Human Rights Education and Student Self-Conception in the Dominican Republic," *Journal of Peace Education* 1, no. 1 (March 2004): 21–36.

8. Betty Reardon, personal communication with author, 23 March 2005.

9. Nguyen My Chau and Tekayosi Terashima, "Global Issues in Understanding: Peace Education in the United States," Gifu University (Japan) *Bulletin (Humanities) of the School of Education*, v. 51, n. 1 (2002), pp. 117–147. I am most grateful to Professor Takayoshi Terashima of Gifu University for making this paper available to me and explaining its context.

10. Robin J. Burns and Robert Aspeslagh, eds., *Three Decades of Peace Education around the World: An Anthology* (New York: Garland Press, 1996), pp. 264–269.

11. "Interview 16: Critical Pedagogy Reloaded," in *Rage and Hope: Interviews with Peter McLaren on War, Imperialism, and Critical Pedagogy*, ed. Peter McLaren (New York: Peter Lang, 2006).

12. Aline M. Stomfay-Stitz, *Peace Education in America, 1828–1990: Sourcebook for Education and Research* (Metuchen, NJ: Scarecrow Press, 1993), passim; quotation p. 343.

13. Marcia L. Johnson, "Trends in Peace Education," *Eric Digest* (1998), ED417123.

14. This is not to suggest that the field is only concerned with conflict resolution curricula; peace education is a diverse field and often cultural needs dictate the theoretical approach across regions and nations. Ian Harris notes five major trends in the twenty-first century: international education, human rights education, development education, environmental education and conflict resolution

education. He notes that conflict resolution is "one of the fastest growing school reforms" in the Western Hemisphere during the early part of the twenty-first century. See Ian Harris, "Peace Education Theory," *Journal of Peace Education* 1, no.1 (March 2004): 5 and 14.

15. United States Institute for Peace / Education Program, "Building Global Peace, Conflict, and Security Curricula at Undergraduate Institutions: A Curriculum Development Guide for Colleges and Universities" (January 2007).

16. George Lopez, "Challenges to Curriculum Development in the Post-Cold War Era," in *Peace and World Security Studies: A Curriculum Guide*, ed. Michael T. Klare (Boulder, CO: Lynne Rienner, 1994), pp. 3–13. In fairness to Lopez, he does not entirely ignore the U.S. role in global arms sales. The point is that his essay does not highlight the disproportionate role that the United States plays in the global arms business and how this arms economy contributes to human rights violations. His general call to develop curricular that tackles militarization is certainly in tune with what this study seeks. More recently, Lopez and his colleagues at the Kroc Institute for International Peace Studies have produced first-rate work regarding the U.S. invasion of Iraq, some of which is available at http://kroc.nd.edu/media/Iraq.shtml. See also Klare's recent *Blood and Oil.*

17. Magnus Haavelsrud, "Target: Disarmament Education," *Journal of Peace Education* 1, no.1 (March 2004): 43; Bhaskar Menon, *Disarmament: A Basic Guide* (New York: United Nations, 2001), pp.10–11. Although published in the early 1980s, a study by Reardon on militarism and peace education is worth consulting. See Betty Reardon, *Militarization, Security and Peace Education* (Valley Forge, PA: United Ministries in Education, 1982).

18. Exact U.S. defense expenditures are a matter of debate. The professional services firm, "Price-WaterhouseCoopers," says that the United States accounts for 47 percent of the global market. Five of the six leading global defense contractors are U.S. companies. See PriceWaterhouseCoopers, *The Defense Industry in the 21st Century: Thinking Global ... or Thinking American?* (London: PriceWater-HouseCoopers, 2005). A respected defense industry news service offers a similar percentage, see Guy Anderson, "US Defense Budget Will Equal ROW Combined with 12 months," *Jane's Defense*, 4 May 2005. Data gathered by the Congressional Research Service shows U.S. defense spending exceeds the combined total of the next twelve highest spenders, including China, Japan, France, UK, Russia, Germany, Italy, Saudi Arabia, Taiwan, South Korea, India and Turkey. See Jeffrey Chamberlin, "Comparisons of U.S. and Foreign Military Spending: Data from Selected Public Sources" (Washington, D.C.: Congressional Research Service), 28 January 2004. The U.S. Department of Defense reports a presidential request for $401.7 billion in discretionary funding for defense in 2005. See "Department of Defense Announces 2005 Budget," (Washington, D.C.: DoD News Release), 23 January 2004, No. 046-04.

19. Two important peace educators, Harris and Morrison, rightly note that "American students in particular need to be aware of the role of the United States as a huge supplier of arms to many smaller nations." See Ian Harris and Mary Lee Morrison, *Peace Education*, 2nd edition (Jefferson, NC: McFarland, 2003), p. 120. Many peace educators acknowledge the need to critique U.S. militarism, but there is little specific discussion on precisely how U.S. arms are used by brutal despots across the globe, which generates cycles of violence. Discussions of U.S. foreign policy are usually abstract, focusing on a general "militarism." Again, this study holds that greater specificity is needed to examine the economic and political roots of U.S. foreign policy.

20. Ian Harris, "Peace Education Theory," *Journal of Peace Education* 1, no. 1, (March 2004): p. 8.

21. Maurice P. Hunt and Laurence E. Metcalf, *Teaching High School Social Studies: Problems in Reflective Teaching and Social Understanding*, 2nd ed. (New York: Harper and Row, 1968), pp. 24–33 and 349–366. Metcalf was concerned with peace education, drafting articles such as "Peace Education within a War System." See also Peter H. Martorella, *Teaching Social Studies in Middle and Secondary Schools*, 3rd ed. (Upper Saddle River, NJ: Prentice Hall, 2001), pp. 24–25 and 271–272.

22. See Ian Harris, Larry J. Fisk, and Carol Rank, "A Portrait of University Peace Studies in North America and Western Europe at the End of the Millennium," *International Journal of Peace Studies* 3, no. 1 (January 1998): 92–93.

23. Johan Galtung, Carl G. Jacobson, and Kai Frithjof Brand-Jacobson, *Searching for Peace: The Road to Transcend*, 2nd ed. (London: Pluto Press, 2002), pp. 74–78.

24. See Michael Henderson, "Acknowledging History as a Prelude to Forgiveness," *Peace Review: Journal of Social Justice* 14, no. 3 (2002): 265–267.

25. The quotation is from *Letter from Birmingham Jail* in Martin Luther King Jr., *Why We Can't Wait* (New York: Signet Classics, 2000).

26. John Synott, "Peace Education as an Education Paradigm: Review of a Changing Field using an Old Measure," *Journal of Peace Education* 2, no. 1 (March 2005): 6. Ian Harris and Mary Lee Morrison, *Peace Education,* 2nd edition (Jefferson, NC: McFarland, 2003), pp. 120–121.

27. Ian Harris and Mary Lee Morrison, *Peace Education,* p. 26.

28. Dave Dellinger, *More Power Than We Know: The People's Movement toward Democracy* (Garden City, NY: Anchor/Doubleday, 1975), p. 316.

29. Henry Giroux, "What Might Education Mean after Abu Ghraib: Revisiting Adorno's Politics of Education," *Comparative Studies of South Asia, Africa and the Middle East* 24, no. 1 (2004): 15–16.

30. Problem-posing inquiries that encourage students to think for themselves is my preferred approach to teaching. However, a word on balance is in order: "Balance" is a rather subjective concept, and one wonders if those calling for it recognize that a truly balanced approach would mean that teaching the Holocaust would include equal attention to the Nazi position as well. Under the rubric "balanced," discussions of terrorism would need to afford equal time to Al Qaeda so that "all sides are represented." Clearly, the discussion over balance is politically motivated as I doubt that its proponents want to give the terrorists equal time. Additionally, few would sink to the level of justifying the Holocaust or offering Nazis "equal time," but who decides what constitutes the proper balance? Regardless, teachers should not rally for any point of view and must always work to create a free and open environment, whereby students feel safe to express a variety of viewpoints without penalty.

31. Alicia Cabezudo and Betty Reardon, *Learning to Abolish War: Teaching toward a Culture of Peace* (New York: Hague Appeal for Peace, 2002), p. 17, 19 and 27. For a brief and reliable introduction to this work and its relationship to the Hague Appeal see Tony Jenkins review in *Journal of Peace Education* 1, no.1 (March 2004): 135–137.

32. Cabezudo and Reardon, *Learning to Abolish War,* p. 20. Andrew Bacevich, *American Empire: The Realities and Consequences of U.S. Diplomacy* (Cambridge, MA: Harvard University Press, 2002), p. 229.

33. For Lincoln quotations and analysis of his spiritual vision, see Mark Noll, *America's God: From Jonathan Edwards to Abraham Lincoln* (Oxford: Oxford University Press, 2002), pp. 430–432. For the "almost chosen people" quotation, see Lucas E. Moral, *Lincoln's Sacred Effort: Defining Religion's Role in American Self-Government* (Lanham, MD: Lexington Books, 2000), pp. 59–60.

34. National Council for the Social Studies, *Expectations for Excellence: Curricular Standards for Social Studies* (Silver Spring, MD: NCSS Publications, 1994).

Chapter 2

1. President Dwight D. Eisenhower, "Farewell Radio and Television Address to the American People," (Abilene, KS: Dwight D. Eisenhower Library), 17 January 1961, available at http://www.eisenhower. archives.gov/farewell.htm. Eisenhower draws our attention to the connection between industry and government; the "revolving door" among big business and the U.S. military is expansive. Consider the following Defense Secretaries: Charles Wilson (1953–1957) served as head of General Motors; Robert McNamara (1961–1968) was president of Ford Motor Company and after the Vietnam catastrophe was awarded the position of president of the World Bank, where he accelerated structural adjustment programs; Frank Carlucci (1987–1989) served as CEO at Sears World Trade, and chairman of the Carlyle Group, which conducted business with the bin Laden family and was awarded defense contracts through United Defense Industries under the second Bush administration. Bush senior also worked for Carlyle. Richard Cheney (1989–1993) is infamous for serving as Halliburton's CEO, a company that won a variety of contracts regarding the reconstruction of Iraq. Donald Rumsfeld (1975–1977 and 2001–2006) was CEO of G.D. Searle and General Instrument Corporation among others. Rumsfeld negotiated a proposed pipeline for Bechtel with Saddam Hussein in the 1980s, a company that employed Reagan's secretary of state, George Shultz, as vice chairman. In 2005, Schultz was listed on the Bechtel Web site among the "Board of Directors" and "Senior Counselor." Riley Bechtel served on Bush junior's export council. The company was awarded, in its own words, "a major" U.S. aid program contract with a value up to $1.8 million. See Secretary of Defense Histories at the Defense Department Web site, http://www.defenselink.mil/specials/secdef-histories/; See "Bechtel Leadership," http://www.bechtel.com/leadership.htm and "U.S. Government's Infrastructure Reconstruction Program," http://www.bechtel.com.iraq.htm. Although the connection between U.S. corporations and the U.S. military is extensive, this author is not arguing that the U.S. wages wars to fill the coffers

of Halliburton and other defense contractors. It is more likely that U.S. planners wish to preserve the global capitalist order that satisfies their quest for power and material status while at the same time accelerating their ideological commitment to free markets as the best hope for democracy and liberty. Indeed, pecuniary self-interest and ideology intersect in U.S. expansionism.

2. Major Ralph Peters, "Constant Conflict," *Parameters: U.S. Army War College Quarterly* (Summer 1997): 4–14. I first learned of this quotation from Susan George's speech, "The Corporate Utopian Dream, The WTO and the Global War System," Seattle, Washington, 29 November 1999.

3. Butler is quoted in the front matter of Hans Schmidt, *Maverick Marine: General Smedley D. Butler and the Contradictions of American Military History* (Lexington: University of Kentucky Press, 1987). See also Smedley D. Butler, *War Is a Racket* (New York: Roundtable Press, 1935).

4. Martin Luther King, Jr., "A Time to Break Silence," in *A Testament of Hope: The Essential Writings and Speeches of Martin Luther king, Jr.*, ed. James Melvin Washington (San Francisco: Harper Collins, 1991), p. 233.

5. Dewey quoted in Robert J. Westbrook, *John Dewey and American Democracy* (Ithaca, NY: Cornell University Press, 1991), pp. 225 and 259.

6. Alex Roland, *Military-Industrial Complex* (Washington, D.C.: Society for the History of Technology and the American Historical Association, 2001), pp. 2–6.

7. Martin Luther King, Jr., "A Time to Break Silence," in *A Testament of Hope: The Essential Writings and Speeches of Martin Luther king, Jr.*, ed. James Melvin Washington (San Francisco: HarperCollins, 1991), pp. 231–244.

8. Telford Taylor, *Nuremberg and Vietnam: An American Tragedy* (New York: Bantam, 1971), p. 185.

9. *U.S. Statutes at Large 90* (1976): 729. Available at http://www.usinfo.state.gov.

10. Noam Chomsky, *The Umbrella of U.S. Power: The Universal Declaration of Human Rights and the Contradictions of U.S. Policy* (New York: Seven Stories Press, 1999), pp. 10–11. Some of the ideas in this paragraph build on, and are derived from, Chomsky's penetrating analysis.

11. Bill Richardson, "Address to the UN Commission on Human Rights" (Geneva, Switzerland), 25 March 1998. President George W. Bush, Press release on Human Rights Day (Washington, D.C.), 10 December 2001.

12. Chomsky quoted in Mark Achbar, ed., *Manufacturing Consent: Noam Chomsky and the Media* (Montreal: Black Rose Books, 1994), p. 154.

13. Dale T. Snauwaert, "Cosmopolitan Democracy and Democratic Education," *Current Issues in Comparative Education* 4, no. 2 (December 2001).

14. See Johan Galtung, "U.S. Hegemony as Fundamentalism," in *Enduring Freedom or Enduring War? Prospects and Costs of the New American Century*, ed. Carl Mirra (Washington, D.C.: Maisonneuve Press, 2005), p. 21.

15. Quotation on the Third World as an economic resource appears in a State Department report according to Noam Chomsky in his "After the Cold War: U.S. Foreign Policy in the Middle East," *Cultural Critique*, no. 19 (Autumn 1991): 17. Bruce Cumings, "Is America an Imperial Power?" *Current History* (November 2003).

16. On Kirkpatrick and encouraging capitalism, see Haynes Johnson, *Sleepwalking through History: America in the Reagan Years* (New York: Anchor Books, 1992), p. 254. Other quotations are from Jeane Kirkpatrick, "Dictatorship and Double Standards," *Commentary* (November 1979).

17. Staughton Lynd, "Reflections on Class in Early America: Personal Reflections," *Labor: Studies in Working-Class History of the Americas* 1, no. 4 (Winter 2004): 31.

18. Betty Reardon, *Militarization, Security and Peace Education* (Valley Forge, PA: United Ministries in Education, 1982), p. 30.

19. Mary Beth Norton et al., *A People and a Nation: Brief Sixth Edition* (Boston: Houghton Mifflin, 2003), p. 490.

20. Truman quoted in Robert Jewett and John Shelton Lawrence, *Captain America and the Crusade against Evil: The Dilemma of Zealous Nationalism* (Grand Rapids, MI: William B. Eerdmans, 2003), p. 259. Schlafly quoted in Walter LaFeber, *The American Age: U.S. Foreign Policy at Home and Abroad since 1898*, vol. 2 (New York: W.W. Norton, 1994), p. 450.

21. "Document 19: Inaugural Address," 20 January 1949, Truman Presidential Museum & Library, Public Papers, online collection, http://www.trumanlibrary.org/calendar/viewpapers.php?pid=1030. Matthew 5:14 taken from *The Saint Joseph Edition of the New American Bible* (New York: Catholic Book Publishing, 1968).

22. "NSC-68: United States Objectives and Programs for National Security" (14 April 1950) in United States Department of State, *Foreign Relations of the United States: 1950,* vol. 1 (Washington, D.C.: Government Printing Office, 1976); available at http://www.fas.org/irp/offdocs/nsc-hst/nsc-68.htm.

23. William Appleman Williams, "The City on a Hill on an Errand into the Wilderness," in *Vietnam Reconsidered,* ed. Harrison E. Salisbury (New York: Harper and Row, 1984), p. 14.

24. Eric Foner, *The Story of American Freedom* (New York: W.W. Norton, 1998), p. 253.

25. "PPS/23: Review of Current Trends in US Foreign Policy," in United States Department of State, *Foreign Relations of the United States: 1948,* vol. 1 (Washington, D.C.: U.S. Government Printing Office, 1972), pp. 510–529. Kennan's report is widely cited in secondary studies. He adds the following, interesting remark regarding the United Nations: "In all areas of the world, we still find ourselves the victims of many of the romantic and universalistic concepts with which we emerged from the recent war. The initial build-up of the UN in U.S. public opinion was so tremendous that it is possibly true, as is frequently alleged, that we have no choice but to make it the cornerstone of our policy in this post-hostilities period. Occasionally, it has served a useful purpose. But by and large it has created more problems than it has solved, and has led to a considerable dispersal of our diplomatic effort. And in our efforts to use the UN majority for major political purposes we are playing with a dangerous weapon which may some day turn against us." The final sentence seems to suggest that the United States will not always adhere to the international norms articulated by the UN, particularly given that Kennan urges policy makers to abandon sentimentality and "unreal objectives" such as human rights.

26. William M. Leary, ed., *Central Intelligence Agency: History and Documents* (University, AL: University of Alabama Press, 1984), pp. 144–145.

27. Frank Kofsky, *Harry Truman and the War Scare of 1948* (New York: St. Martin's, 1993), pp. 250–251.

28. Kofsky, *Harry Truman and the War Scare of 1948,* p. 149.

29. Quoted in Jack Nelson-Pallmeyer, *School of Assassins* (Maryknoll, NY: Orbis Books, 1999), p. 38.

30. Statement regarding scaring the American people was made by Arthur Vandenberg, then Chairman of the Senate Foreign Relations Committee. For the Vandenberg and Acheson quotations, see Walter LaFeber, *The American Age: U.S. Foreign Policy at Home and Abroad,* vol. 2 (New York: W.W. Norton, 1994), p. 477. Acheson's original quote is in Dean Acheson, *Present at the Creation: My Years in the State Department* (New York: W.W. Norton, 1969), p. 219.

31. Truman quotations in "Document 42. Address on Foreign Policy at the George Washington National Masonic Memorial," 22 February 1950. And, "Document 232. Radio and Television Report to the American People on the Situation in Korea," 1 September 1950, both available at http://www.trumanlibrary.org.

32. Acheson quoted in Bruce Cumings, "The New Danger in Korea," in *Enduring Freedom or Enduring War? Prospects and Costs of the New American Century?* ed. Carl Mirra (Washington, D.C.: Maisonneuve Press), pp. 72–73.

33. Budget estimates are in 1982 dollars. See Robert Higgs, "U.S. Military Spending in the Cold War Era: Opportunity, Costs, Foreign Crisis and Domestic Constraints," *Cato Institute Analysis No. 114,* 30 March 1998.

34. Eisenhower, "First Inaugural Address," 20 January 1953, *Dwight D. Eisenhower Library* http://www.eisenhower.archives.gov/1stinaug.htm.

35. Dulles quoted in Charles Hund, ed., *A Treasury of Great American Speeches: Our Country's Life and History in the Words of its Great Men* (New York: Hawthorn Books, 1959), pp. 261–267.

36. Data on religious growth in Mary Beth Norton et al. *A People and A Nation* (Boston: Houghton Mifflin Company, 2003), p. 504. The DeMille quotation is in the film, *The Ten Commandments, 40th anniversary videocassette edition* (Hollywood, CA, 1995). According to the film's introduction, DeMille's overture was included in the 1956 edition. I viewed the film after consulting Glenn Whitehoue's "Go Down to L.A. Land: Hollywood and God's New Israel," *Journal of Religion and Society* 3 (2001). This paragraph follows Whitehouse's article.

37. See Billy Graham, *Just as I Am: The Autobiography of Billy Graham* (San Francisco: Harper-Collins, 1997), pp. 191–192 and 199. George H. Bush called Graham "America's Pastor," according to Harold Bloom, "The Preacher," *Time,* 14 June 1999.

38. Graham, *Just as I* Am, pp. 202–204. Documents related to the Prayer Breakfast are stored at the Billy Graham Center Archives, Bushwell Library of Wheaton College, Wheaton, Illinois.

39. Reverend George M. Docherty, "Under God" sermon preached at New York Avenue Presby-terian Church, 7 February 1954, the full text is available at the church's Web page http://www.nyapc.org and in the *Congressional Record*.

40. Eisenhower quoted in William J. Federer, ed., *America's God and Country: Encyclopedia of Quotations* (Coppell, TX: Fame Publishing, 1994), p. 226.

41. Billy Graham, *Just as I Am*, p. 382.

42. Mark J. Gasiorowski, "The 1953 Coup d'etat in Iran," *International Journal of Middle Eastern Studies* 19, no. 3 (1987): 261–286. See also Stephen Kinzer, *All the Shah's Men: An American Coup and the Roots of Middle East Terror* (Hoboken, NJ: John Wiley and Sons, 2004). The spelling of Mossadegh's name varies in English-language sources. Quotations in this book may contain varia-tions that differ from the author's spelling of the Iranian leader's name.

43. Zahedi quoted in Donald Wilber, "Overthrow of Premier Mossadeq of Iran," Central Intel-ligence Agency Clandestine Service Historical Paper, no. 208 (October 1969).

44. Kermit Roosevelt, *Countercoup: The Struggle for the Control of Iran* (New York: McGraw Hill, 1979), p. 199.

45. Stephen Ambrose, *Ike's Spies* (Jackson: University Press of Mississippi, 1999), p.198.

46. Eisenhower quoted in John Prados, *President's Secret Wars: CIA and Pentagon Covert Opera-tions from World War II through the Persian Gulf War* (Chicago: Ivan R. Dee, 1996), p. 95.

47. Dulles quoted in William Blum, *Killing Hope: U.S. Military and CIA Interventions since World War II* (Monroe, ME: Common Courage, 1995), p.167.

48. Information on antitrust case in U.S. Senate, Report to the Committee on Foreign Relations, *Multinational Oil Corporations and U.S. Foreign Policy* (Washington, D.C.: U.S. Government Print-ing Office, 1975).

49. See William Blum, *Killing Hope*, p. 71.

50. John Tirman, *Spoils of War* (New York: The Free Press, 1997), pp. 32–33.

51. Background information located in Gerald Haines, *CIA and Guatemala Assassination Propos-als 1952–54* (CIA History Staff Analysis, June 1995) and Stephen Ambrose, *Ike's Spies*, pp. 215–234.

52. Dwight D. Eisenhower, *Mandate for Change: The White House Years, 1953–1956* (Garden City, NY: Doubleday, 1963), pp. 421–423. For background on the United States and Guatemala, consult Stephen Schlesinger and Stephen Kinzer, *Bitter Fruit: The Story of the American Coup in Guatemala* (Cambridge, MA: Harvard University Press, 1999), and Piero Gleijeses, *Shattered Hope: The Guatemalan Revolution and the United States, 1944–1954* (Princeton, NJ: Princeton University Press, 1991).

53. See Stephen Schlesinger and Stephen Kinzer, *Bitter Fruit: The Story of the American Coup in Guatemala* (Cambridge, MA: Harvard University Press, 1999), pp. 49–63.

54. Hunt quoted in Stephen Ambrose, *Ike's Spies*, p. 218. Eisenhower quoted in Eisenhower, *Man-date for Change*, p. 421.

55. Nixon quoted in David F. Schmitz, *Thank God They're on Our Side: The United States and Right-Wing Dictatorships, 1921–1965* (Chapel Hill: University of North Carolina Press, 1999), pp. 196–197.

56. Jane Franklin, *Cuba and the United States: A Chronological History* (Chicago: Ocean Press, 1997) and John Prados, *President's Secret Wars*, pp. 172–174.

57. Bonsal quoted in Walter LaFeber, *Inevitable Revolutions: The United States in Central America* (New York: W.W. Norton, 1984), pp. 142–143.

58. Arthur Schlesinger, "Memorandum for the President, Subject: Cuba: Political, Diplomatic and Economic Problems" (NSC-Declassified, April 11, 1972).

59. Fidel Castro, "We Must Defend Our Country" (Havana: Havana Domestic Service), 23 April 1961. Available at http://www.marxists.org.

60. Department of Defense — Joint Chiefs of Staff — Memorandum for the Secretary of Defense, "Justification for US Military Intervention in Cuba" (13 March 1962). For information concerning Robert Kennedy and Cuba, see John Trumpbour, ed., *How Harvard Rules: Reason in the Service of Empire* (Boston: South End Press, 1989), pp. 77–78.

61. The inaugural addresses of John F. Kennedy and Lyndon Johnson are reprinted in *Inaugural Addresses of the Presidents of the United States: Grover Cleveland (1885) to George W. Bush (2001)* (Bed-ford, MA: Applewood Books, 2001).

62. *Public Papers of the Presidents of the United States of America: John F. Kennedy, 1961* (Washing-ton, D.C.: U.S. Government Printing Office, 1962), pp. 305–306.

63. John Prados, "40th Anniversary of the Gulf of Tonkin Incident," 4 August 2004, http://www.gwu.edu, accessed on June 5, 2005. Marilyn Young, *The Vietnam Wars, 1945–1990* (New York: Harper Perennial, 1991), pp. 116–123.

64. *Senate Select Committee to Study Governmental Operations with Respect to Intelligence Activities: Foreign and Military Intelligence,* Book 1 (Washington, D.C.: U.S. Government Printing Office, 1976), pp. 27–28.

65. Quotations from Henry Steel Commager, "The Defeat of America," *New York Review of Books,* 12 June 1975.

66. Staughton Lynd, "Civil Liberties in Wartime," paper presented at the "Civil Liberties and War" Workshop at the State University of New York, Stony Brook, Long Island, 19 June 1966.

67. Information in this paragraph derived from Matthew Rinaldi, "The Olive-Drab Rebels: Military Organizing during the Vietnam War," *Radical America* 8, no. 3 (May–June 1974): 17–18, 22, 27, and 30. David Cortright, *Soldiers in Revolt: GI Resistance during the Vietnam War* (Chicago: Haymarket Books, 2005).

68. Information on Fortunato and Ali in Alice Lynd, *We Won't Go: Personal Accounts of War Objectors* (Boston: Beacon Press, 1968), pp. xv, 76–81 and 226–229. On the "prayer-in," see Rinaldi, "The Olive-Drab Rebels: Military Organizing during the Vietnam War," *Radical America* 8, no. 3 (May–June 1974): 23.

69. Inaugural address of Richard Milhous Nixon in *Inaugural Addresses of the Presidents of the United States: Grover Cleveland (1885) to George W. Bush (2001)* (Bedford, MA: Applewood Books, 2001). "Remarks at the Presidential Prayer Breakfast," 5 February 1970, Public Papers of Richard M. Nixon. On the shift of the God's New Israel metaphor from international to domestic issues, see Conrad Cherry, ed. *God's New Israel: Religious Interpretations of American Destiny* (Chapel Hill: University of North Carolina Press, 1998), pp. 305–308.

70. King quoted in Sheryl McCarthy, "King's Words on War Still Ring True Today," *Newsday,* 19 January 2004, p. A21.

71. Charles Long, *Significations: Signs, Symbols and Images in the Interpretation of Religion* (Philadelphia: Fortress Press, 1986), pp. 148–155. The U.S. Army marks the start of the Vietnam War on 11 December 1961 according to Staughton Lynd in "Vietnam and Iraq," *Radical Historians Newsletter,* no. 88 (December 2003): 5.

72. Potter quoted in Douglas Sloan, *Faith and Knowledge: Mainline Protestantism and American Higher Education* (Louisville: John Knox Press, 1994), p. 153.

73. Gregory Nevala Calvert, *Democracy from the Heart: Spiritual Values, Decentralism and Democratic Idealism in the Movement of the 1960s* (Eugene, OR: Communitas Press, 1991), p. xvi.

74. Tom Engelhardt, *The End of Victory Culture: Cold War America and the Disillusioning of a Generation* (New York: Basic Books, 1995), pp. 274–275.

75. Robert S. McNamara, *In Retrospect: The Tragedy and Lessons of Vietnam* (New York: Times Books, 1995), p. 333.

76. Tom Engelhardt, *The End of Victory Culture,* p. 274.

77. President Ford quoted in Sheldon Wolin, "The Meaning of Vietnam," *New York Review of Books,* 12 June 1975, p. 23.

78. *Senate Select Committee to Study Governmental Operations,* pp. 563–565.

79. George Bush, Sr., "Inaugural Address," 20 January 1989 reprinted in *Inaugural Addresses of the Presidents of the United States: Grover Cleveland (1885) to George W. Bush (2001)* (Bedford, MA: Applewood Books, 2001).

80. Ingersoll quoted in Lloyd Gardner, *Imperial America: American Foreign Policy since 1898* (New York: Harcourt Brace Jovanovich, Inc. 1976), p. 6. On Vietnam and corporations, see Richard J. Barnett, *The Roots of War: The Men and Institutions behind U.S. Foreign Policy* (Baltimore, MD: Penguin Books, 1973), pp. 189–191.

81. Wilson quoted in Mohammad Yousef and Mark Adkin, *The Bear Trap: Afghanistan's Untold Story* (London: Leo Cooper, 1992), p. 62.

82. See "Interview with Zbigniew Brzezinski," *Le Nouvel Observateur,* 15 January 1998 translated from French by William Blum, available in Blum *Rogue State,* pp. 4–5.

83. Brzezinski quoted in *Le Nouvel Observateur,* 15 January 1998. See William Blum, *Rogue State,* pp. 4–5. Douglas Little, a respected historian of U.S. diplomacy, also cites Brzezinski's provocation of the Soviets, see Douglas Little, *American Orientalism: The United States and the Middle East since 1945* (Chapel Hill: University of North Carolina Press, 2002), p. 152.

84. George Kennan quoted in Howard Zinn, *A People's History of the United States* (New York: Harper Collins, 1999), p. 592. For background on the Afghanistan intervention and Reagan quotation, see Stephen Galster, "The Afghan Pipeline," *Covert Action Quarterly*, no. 30 (Summer 1998): 55–60.

85. United Nations, International Court of Justice, *Case concerning the Military and Paramilitary Activities in and Against Nicaragua (Nicaragua v. United States of America)*, Judgment 27 June 1986, available at http://www.icj-cij.org/icjwww/idecisions/isummaries/isummaries/inussummary860627.htm.

86. Peter Kornbluh and Malcolm Byrne, eds., *The Iran-Contra Scandal: The Declassified History, A National Security Archives Documents Reader* (New York: The New Press, 1993), pp. xx and 374–375.

87. Kornbluh and Byrne, eds., *The Iran-Contra Scandal: The Declassified History, A National Security Archives Documents Reader*, p. 378.

88. Paul Kengor, *God and Ronald Reagan: A Spiritual Life* (New York: Regan Books, 2004), p. 89.

89. "Presidential Candidate Ronald Reagan Vows a National Crusade to Make America Great Again," Speech at the Republican National Convention 17 July 1980, reprinted in *In Our Own Words: Extraordinary Speeches of the American Century*, eds. Robert Torricelli and Andrew Carroll (New York: Kodansha International, 1999), p. 345.

90. Ronald Reagan, "Farewell Address," reprinted in *Representative American Speeches, 1988–89*, vol. 61, no. 6, ed. Owen Peterson (New York: H.W. Wilson, 1989), p. 13. The *Washington Post* article regarding Reagan's speech is cited in this reference volume, p. 9.

91. Kengor, *God and Ronald Reagan*, p. 221.

92. On Ortega, see Karl Grossman, *Nicaragua: America's New Vietnam?* (Sag Harbor, NY: Permanent Press, 1984), p. 118. On the Puebla Institute, see Russ Bellant, "Secretive Puebla Institute has Ties to the CIA," *National Catholic Reporter*, 18 November 1988.

93. Miguel D' Escoto, interviewed by Amy Goodman on *Democracy Now!* radio program, 8 June 2006.

94. Archbishop Oscar Romero, *Voice of the Voiceless: The Four Pastoral Letters and Other Statements* (Maryknoll, NY: Orbis, 1994), pp. 188–189.

95. On the role of D'Abuisson, see Boutros Boutrous-Ghali, "Letter date 29 March 1993 from the Secretary Council transmitting the report presented on 15 March 1993 by the Commission of Truth," in *United Nations and El Salvador, 1990–1995*, vol. 4 (New York: United Nations Blue Book Series, 1995), pp. 354–360. Robert White, "Too Many Spies, Too Little Intelligence," in *National Insecurity: U.S. Intelligence after the Cold War*, ed. Craig Eisendrath (Philadelphia: Temple, 2000), pp. 46–53.

96. Senator Tom Harkin, "Forward," in *National Insecurity*, p. vii.

Chapter 3

1. Robert McNamara, *In Retrospect*, p. 323.

2. Williams quoted in Paul Buhle and Edward Rice-Maximin, *William Appleman Williams: The Tragedy of Empire* (New York: Routledge, 1995), pp. 183–184.

3. James Melvin Washington, ed., *Conversations with God: Two Centuries of Prayer by African Americans* (New York: HarperCollins, 1994), p. xxvii.

4. William Appleman Williams, *The Tragedy of American Diplomacy* (New York: W.W. Norton & Company, 1972), p. 310.

5. Bundy quoted in Roy F. Baumeister, *Evil: Inside Human Violence and Cruelty* (New York, W.H. Freeman, 1999), p. 305. Baumeister's superb study addresses the importance of acknowledging guilt in preventing violent behavior. Many of his insights bear directly on my analysis on the role of guilt in U.S. foreign policy, although Baumeister does not mention American policy in his work.

6. June Price Tangney and Ronda L. Dearing, *Shame and Guilt* (New York: The Guilford Press, 2002), p. 3. Tangney and Dearing are not concerned with group psychology or foreign policy behavior, yet they offer valuable insights as to the role of shame in violence and projections. There are numerous studies that document the link between unacknowledged guilt, shame and violence. They include Silvan Tomkins, *Affect, Imagery and* Consciousness (New York: Springer, 1963); Willard Gaylin, *The Rage Within: Anger in Modern Life* (New York: Simon and Schuster, 1984); and James Gilligan, *Violence: Reflections on a National Epidemic* (New York: Vintage, 1996). Tomkins and Gaylin discover a connection between shame and violence. James Gilligan's study finds that shame leads to

anger and offers three general criteria among violent criminals, whereby shame becomes a catalyst to violence. First, the shame must be concealed behind a "defensive mask of bravado [and] arrogance." Second, the perpetrator must remain unaware of vital emotions such as guilt; and third, perpetrators must remain unaware of alternatives to violence. As we shall see, this framework closely matches U.S. foreign policy behavior. For a discussion of the literature on shame and violence see Thomas Scheff, "Male Emotions/Relationships and Violence: A Case Study," available at http://www.soc.ucsb.edu/faculty/Scheff. My analysis here is indebted to Scheff's book and article.

7. Riita Wahlstrom, "Peace Education Meets the Challenge of the Cultures of Militarism," *Peace Education Miniprints,* no. 11. Lund University (Sweden), Malmö School of Education (March 1991), pp. 17–18.

8. Tangney and Dearing, *Shame and Guilt,* pp. 1–2.

9. Robert Jay Lifton, *Super Power Syndrome: America's Apocalyptic Confrontation with the World* (New York: Thunder's Mouth Press, 2003), pp. 47–48.

10. Franco Fornari, *The Psycho-analysis of War* (New York: Anchor Books, 1974), p. ix.

11. Thomas Scheff, *Bloody Revenge: Emotions, Nationalism and War* (1994, reprint, Lincoln, NE: iUniverse, 2000); Bertrand Russell, *Why Men Fight* (New York: The Century Company, 1916); James Halpern and Ilsa Halpern, *Projections: Our World of Imaginary Relationships* (New York: Seaview/Putnam, 1983); Franklin Ford, *Political Murder: From Tyrannicide to Genocide* (Cambridge, MA: Harvard University Press, 1985); Helen Block Lewis, *Shame and Guilt in Neurosis* (New York: International Universities Press, 1971). Again, I am indebted to Scheff's writings in my background discussion on shame.

12. My discussion here on chosenness and archetypes follows Johan Galtung, "Global Projections of Deep-Rooted U.S. Pathologies," Institute for Conflict Analysis and Resolution: Occasional Paper 11 (October 1996).

13. Russell E. Richey and Donald G. Jones, eds., *American Civil Religion* (New York: Harper and Row, 1974), pp. 14–18.

14. Robert Bellah, "Civil Religion in America," in *American Civil Religion,* eds. Russell Richey and Donald Jones (New York: Harper and Row, 1974), p. 40.

15. Lincoln quoted in Vine Deloria, Jr., *For This Land: Writings on Religion in America* (New York: Routledge, 1999), p. 166.

16. Robert Jewett and John Shelton Lawrence, *Captain America and the Crusade against Evil: The Dilemma of Zealous Nationalism* (Grand Rapids, MI: William B. Eerdmans, 2003). Cornel West, *Democracy Matters: Winning the Fight against Imperialism* (New York: Penguin Books, 2004).

17. Johan Galtung, "Global Projections of Deep-Rooted U.S. Pathologies," Institute for Conflict Analysis and Resolution: Occasional Paper 11 (October 1996), p. 51.

18. Eric Hoffer, *The True Believer* (New York: Perennial Classics, 2002), pp. 95–96. For a sharp critique of *The True Believer,* see Paul Breines, "Would You Believe? An Introductory Critique of the True Believer," and Peter Wiley, "Eric Hoffer and Cold War Ideology," a pamphlet of the Radical Education Project (Ann Arbor, MI: n.d.), likely published in the late 1960s.

19. See Anders Stephanson, *Manifest Destiny: American Expansion and the Empire of the Right* (New York: Hill and Wang, 1995); Conrad Cherry, ed. *God's New Israel: Religious Interpretations of American Destiny* (Englewood Cliffs, NJ: Prentice Hall, 1971).

20. Bradford quoted in Herbert Aptheker, *The Colonial Era* (New York: International Publishers, 1979), p. 20; Winthrop quoted in Stephason, *Manifest Destiny,* p. 11.

21. Robert Bellah, *The Broken Covenant: American Civil Religion in Time of Trial* (New York: Seabury Press, 1975), pp. 3, 13, and 24. Information on early colonies is from Bellah's book.

22. Mark A. Beliles and Stephen K. McDowell, *America's Providential History* (Charlottesville, VA: Providence Foundation, 1989), p. 147.

23. Information on Jefferson and Deism in Jon Butler, *Awash in a Sea of Faith: Christianizing the American People* (Cambridge, MA: Harvard University Press, 1992), pp. 219–220, 294. Ben Franklin also wrote about Jesus that he "had some Doubts as to his Divinity." See Mark A. Knoll, "Evangelicals in the American Founding and Evangelical Political Mobilization Today," in *Religion and the New Republic: Faith in the Founding of America,* ed. James H. Hutson (Oxford: Rowman and Littlefield, 2000), p. 138.

24. Frank Lambert, *The Founding Fathers and the Place of Religion in America* (Princeton, NJ: Princeton University Press, 2003), pp. 2–4.

25. Mark A. Knoll, "Evangelicals in the American Founding and Evangelical Political Mobilization Today," in *Religion and the New Republic: Faith in the Founding of America,* ed. James H. Hutson (Oxford: Rowman and Littlefield, 2000), pp. 137–138.

26. Quotation on the "whole boundless continent" is John O' Sullivan in Frederick Merk, *Manifest Destiny and Mission in American History* (Cambridge, MA: Harvard University Press, 1995), p. 46. McKinley quoted in Thomas Bailey, *A Diplomatic History of the American People*, 10th ed. (Englewood Cliffs, NJ: Prentice Hall, 1980), pp. 473–474. Beveridge quoted in Richard W. Van Alstyne, *The Rising American Empire* (New York: W.W. Norton & Company, 1974), p. 187.

27. Winthrop Jordon, *White over Black: American Attitudes toward the Negro 1550–1812* (Baltimore: Penguin Books, 1969), pp. 220–221.

28. Charles Long, *Significations: Signs, Significations, and Images in the Interpretation of Religion* (Philadelphia: Fortress Press, 1986), p. 83; Owen Barfield, *History in English Words* (Hudson, NY: Lindisfarne Press, 1967), p. 179.

29. General Colin Powell, "2000 Republican National Convention Address"; Senator John McCain, "2000 Republican National Convention Address," available at http://www.csmonitor.com.

30. The Defense Science Board study was written for the U.S. undersecretary of defense and is cited in Chalmers Johnson, *Blowback: The Cost and Consequences of American Empire* (New York: Henry Holt and Company, 2000), p. 9; *Human Rights and Security Assistance: An Amnesty International USA Report on Human Rights Violations in Countries Receiving U.S. Security Assistance* (Washington, D.C.: AIUSA, May 1996), p. 1.

31. F. Kraupl Taylor and J.H. Rey, "The Scapegoat Motif in Society and Its Manifestations in a Therapeutic Group," *International Journal of Psychoanalysis* 34 (1953): 253–263.

32. Baumeister, *Evil: Inside Human Violence and Cruelty*, pp. 135–137, passim.

33. The quotation is from Al Gore in "First in the Nation: A New Hampshire Town Meeting," *CNN.com*, 27 October 1999.

34. Bush quoted in William Blum, *Rogue State: A Guide to the World's Only Superpower* (Monroe, Maine: Common Courage Press, 2000), p. 227.

35. Ervin Staub, *The Roots of Evil: The Origins of Genocide and Other Group Violence* (Cambridge: Cambridge, 1989), p. 241.

36. Staub, *The Roots of Evil*, p. 252.

37. Quoted in Halpern and Halpern, *Projections*, p. 151.

38. "Presidential Candidate Ronald Reagan Vows a National Crusade to Make America Great Again," Speech at the Republican National Convention 17 July 1980, reprinted in Robert Torricelli and Andrew Carroll, eds., *In Our Own Words: Extraordinary Speeches of the American Century* (New York: Kodansha International, 1999), p. 343.

39. Melanie Klein, *The Writings of Melanie Klein*, Vol. 3: *Envy and Gratitude and Other Works, 1946–1963* (New York: The Free Press, 1975), pp. 141–175.

40. See Saul Scheidlinger, "Presidential Address: On Scapegoating in Group Psychotherapy," *International Journal of Group Psychotherapy* 32, no. 2 (April 1982): 132–133.

41. Lawrence Leshaun, *The Psychology of War: Comprehending Its Mystique and Its Madness* (New York: Helios Press, 2002), pp. 35–58.

42. Else Hammerich, "Working with Conflicts of Zone 1: The Example of the War on Terrorism," *The Transnational Foundation for Peace and Future Research*, 12 December 2001, available at http://www.transnational.org/Forum/meet/2001/ElseH_ConflictsTerrorism.html.

43. Hussein quoted in Lawrence Leshaun, *Psychology of War*, p. 59; Bush quoted in *Z Magazine*, "Quotations," available at http://www.zmag.org.

44. For information on newspaper stories, Koppel and Gulf War bombings see, Ramsey Clark, *War Crimes: U.S. War Crimes in the Gulf* (New York: International Action Center, 1992), pp. 62–68, and 145.

45. Lt. Col. Dave Grossman, *On Killing: The Psychological Cost of Learning to Kill in War and Society* (Boston: Back Bay Books, 1996), pp. 1–4 and 256.

46. Sergeant Martin Smith, "Learning to Be a Lean, Mean Killing Machine: Structured Cruelty," *Counterpunch*, 20 February 2007. I wish to thank Rosalyn Baxandall for alerting me to this article.

47. Peter McLaren, "George Bush, Apocalypse Sometime Soon, and the American Imperium," *Cultural Studies / Critical Methodologies* 2, no. 3 (2002): 332.

48. Giuliani quoted in Jerry L. Martin and Anne D. Neal, "Defending Civilization: How Our Universities Are Failing America and What Can Be Done about It," A Project of the Defense of Civilization Fund, American Council of Trustees and Alumni (November 2001), p. 4.

49. Johan Galtung, "Moderates All over the World Unite," Speech to the German Peace Movement, Cologne, Germany, 14 September 2002, available at http://www.transcend.org . On U.S. threats to attack Afghanistan, see Jonathan Steele, Ewen MacAskill, Richard Norton-Taylor and Ed Harri-

man, "Threat of US strikes passed to Taliban weeks before NY attack," *The Guardian*, 22 September 2001. It is not entirely clear if it was U.S. official policy to warn of strikes, but a former U.S. ambassador who was present at a meeting attended by various diplomats is quoted in the article as saying, "I think there was some discussion of the fact that the United States was so disgusted with the Taliban that they might be considering some military action." Other U.S. representatives maintain that the discussion of military strikes was only "in passing." Pakistani officials, however, felt the mention of strikes was significant enough to pass the information to the Taliban regime in Afghanistan.

50. Dinesh D'Sousa, *What's So Great about America*, pp. 192–193 and Samuel Huntington, *The Clash of Civilizations and the Remaking of World Order* (New York: Simon and Schuster, 1996), pp. 311–312.

51. Chambliss quoted in William Bennett, *Why We Fight: Moral Clarity and the War on Terrorism* (New York: Doubleday, 2002), p. 74.

52. Pippa Norris and Ronald Inglehardt, "Islam and the West: Testing the Clash of Civilizations Thesis," John F. Kennedy School of Government, Harvard University, Faculty Research Working Paper Series, #RWP02-015 (April 2002), pp. 1–5.

53. Michel J. Crozier, Samuel P. Huntington and Joji Watanuki, *The Crisis of Democracy: Report on the Governability of Democracies to the Trilateral Commission* (New York: New York University Press, 1975), pp. 98, 114.

54. "Governor George W. Bush: A Distinctly American Internationalism," speech at Ronald Reagan Presidential Library, Simi Valley, California, 19 November 1999. Rumsfeld quoted in "Empire Snaps Back," *The Progressive* (June 2003). Official from Clinton years quoted in *U.S. Department of State Daily Briefing* (DPB#65), 29 April 1997.

55. Niall Ferguson, "An Empire in Denial: The Limits of US Imperialism," *Harvard International Review* 25, no. 3 (2003): 64–69. Andrew Bacevich, ed., *The Imperial Tense: Prospects and Problems of American Empire* (Chicago: Ivan R. Dee Publishers, 2003), p. xiii.

56. Robert Jervis, "Compulsive Empire," *Foreign Policy* (July–August 2003): 83–87.

57. Max Boot, "Washington Needs a Colonial Office," *The Financial Times*, 2 July 2003; Charles Krauthammer, "The Unipolar Era," in Bacevich *Imperial Tense*, p. 47. Information on Gray in Alan Murray, "Political Capital," *Wall Street Journal*, 15 July 2003; James Rubin, "Stumbling into War," *Foreign Affairs* 82, no. 5 (2003): 55.

58. Graham Evans and Jeffrey Newham, *The Penguin Dictionary of International Relations* (London: Penguin Books, 1998), pp. 244–245. J.A. Hobson, *Imperialism: A Study* (New York: Cosimo, Inc, 2005), p. 368. Johan Galtung, "The Fall of the U.S. Empire," 16 September 2003, www.transcend.org.

59. Donald L. Nathanson, *Shame and Pride: Affect, Sex and the Birth of the Self* (New York: W.W. Norton and Company, 1992), p. 364.

60. Baumeister, *Evil: Inside Human Violence and Cruelty*, p. 94.

61. John Dower, "An Aptitude for Being Unloved: War and Memory in Japan," in *Crimes of War: Guilt and Denial in the Twentieth Century*, eds. Omar Bartov, Atina Grossman, and Mary Nolan (New York: The New Press, 2002), p. 227. Dower offers a brilliant analysis of the Japanese "acute sense of victimization," during World War II. He adds that the Japanese were not alone "in conveying such victim consciousness through highly evocative, proper-name catch phrases. 'Remember Hiroshima' has its obvious American analogue in 'Remember Pearl Harbor.'"

62. Omar Bartov, Atina Grossman, and Mary Nolan, eds., *Crimes of War: Guilt and Denial in the Twentieth Century* (New York: The New Press, 2002), xxiii.

63. James C. Thompson, "How Could Vietnam Happen? An Autopsy," *The Atlantic Monthly* (April 1968). For a discussion of Thompson, see Tom Engelhardt, *The End of Victory Culture: Cold War America and the Disillusioning of a Generation* (New York: Basic Books, 1995), pp. 13–14. See also H. Bruce Franklin, *M.I.A or Mythmaking in America* (Chicago: Lawrence Hill Books, 1992).

64. Martin Luther King, Jr., "A Time to Break Silence," in *A Testament of Hope: The Essential Writings and Speeches of Martin Luther King, Jr.*, ed. James Melvin Washington (San Francisco: HarperCollins, 1991), pp. 231–244. For Chomsky's comment that the phrase regarding the United States invading South Vietnam sounds "very strange." See James Peck, ed. *The Chomsky Reader* (New York: Pantheon Books, 1987), p. 34.

65. National Park Service, Department of the Interior, http://www.nps.gov/vive.

66. Rudolph Giuliani quoted on *CBS News* (15 October 2001) 5:13pm EST.

67. President George Bush, "Address to the Nation" (Washington, D.C.: Office of the Press Sec-

retary) 20 September 2001, available at http://www.whitehouse.gov. Jerry L. Martin and Anne D. Neal, "Defending Civilization: How Our Universities Are Failing America and What Can Be Done about It," A Project of the Defense of Civilization Fund, American Council of Trustees and Alumni (November 2001), p. 5.

68. The victim's statements can be found at the War Resister's League Web page, http://www.wrl.org.

69. Jennifer Roback Morse, "Battered America," *Hoover Institute Weekly Essays* (26 November 2001).

70. See the full page advertisement from AVOT in the *New York Times* (10 March 2002), p. 7. The organization lists William Bennett and former CIA director, James Woolsey, as senior advisors.

71. Jerry L. Martin and Anne D. Neal, "Defending Civilization: How Our Universities Are Failing America and What Can Be Done about it," A Project of the Defense of Civilization Fund, American Council of Trustees and Alumni (November 2001), p. 7.

Chapter 4

1. Peter McLaren, "George Bush, Apocalypse Sometime Soon, and the American Imperium," *Cultural Studies / Critical Methodologies* 2, no. 3 (2002): 327–328.

2. George W. Bush, *A Charge to Keep* (New York: Perennial, 1999), pp. 6, 44–45 and 136.

3. For quotation, see Gustav Niebuhr, "The 2000 Campaign: The Religious Issue; Lieberman Is Asked to Stop Invoking Faith in Campaign," *New York Times*, 29 August 2000. Also, "What the U.S. Media Is Saying," *Guardian* (London), 7 March 2000.

4. For Time/CNN poll, see Nancy Gibbs, "Apocalypse Now," *Time*, 1 July 2002. Information on Rove in Howard Fineman, "Bush and God," *Newsweek*, 10 March 2003. "Interview with E.J. Dionne," *PBS: The Jesus Factor*, available at http://www.pbs.org/wgbh/pages/frontline/shows/jesus/interviews/dionne.html, accessed on 15 September 2004.

5. Doug Wead interview on *PBS Frontline*, "The Jesus Factor," 2004; transcript available at http://www.pbs.org/wgbh/pages/frontline/shows/jesus/president/spirituality.html.

6. See Ayelish McGarvey, "As God Is His Witness," *The American Prospect*, 19 October 2004 at http://www.prospect.org; "Bush's Messiah Complex," *The Progressive* (February 2003); Thomas M. Freiling, ed., *George W. Bush on God and Country* (Washington, D.C.: Allegiance Press, 2004), p. 10; Stephen Mansfield, *The Faith of George W. Bush* (New York: Tarcher/Penguin, 2003), p. 147.

7. Freiling, ed., *George W. Bush on God and Country*, p. 9.

8. Information on Bush's background and Andover in J. H. Hatfield, *Fortunate Son: George W. Bush and the Making of an American President* (New York: Soft Skull Press, 2002), see p. 19 for quotation on Chapel service. Other background material on his early life in George W. Bush, *A Charge to Keep*, pp. 1, 15, 18 and 47.

9. Although massive student unrest was not characteristic of Bush's years at Yale (1964–1968), it was still a period of rising discontent. Yale chaplain William Sloane Coffin was well known for his anti-draft activity. Bush also majored in history and may have noticed that Yale history professor Staughton Lynd traveled to North Vietnam in 1965 in a highly publicized and controversial trip. Coffin's biographer, historian Warren Goldstein, offers the following interpretation of Bush's (and Cheney who also attended Yale) political apathy. "Coffin argued that one could learn something about the candidates by paying attention to how they responded to the social issues of their college years, and that two of them — George W. Bush and Dick Cheney — in effect flunked that test. After all, the two great issues during his tenure, civil rights and the war in Vietnam, absorbed the energies, money, concerns, and worries of thousands of Yale students at that time. Why not future presidents and vice-presidents?" See Warren Goldstein, *William Sloane Coffin, Jr.: A Holy Impatience* (New Haven, CT: Yale University Press, 2004), p. 316. Bush alleges that he met Coffin while at Yale, and the liberal pastor derided Bush senior, saying that he lost to a better man in his failed Senate campaign in 1964. See Paul Kengor, *God and George W. Bush: A Spiritual Life* (New York: Regan Books, 2004), p. 14.

10. George W. Bush, *A Charge to Keep*, p. 48.

11. George W. Bush, *A Charge to Keep*, pp. 49–50.

12. See David Barstow, "In Haze of Guard Records, a Bit of Clarity," *New York Times*, 15 February 2004, p. 24. As for Bush's reluctance to serve in Vietnam, one biographer claims that Bush's National Guard application contained a box that read "do not volunteer" for oversees duty, which

was checked off. See J. H. Hatfield, *Fortunate Son: George W. Bush and the Making of an American President* (New York: Soft Skull Press, 2002), p. 39.

13. George W. Bush, *A Charge to Keep*, pp. 56, 79 and 82.

14. George W. Bush, *A Charge to Keep*, p. 86.

15. George W. Bush, *A Charge to Keep*, pp. 62–63. For an interesting article on Bush's early oil dealings, see David Armstrong, "Oil in the Family: George W. Bush and His Slippery Friends," *Texas Observer*, 12 July 1991, pp. 12–15.

16. Quotations in this paragraph are from George W. Bush, *A Charge to Keep*, p. 136. After Graham planted the mustard seed, it appears that Bush continued drinking and engaged in reckless, aggressive behavior. One evening, as the story goes, he noticed *Wall Street Journal* columnist Al Hunt in a restaurant. Bush walked to the table and told Hunt, who criticized Bush senior during his 1988 presidential campaign, that the journalist was "a fucking son of a bitch." Incidents like these are what critics interpret as Bush's insincerity. If the religious experience with Graham was so profound, Bush said "it sparked a change in my heart," then one might expect some modification of Bush's behavior. Again, it is impossible to gauge Bush's theological sincerity, but such incidents provide ammunition to his doubters. See J. H. Hatfield, *Fortunate Son: George W. Bush and the Making of an American President* (New York: Soft Skull Press, 2002), pp. 73–74. Paul Kengor's sympathetic account of Bush's faith also discusses the Hunt incident, noting that Bush was still "lost" at the time; see his *God and George W. Bush: A Spiritual Life* (New York: Regan Books, 2004), p. 24.

17. George W. Bush, *A Charge to Keep*, p. 132.

18. Quote from George W. Bush, *A Charge to Keep*, p. 136. J.H. Hatfield calls Bush's decision to stop drinking and the Graham meeting "defining moments," in *Fortunate Son: George W. Bush and the Making of an American President* (New York: Soft Skull Press, 2002), pp. 71–72. David Aikman claims that Bush's closest friends consider the Graham meeting "the absolutely decisive event," in Bush's salvation in *A Man of Faith: The Spiritual Journey of George W. Bush* (Nashville: W Publishing Group, 2004), p. 75.

19. George W. Bush, *A Charge to Keep*, pp. 136–137.

20. See "Christian Leaders Take a Stand for Morality on Election," *Family.org—A Web site of Focus on the Family*, 8 October 2004, available at http://www.family.org.

21. Bruce Lincoln, "The Theology of George W. Bush," *Christian Century*, 5 October 2004. Ron Suskind, "Without a Doubt," *New York Times Magazine*, 17 October 2004.

22. David D. Kirkpatrick, "In Secretly Taped Conversations, Glimpses of the Future President," *New York Times*, 20 February 2005, pp. 1, 26.

23. Kirkpatrick, "In Secretly Taped Conversations, Glimpses of the Future President," *New York Times*, 20 February 2005, pp. 1, 26.

24. George W. Bush, *A Charge to Keep*, pp. 44–45.

25. The April 1995 memo and Jesus Day proclamation were discussed on "The Jesus Factor," *PBS Frontline*, 2004. Available online at http://www.pbs.org/wgbh/pages/frontline/shows/jesus/readings/jesusdaymemo.html.

26. The description of the Craig sermon and quotations in this paragraph are in George W. Bush, *A Charge to Keep*, pp. 1 and 9–10.

27. Paul Kengor, *God and George W. Bush: A Spiritual Life* (New York: Regan Books, 2004), pp. x–xi.

28. Richard Land quoted on *PBS Frontline*, "The Jesus Factor," 2004. Transcript available online at http://www.pbs.org/wgbh/pages/frontline/shows/jesus/etc/synopsis.html.

29. Frank Bruni, "For Bush, a Mission and Defining Moment," *New York Times*, 22 September 2001.

30. This much publicized statement appears in many sources, and brief footage of the debate is featured in the documentary, *George W. Bush: Faith in the White House* (New York: Good Times Entertainment, 2004).

31. "President Bush Meets with National Security Team" (Washington, D.C.: Office of the Press Secretary), 12 September 2001, available at http://www.whitehouse.gov. I am indebted to Richard Van Alstyne, who describes early American leaders as Old Testament prophets.

32. Bush quoted in Jim Garamone, "Memorial Service Honors Pentagon Victims," *Armed Forces Information Service News Article*, 11 October 2001. See also Bush's speech at www.whitehouse.gov.

33. Wendy S. Ross, "Memorial Services Mark Six Month Anniversary of 9/11 Attacks" (Caracas, Venezuela: Embassy of the United States, Public Affairs Press Release), 11 March 2002, http://embajadausa.orgve/wwwh1731.html.

34. "Remarks by the President upon Arrival at the South Lawn" (Washington, D.C.: Office of the Press Secretary), 16 September 2001, http://www.whitehouse.gov/news/releases/2001/09/20010916-2.html.

35. Ron Suskind, "Without a Doubt," *New York Times Magazine*, 17 October 2004.

36. Powell quoted in "Remarks by Secretary of State Colin L. Powell at the 2004 Annual Kennan Institute Dinner, Woodrow Wilson Institute for International Scholars" (Washington, D.C.: National Press Club), 15 March 2004, http://www. usembassy.it/file2004_03/alia/a4032606.htm. "Powell Slips, 'Crusade' Re-enters US Lexicon on War," *Agence France Press*, 23 March 2004.

37. Frum is quoted in "Bush's Messiah Complex," *The Progressive* (February 2003).

38. Elisabeth Bumiller, "America as Reflected in Its Leader," *New York Times*, 6 January 2002, p. 3.

39. Andrew Jacobs, "Peace Signs Amid Calls for War," *New York Times*, 20 September 2001.

40. Frank Bruni, "For Bush, a Mission and Defining Moment," *New York Times*, 22 September 2001.

41. "President George W. Bush, the Bible and Israel," *Yediot Achronot Israeli News*, 11 January 2001.

42. William J. Bennett, *Why We Fight: Moral Clarity and the War on Terrorism* (New York: Doubleday, 2002), pp. 44–45 and 129–130.

43. Dinesh D'Souza, *What's So Great about America* (Washington, D.C.: Regnery Publishing, 2002), pp. 89 and 192.

Chapter 5

1. Amnesty International, Memorandum to the U.S. government, "USA: Treatment of Prisoners in Afghanistan and Guantanamo Bay Undermines Human Rights," 15 April 2002, Amnesty International Index: AMR 51/054/2002.

2. Report of the Defense Science Board Task Force on Strategic Communication (Washington, D.C.: Office of the Under Secretary of Defense for Acquisition, Technology and Logistics, September 2004), p. 35.

3. Cora Weiss, introductory remarks in Alicia Cabezudo and Betty Reardon, *Learning to Abolish War: Teaching toward a Culture of Peace*, p. 4.

4. Report of the Defense Science Board Task Force on Strategic Communication (Washington, D.C.: Office of the Under Secretary of Defense for Acquisition, Technology and Logistics, September 2004), p. 46.

5. Henry Giroux, "Democracy, Freedom and Justice after September 11: Rethinking the Role of Educators and the Politics of Schooling," *Teachers College Record* 104, no. 6 (September 2002): 1158.

6. Bacevich quoted in an interview by Taylor McNeil in "Seduced by War," *Bostonia* (Winter 2004–2005): 21.

7. IAEA Update Report for the Security Council Pursuant to Resolution 1441 (2002). For a further discussion of this matter, see the section in this chapter "Iraq and Historical Accuracy: A Task for Peace Educators." The full quotation from the CIA report is: "Although Saddam probably does not yet have nuclear weapons or sufficient material to make any, he remains intent on acquiring them." See Central Intelligence Agency, "Iraq's Weapons pf Mass Destruction Programs" (October 2002), p. 1.

8. David Barstow and Robin Stein, "Under Bush, a New Age of Prepackaged News," *New York Times*, 13 March 2005.

9. Kevin R. Kosar, *Public Relations and Propaganda: Restrictions on Executive Agency Activities* (Washington, D.C.: Congressional Research Service), 8 February 2005. Order Code RL32750.

10. Biographical information on Williams's appearances in the media, his independence and description as one of the "most recognizable" conservatives at "The Right Side with Armstrong Williams: Biography, Core Pages," http//www.Armstrong Williams.com, accessed on 20 March 2005.

11. No Child Left Behind, http://www.ed.gov.policy/elsec/leg/esea02/pgl12.html, accessed on 20 March 2005. For a succinct discussion on how the No Child Left Behind Act aids military recruitment and is not simply offering the armed services the same access as colleges to information as is often claimed, see Leah Wells, "No Child Left Behind by Military Recruiters," *Alternet*, 9 December 2002, http://www.alternet/story/14716/, accessed on 20 March 2005. Wells is the peace education coordinator at the Nuclear Age Peace Foundation who also notes that the 2003 Department of Education budget proposal was $56.5 billion compared to the Department of Defense budget of $396 billion at the time. On the purpose of No Child Left Behind, see *No Child Left Behind: A Tool Kit for Teachers* (Jessup, MD: Ed Pubs., Educational Publications Center, 2004), p. 1.

12. Amy Goldstein, "Paige Calls NEA a 'Terrorist' Group," *Washington Post*, 24 February 2004, p. A19.

13. Michael Apple, "Patriotism, Pedagogy and Freedom: On the Educational Meanings of September 11th," *Teachers College Record* 104, no. 8 (December 2002): 1,767.

14. Joel Spring, *Education and the Rise of the Corporate State* (Boston: Beacon Press, 1972). David Nasaw, *Schooled to Order: A Social History of Public Schooling in the United States* (Oxford: Oxford University Press, 1979). Thorstein Veblen, *The Higher Learning in America: A Memorandum on the Conduct of Universities by Business Men* (New York: Huebsch), republished by Cosimo in 2005. Robert J. Westbrook, *John Dewey and American Democracy* (Ithaca, NY: Cornell University Press, 1991), p. 507.

15. Peter Knecht, managing editor and Peter Freeman, editor, "Background Notes: Afghanistan," United States Department of State, Bureau of Public Affairs, Office of Public Communication, Department of State Publication 7795-Background Notes Series (Washington, D.C.: U.S. Government Printing Office, July 1994).

16. John Barber, "Wounded and Left on Afghanistan's Plains," *Toronto Globe and Mail*, 29 September 2001.

17. Carl Mirra, ed. *Enduring Freedom or Enduring War? Prospects and Costs of the New American Century* (Washington, D.C.: Maisonneuve Press, 2005), pp. 135–136.

18. Zalmay Khalilzad, "Afghanistan: Time to Reengage," *Washington Post*, 7 October 1996. See also Kim Seagupta and Andrew Gumbell, "New U.S. Envoy to Kabul Lobbied for Taleban Oil Rights," *New Zealand Herald*, 11 January 2002.

19. On support for the United Front, see Kenneth Katzman, "Afghanistan: Current Issues and U.S. Policy Concerns" (Washington, D.C.: Congressional Research Service Report), 15 November 2001. On international agencies and human rights, see Human Rights Watch Backgrounder, "Military Assistance to Afghanistan," 5 October 2001.

20. Human Rights Watch, "All Our Hopes Are Crushed: Violence and Repression in Western Afghanistan," *Human Rights Watch* 14, no. 2 (November 2002). Rumsfeld quoted on p. 3. Information on Herat and Khan, pp. 4–6. Support for Khan eventually evaporated.

21. Mehmooda Shekiba, "The Miracle or Mockery of Afghanistan?" *Seattle Times*, 4 October 2005.

22. Human Rights Watch, "Key Areas of Concern: The Threat from Taliban and Other Insurgent Forces," *Human Rights Watch*, 15 September 2005.

23. "President Says Saddam Hussein Must Leave Iraq within 48 Hours: Remarks by the President in Address to the Nation" (Washington, D.C.: Office of the Press Secretary), 17 March 2003, http://www.whitehouse.gov/news/releases/2003/03/20030317-7.html. Bush often ends his speeches with "may God continue to Bless America," a not so subtle homage to chosenness, the notion that God's blessing of the United States is longstanding and ongoing.

24. "President Says Saddam Hussein Must Leave Iraq within 48 Hours: Remarks by the President in Address to the Nation" (Washington, D.C.: Office of the Press Secretary) 17 March 2003 http://www.whitehouse.gov/news/releases/2003/03/20030317-7.html.

25. "President Bush's Victory Celebration, Remarks by President Bush from the U.S.S. *Abraham Lincoln*," 1 May 2003.

26. "President's Remarks at the United Nations General Assembly" (Washington, D.C.: Office of the Press Secretary) 12 September 2002 http://www.whitehouse.gov/news/releases/2002/09/20020912-1.html.

27. See Sidney Blumenthal, "The Religious Warrior of Abu Ghraib: An Evangelical US General Played a Pivotal Role in Iraqi Prison Reform," *Guardian*, 20 May 2004.

28. Ted Nuget's reflections are in Ted Nuget, "Salute to the Spirit-Wild Warriors," at www.tednugent.com/salute.shtml. See also David de Sola, "The Politics of Music," *CNN.com*, 20 August 2004.

29. See Dennis Prager, "America Is a Light in This Dark World," in *Spiritual Perspectives on America's Role as Superpower* (Woodstock, VT: Sky Light Paths Publishers, 2003), pp. 66–71.

30. David D. Kirkpatrick, "Battle Cry of Faithful Pits Believers and Unbelievers," *New York Times*, 31 October 2004, p. 22.

31. "Full Text of Remarks by Rudy Giuliani," prepared for delivery at the 2004 Republican National Convention, 30 August 2004, *USA Today* http://www.usatoday.com/news/politicselections/nation/president/2004-08-30giulianifulltext_x.htm.

32. Reverend Max Lucado, "Benediction: Remarks as Prepared for Delivery at the 2004 Republican National Convention on Monday, August 30, 2004," available at http://www.prnewswire.com/cgi-bin/micro_stories.pl?ACCT=919633&TICK=REPS04&STORY=/www/story/08-30-2004/0002241059&EDATE=Aug+30,+2004.

33. "Full Text of Remarks by Senator Zell Miller," prepared for delivery at the 2004 Republican National Convention, *USA Today*, 1 September 2004, http://www.usatoday.com/news/politicselections/nation/president/2004-09-01-miller-text_x.htm.

34. "Full Text of Remarks by Arnold Schwarzenegger," prepared for delivery at the 2004 Republican National Convention, *USA Today* 31 August 2004 http://www.usatoday.com/news/politicselections/nation/president/2004-08-31-schwarzeneggerfulltext_x.htm.

35. "Americans Still Dour on U.S. Economy," *Gallup Poll*, 17 July 2006, http://poll.gallup.com/content/default.aspx?ci=23782. See also, "Poll: Fix the Economy First," CBS News, 7 January 2003, http://www.cbsnews.com/stories/2003/01/07/opinion/polls/main535547.shtml.

36. Cardinal Egan, "Benediction: Remarks as Prepared for Delivery at the 2004 Republican National Convention on Thursday, September 2," available at http://www.prnewswire.com/cgi-bin/micro_stories.pl?ACCT=919633&TICK=REPS04&STORY=/www/story/09-02-2004/0002243632&EDATE=Sep+2,+2004.

37. "President's Remarks at the 2004 Republican National Convention," 2 September 2004, http://www.whitehouse.gov/news/releases/2004/09/20040902-2.html.

38. Project for the New American Century, "Statement of Principles," 3 June 1997. "Rebuilding America's Defenses: Strategy, Forces and Resources for a New Century," *A Report of the Project for a New Century* (September 2000), pp. 4 and 75. Both documents are available at http://www.newamericancentury.org.

39. The quotations on the secular ideology of the neoconservatives and its relation to Bush's messianic discourse is from an excellent article by Andrew J. Bacevich and Elizabeth H. Prodromou, "God Is Not Neutral: Religion and U.S. Foreign Policy after 9/11," *Orbis: A Journal of World Affairs* 48, no. 1 (Winter 2004): 43–54. They compare Bush's good and evil rhetoric to neoconservative notions of democracy against dictatorship.

40. Bush quoted in "Bush raps 'revisionist historians' on Iraq," *CNN.com*, posted 16 June 2003.

41. This section is based on Staughton Lynd and Carl Mirra, "I Am a Revisionist Historian," *ZNet*, 16 March 2006, available at http://www.zmag.org/content/showarticle.cfm?SectionID=15&ItemID=9913.

42. "President Commemorates Veterans Day, Discusses War on Terror," Tobyhanna Army Depot, Tobyhanna, Pennsylvania, 11 November 2005, http://www.whitehouse.gov/news/releases/2005/11/print/20051111-1.html.

43. Scott Shane and Daniel Sanger, "Bush Panel Finds Big Flaws Remain in U.S. Spy Efforts," *New York Times*, 1 April 2005, p. A10.

44. "Blix: U.S. Leaned on Us," *Newsday*, 12 June 2003, p. A48.

45. "President Commemorates Veterans Day, Discusses War on Terror," Tobyhanna Army Depot, Tobyhanna, Pennsylvania, 11 November 2005, http://www.whitehouse.gov/news/releases/2005/11/print/20051111-1.html.

46. "President Says Saddam Hussein Must Leave Iraq within 48 Hours: Remarks by the President in Address to the Nation" (Washington, D.C.: Office of the Press Secretary), 17 March 2003.

47. IAEA Update Report for the Security Council Pursuant to Resolution 1441 (2002).

48. "No Evidence of Nuclear Weapons Program: ElBaradei," *Sydney Morning Herald*, 8 March 2003.

49. Secretary Colin L. Powell, "Press Remarks with Foreign Minister of Egypt Amre Moussa," *U.S. Department of State*, 24 February 2001, http://www.state.gov/secretary/rm/2001/933.htm.

50. "President Delivers State of the Union," 28 January 2003, http://www.whitehouse.gov/news/releases/2003/01/20030128-19.html.

51. Dana Priest and Karen DeYoung, "CIA Questioned Documents Linking Iraq, Uranium Ore," *Washington Post*, 22 March 2003. See also "Report on the U.S. Intelligence Community's Prewar Intelligence Assessments on Iraq," Select Committee on Intelligence, United States Senate, 7 July 2004. The report finds numerous agencies challenging the documents regarding the Nigerian uranium sale to Iraq. The responses included that it was "highly suspect"; "lacks crucial details"; and was "completely implausible."

52. Jeanne Cummings, "Security Advisers Now Share Blame in Intelligence Row," *Wall Street Journal*, 23 July 2003, p. A4. Note that the CIA's initial challenge led to the removal of the uranium claim from an October speech. See Ken Fireman, "Warning Unheeded," *Newsday*, 23 July 2003.

53. Mark Danner, "The Secret Way to War," *The New York Review of Books*, 9 June 2005.

54. Danner, "The Secret Way to War," *The New York Review of Books*, 9 June 2005. This quota-

tion is from the infamous Downing Street memo. For more details and responses to Bush support-ers, visit http://www.downingstreet.org, which explains that, "The Downing Street Memo is actu-ally meeting minutes transcribed during the British Prime Minister's meeting on July 23, 2002. Published by *The Sunday Times* on May 1, 2005 it was the first hard evidence from within the UK or US governments that exposed the truth behind how the Iraq war began."

55. See Stephen Shalom, "Iraq White Paper," for reference and more details in *Enduring Freedom or Enduring War? Prospects and Costs of the New American 21st Century*, ed. Carl Mirra (Washington, D.C.: Maisonneuve Press, 2005), pp. 173–176.

56. Shalom, "Iraq White Paper," p. 174.

57. "U.S. Troops in Iraq: 72% Say End the War in 2006," *Zogby International*, 28 February 2006, http://www.zogby.com/news/ReadNews.dbm?ID=1075. To be sure, withdrawal does not mean aban-donment. See Johan Galtung, "Human Needs, Humanitarian Intervention, Human Security and the War in Iraq" (February 2004), posted at http://www.transcend.org.

58. Sean Rayment, "Secret MoD Poll: Iraqis Support Attacks on British Troops," *Sunday Tele-graph*, 23 October 2005.

59. "Iraqis Not So Happy," *Newsday*, 29 September 2003, p. A12. Furthermore, the Brookings Institute identifies a February 2005 poll in which 71 percent of Iraqis "oppose the presence of Coali-tion forces in Iraq." For this poll and several others with similar data, see Abigail Fuller and Neil Woll-man, "Should the U.S. Withdraw? Let the Iraqi People Decide," *Professors for Peace*, 13 October 2005.

60. Christopher Preble, *Exiting Iraq: Why the U.S. Must End the Military Occupation and Renew the War against Al Qaeda* (Washington, D.C.: Cato Institute, 2004), pp. 2, 34 and 66.

61. See David Armstrong, "Dick Cheney's Song for America," *Harper's Magazine*, October 2002. *PBS* also aired a program that addressed the DPG in 2003. Cheney and Wolfowitz deny any knowl-edge of this version of the draft and a revised version was circulated after news reports on the DPG surfaced.

62. William R. Polk, "A Time for Leaving," *The American Conservative*, 17 January 2005. Preble, *Exiting Iraq*, p. 31.

63. William Appleman Williams, *The Tragedy of American Diplomacy* (New York: W.W. Norton, 1972), p. 10.

64. On Order 39 and Iraqis, see Naomi Klein, "Baghdad Year Zero," *Harper's Magazine* (Septem-ber 2004).

65. Klein, "Baghdad Year Zero," *Harper's Magazine* (September 2004).

66. Paul Alexander, "Seven Retired Military Leaders Discuss What Has Gone Wrong in Iraq," *Rolling Stone*, 2 November 2004. This article was sent to me via e-mail from the Professors for Peace.

67. On Syria and Iran, see Douglas Little, *American Orientalism: The United States and the Mid-dle East since 1945* (Chapel Hill: University of North Carolina Press, 2002), pp. 52–58. Eisenhower quoted as saying a "campaign of hatred against us, not by the governments but by the people" in the context of the Lebanon intervention in Little, *American Orientalism*, p. 136. Information on Kurds derived from William Blum, *Killing Hope* (Monroe, ME: Common Courage Press, 1995). See also Douglas Little, "Cold War and Covert Action: The United States and Syria, 1945–1958," *Middle East Journal* 44, no. 1 (Winter 1990): 51–75.

68. Bush quoted in Preble, *Exiting Iraq*, p. 66.

69. At *Slate.com*, Fred Kaplan challenged the Lancet study in an article titled, "100,000 Dead — or 8,000 — How Many People Have Died as a Result of the Iraq War," 29 October 2004. On tor-ture, see Mark Danner, *Torture and Truth: America, Abu Ghraib, and the War on Terror* (New York: New York Review of Books, 2004), pp. 251–275. On air strikes, see Human Rights Watch, "Off Tar-get: The Conduct of the War and Civilian Casualties in Iraq" (2003), available at: http://www.hrw.org. On the UN Assistance Mission figures, see Nancy Benac, "Americans Underestimate Iraqi Death Toll," *Associated Press*, 24 February 2007.

70. This paragraph follows Johan Galtung, "Human Needs, Humanitarian Intervention, Human Security and the War in Iraq" (February 2004), posted at http://www.transcend.org.

71. On Bush's regret, see "Bush Rethinks His Tough Talk," *Newsday*, 15 January 2005. Quota-tions in George W. Bush, *A Charge to Keep*, pp. 50, 55 and 240.

72. Clergy quoted in David D. Kirkpatrick, "Battle Cry of Faithful Pits Believers and Unbeliev-ers," *New York Times*, 31 October 2004, p. 22.

73. This paragraph follows Les T. Csorba, "President Bush, part 2," *Newsday*, 21 January 2005, p. A45. Information concerning Bush's mention of freedom forty-four times in "A Global Strategy

of Freedom," *Newsday*, 21 January 2005, p. A56. Bush's Second Inaugural Address (Washington, D.C.), 20 January 2005.

74. Bush's Second Inaugural Address (Washington, D.C.), 20 January 2005.

75. Csorba, "President Bush, part 2," *Newsday*, 21 January 2005.

76. Peggy Noonan, "Way Too Much God," *Wall Street Journal*, 21 January 2005.

77. Quoted in Bonnie Goodman, "What Historians Thought of President Bush's 2nd Inaugural Address: Excerpts," *History News Network*, 22 January 2005.

78. Cornel West, "Exiles from a City and from a Nation," *The Observer* 11 September 2005.

79. See Timothy McDonald, "He Came Not to Praise King But...," *Los Angeles Times*, 19 January 2004. Information about protest sign from "Crowds Protest Bush Visit to MLK Tomb," *MSNBC.com*, 15 January 2004.

80. Information concerning first female AME bishop as well as King III and Franklin quoted in "War Protests Mark King Day," *Associated Press*, 19 January 2004.

81. Shuttlesworth and SCLC quotations are from Southern Christian Leadership Conference statement, "SCLC Question the Integrity of Bush's Decision to Lay a Wreath on King's 75th Birthday," available at http://www.sclcnational.org. Shuttlesworth has since resigned from his position, citing internal problems. Although the organization has internal differences, staff seem united in their suspicion of Bush's questionable visit to King's tomb.

82. "Gallup International Poll on Terrorism in the U.S. (figures)," n.d., (c. October 2001), http://www.gallup-international.com/terrorismpoll_figures.htm. See also Galtung, "September 11: Diagnosis, Prognosis, Therapy," available at http://www.transcend.org.

Chapter 6

1. George W. Bush, *National Security Strategy of the United States of America*, 20 September 2002, available at http://www.whitehouse.gov/nsc/nss.pdf.

2. International Criminal Court, "Frequently Asked Questions," available at http://www.icc-cpi.int/about/ataglance/faq.html#faq1.

3. For information on the formation of the ICC, see United Nations "Setting the Record Straight: The International Criminal Court" (New York: UN Department of Public Information, October 1998). On Canada's support, consult, "Canada and the ICC," http://209.217.98.9/english/08_canadaICC_e/08_canadaICC_e.htm.

4. George W. Bush, *National Security Strategy of the United States of America*, 20 September 2002, available at http://www.whitehouse.gov/nsc/nss.pdf. On Europe, see "Remarks of European Delegates to the Preparatory Commission," 25 September 2001, compiled by the Washington Working Group on the International Criminal Court.

5. Sarah B. Sewell and Carl Kayson, eds., *The United States and the International Criminal Court* (Boston: Rowman and Littlefield Publishers, 2000), pp. 67–68.

6. Marc Grossman, "American Foreign Policy and the International Criminal Court," Remarks to the Center for Strategic Studies, Washington, DC, 6 May 2002.

7. Henry Kissinger, "The Pitfalls of Universal Jurisdiction," *Foreign Affairs* (July–August 2001), available at http://www.foreignaffairs.org. Marc Grossman, "American Foreign Policy and the International Criminal Court." Robert Hirshon, "Letter to the President," May 2002, available at http://www.fed-soc.org/Publications/barwatchbulletin/barwatchmay2002.htm.

8. "Negroponte Calls Exemption for U.N. Peacekeepers a First Step," U.S. State Department, Washington File, 13 July 2002. Canadian ambassador quoted in "Canadian Ambassador Attacks ICC Exemption for the US," Canadian Broadcasting Corporation, 13 July 2002. Elie Wiesel, "Letter to Honorable Benjamin Gilman," 19 September 2000, available at http://www.igc.org/icc/html/wiesel20000919.html.

9. David J. Scheffer, "Statement before the House International Relations Committee," Washington, D.C., 26 July 2000, available at http://www.state.gov/www/policy_remarks/2000/000726_scheffer_service.html.

10. Information on Status of Force Agreements in Scheffer, "Statement before the House International Relations Committee." Bush quoted in *National Security Strategy of the United States of America*, 20 September 2002, available at http://www.whitehouse.gov/nsc/nss.pdf. Comments from European Parliament quoted in Washington Working Group on the International Criminal Court.

11. Mike Kitzman, "International Criminal Court," *H-Diplo*, 16 August 2002. Kofi Annan,

"Letter to Colin Powell, July 3, 2002," Press Release NGO Coalition for the ICC, 9 July 2002.

12. Dana Priest, "U.S. Military Trains Foreign Troops," *Washington Post*, 12 July 1998, p. A01.

13. Leslie Wayne, "America's for Profit Secret Army," *New York Times*, 13 October 2002, pp. 1 and 10–11.

14. Wayne, "America's for Profit Secret Army," *New York Times*, 13 October 2002, p. 10.

15. U.S. State Department, "Security Companies Doing Business in Iraq," http://travel.state.gov/travel/cis-partw/cis/cis-1763.html. Lynda Hurst, "The Privatization of Abu Ghraib," *Toronto Star*, 16 May 2004.

16. Ken Silverstein, "Privatizing War: How Affairs of State Are Outsourced to Corporations beyond Public Control," *The Nation*, 28 July 1997.

Chapter 7

1. John Perkins, *Confessions of an Economic Hit Man* (San Francisco: Berrett-Koehler Publishers, 2004), pp. 127–128.

2. Howard Zinn, "The Power and the Glory: Myths of American Exceptionalism," *The Boston Review: A Political and Literary Forum* (Summer 2005). We should note that Garrison employs sexist language that is problematic and should think and speak in terms of "My country is the world. My countrywomen and men are humankind."

3. The Keller quotation is from her speech "Strike against War" in 1916. See Lois Einhorn, *Helen Keller, Public Speaker: Sightless but Seen, Deaf but Heard* (Westport, CT: Greenwood Press, 1998), p. 30. The entire speech is reprinted in Howard Zinn and Anthony Arnove, eds., *Voices of a People's History of the United States* (New York: Seven Stories Press, 2004), pp. 284–288.

4. Douglas Sloan, *Insight-Imagination: The Emancipation of Thought and the Modern World* (Westport, CT: Greenwood Publishing Group, 1983), pp. 197–198.

5. My thoughts in this chapter were sharpened and clarified by Staughton Lynd, see especially Lynd, *The Intellectual Origins of American Radicalism* (New York: Vintage Books, 1969), pp. 130–159. I owe much to his analysis of Paine's famous remark that, "My country is the world."

6. Teachers College, Columbia University, Peace Education Center, "Action Research — Exploring New Terrain in the Field: The Spiritual and Ethical Foundations of Peace Education," http://www.tc.columbia.edu/PeaceEd/activities/research.htm.

7. Helen Merrell Lynd, *On Shame and the Search for Identity* (New York: John Wiley and Sons), p. 35.

8. For George W. Bush's Second Inaugural Address, see "President Bush Sworn-In to Second Term," 20 January 2005, http://www.whitehouse.gov/inaugural. Bakunin quoted in Noam Chomsky, *Chomsky on Anarchism* (Oakland, CA: AK Press, 2005), p. 155.

9. Interview of Staughton Lynd in Henry Abelove et al., *Visions of History* (New York: Pantheon Books, 1983), pp. 160–161.

10. John Dewey, *The Public and Its Problems* (Athens, OH: Swallow Press/Ohio University Press, 1954), pp. 170–171.

11. Helen Merrell Lynd, *On Shame and the Search for Identity*, pp. 215–217.

12. My thoughts on the American tradition in this paragraph are based on Staughton Lynd, *Intellectual Origins of American Radicalism* (New York: Vintage Books, 1969), pp. v–vi.

13. Lynd, *Intellectual Origins of American Radicalism*, p. 173.

14. SNCC Statement of Purpose reprinted in Clayborne Carson, *In Struggle: SNCC and the Black Awakening of the 1960s* (Cambridge, MA: Harvard University Press, 1981), pp. 23–24.

15. Quotation and information on SNCC in this paragraph taken from Michael Ferber and Staughton Lynd, *The Resistance* (Boston: Beacon Press, 1971), pp. 30–32.

16. Dale T. Snauwaert, "Cosmopolitan Democracy and Democratic Education," *Current Issues in Comparative Education* 4, no. 2 (December 2001).

17. Martin Luther King Jr., *Why We Can't Wait* (New York: Signet Classics, 2000), p. 65.

18. See Douglas Sloan, "A Postmodern Vision of Education for a Living Planet," in *Postmodern Politics for a Planet in Crisis: Policy, Process, and Presidential Vision*, eds. David Ray Griffin and Richard Falk (New York: State University of New York Press, 1993), p. 121.

19. Albert Einstein, *Ideas and Opinions* (New York: Three Rivers Press, 1982), p. 38.

20. Richard Falk, "Religion and Politics: Verging on the Postmodern," in *Sacred Interconnections: Postmodern Spirituality, Political Economy, and Art*, ed. David Ray Griffin (Albany: State University of New York Press, 1990), p. 84.

21. Richard Falk and David Ray Griffin, "The 'Vision Thing,' the Presidency, and the Ecological Crisis, or the Greenhouse Effect and the 'White House Effect,'" in *Postmodern Politics for a Planet in Crisis: Policy, Process and Presidential Vision*, eds. David Ray Griffin and Richard Falk (New York: State University of New York Press, 1993), p. 80.

22. David Ray Griffin, "Introduction: From Modern to Postmodern Politics," in *Postmodern Politics for a Planet in Crisis: Policy, Process and Presidential Vision*, eds. David Ray Griffin and Richard Falk (New York: State University of New York Press, 1993), pp. 4–5.

23. Douglas Sloan, "A Postmodern Vision of Education for a Living Planet," in *Postmodern Politics for a Planet in Crisis: Policy, Process, and Presidential Vision*, eds. David Ray Griffin and Richard Falk (New York: State University of New York Press, 1993), p. 119.

24. Information on Carl Rogers and a detailed discussion of the role of "other-oriented" empathy in accepting guilt is located in June Price Tangney and Ronda L. Dearing, *Shame and Guilt* (New York: The Guilford Press, 2002), pp. 78–89. See also Roy F. Baumeister, *Evil: Inside Human Violence and Cruelty* (New York: W.H. Freeman, 1999), p. 312 and passim.

25. Thomas Scheff, *Bloody Revenge: Emotions, Nationalism and War* (1994, reprint, Lincoln, NE: iUniverse, 2000), pp. 142–143.

26. The threefold process is associated with philosopher Rudolf Steiner and is practiced in holistic schools, especially the Waldorf movement that has over seven hundred schools worldwide. I am also following Owen Barfield's discussion of the threefold process in *Saving the Appearances: A Study in Idolatry* (Middletown, CT: Wesleyan, 1988), pp. 140–141. Indeed, we need not agree with every aspect of Barfield and Steiner's work to embrace holistic teaching strategies.

27. See David Steindl-Rast, *Gratefulness, the Heart of Prayer* (Ramsey, NJ: Paulist Press, 1984), p. 163. Eric Fromm, *The Art of Loving* (New York: Harper and Row, 1956), p. 50. Philosopher Owen Barfield also explains that threefold thinking is inseparable from love, see his *Rediscovery of Meaning and Other Essays* (Middletown, CT: Wesleyan, 1977), pp. 222–223.

28. Douglas Sloan, *Insight-Imagination: The Emancipation of Thought and the Modern World* (Westport, CT: Greenwood Publishing Group, 1983), pp. 202–207.

29. Eugene Schwartz is a lecturer on Waldorf Education; for further discussion and examples of the threefold process, see John Alexandra, *Mephistopheles' Anvil: Forging a More Humane Future* (Spring Valley, NY: Rose Harmony Publications, 1996), pp. 148–170.

30. Peter McLaren, "Unthinking Whiteness: Rearticulating Diasporic Practice," in *Revolutionary Pedagogies: Cultural Politics, Instituting Education and the Discourse of Theory*, ed. Peter Trifonas (New York: Routledge, 2000), p. 165. Henry A. Giroux, *Disturbing Pleasures: Learning Popular Culture* (London: Routledge, 1994), pp. 29–30.

31. Paulo Freire, *Pedagogy of the Oppressed: New Revised 20th Anniversary Edition* (New York: Continuum Press, 1998), p. 70. On the dialogic encounter as a meeting between humans, see Ira Schor and Paulo Freire, "What Is the 'Dialogical Method of Teaching?" *Journal of Education* 169, no. 3 (1987): 13.

32. For details on critical pedagogy's religious roots and its general link to U.S. colonialism, see Enrique Dussel, *A History of the Church in Latin America: Colonialism to Liberation* (Grand Rapids, MI: Eerdmans Publishing Company, 1981), pp. 148–152.

33. Freire quoted in Blanca Facundo, "How Is Freire Seen in the United States," http://www.uow.edu/arts/sts/bmartin/dissent/documents/Facundo/section2/html.

34. Paulo Freire, *The Politics of Education: Culture, Power and Liberation* (Granby, MA: Bergin and Garvey, 1985), p. 139.

35. John Dewey, *The Public and Its Problems* (Athens, OH: Swallow Press Books/Ohio University Press, 1954), p. 170.

36. Maxine Greene, "In Search of a Critical Pedagogy," *Harvard Educational Review* 56, no. 4 (November 1986): 427–441. To be sure, I very much admire the work of Freire and he remains important to any critical pedagogy project and I am equally indebted to the historical courage and commitment of all those associated with Latin American liberation theology. It seems to me, however, that U.S. children would benefit from sharing in similar examples in their own tradition in addition to the courageous Latin American movements.

37. "Teachers Manual: 1964 Mississippi Freedom Schools," (COFO Publication) in Staughton Lynd Papers, State Historical Society of Wisconsin, Box 4, Folder 13.

38. "1964 Platform of the Mississippi Freedom School Convention: August, 6th, 7th, 8th Meridian Mississippi," in Staughton Lynd Collection, Kent State University Special Collections, Box 6, Folder 3. Staughton Lynd, "Freedom Schools: Concept and Organization," *Freedomways* (April 1965).

39. William Appleman Williams, "The City on a Hill and an Errand into the Wilderness," in *Vietnam Reconsidered*, ed. Harrison Salisbury (New York: Harper and Row, 1984), pp. 11–14. On religion as community, see Paul Buhle and Edward Rice-Maximin, *William Appleman Williams: The Tragedy of Empire* (New York: Routledge, 1995), p. 232.

40. Williams Appleman Williams, "The Empire at Bay," in *A William Appleman Williams Reader*, ed. Henry Berger (Chicago: Ivan R. Dee Publishers, 1992), pp. 364 and 371.

41. William Appleman Williams, *The Contours of American History* (Chicago: Quadrangle Books, 1966), pp. 6–9.

42. Williams Appleman Williams, "The Empire at Bay," in *A William Appleman Williams Reader*, ed. Henry Berger (Chicago: Ivan R. Dee Publishers, 1992), p. 375.

43. Peter McLaren and Ramin Farahmandpur, "Critical Revolutionary Pedagogy at Ground Zero," in *Education as Enforcement: The Militarization and Corporatization of Schools*, eds. Kenneth J. Saltman and David A. Gabbard (New York: Routledge Falmer, 2003), pp. 311–326.

44. Birgit Brock-Utne, "The Challenges for Peace Educators at the End of a Millennium," *International Journal of Peace Studies* 1, no. 1 (January 1996).

45. Staughton Lynd and Alice Lynd, eds., *Nonviolence in America: A Documentary History* (Maryknoll, NY: Orbis Books, 2002), p. xii.

46. Marvin J. Berlowitz, Nathan A. Long, and Eric Jackson, "The Exclusion and Distortion of African American Perspectives in Peace Education," *Educational Studies* 39, no. 2 (2006).

47. Staughton Lynd and Alice Lynd, eds., *Nonviolence in America*, p. xxxv.

48. Gene Sharp, *There Are Realistic Alternatives* (Boston: Albert Einstein Institution, 2003), pp. 5–7, quotation on p. 8.

49. Michael Bar-Zohar, *Beyond Hitler's Grasp: The Heroic Rescue of Bulgaria's Jews* (Holbrook, MA: Adams Media, 1998), p. vii. It is estimated that there were roughly 50,000 Jewish people in Bulgaria at the time.

50. Tzvetan Todorov, *The Fragility of Goodness: Why Bulgaria's Jews Survived the Holocaust* (Princeton, NJ: Princeton University Press, 2003), p. 43.

51. Michael Bar-Zohar, *Beyond Hitler's Grasp*, p. ix.

52. See Daniel Rosenberg, "The Holocaust and Business as Usual: Congressional Source Materials," *The Reference Librarian*, no. 61/62 (1998): 99–111. Rosenberg relies on congressional hearings that uncovered and put a stop to U.S. business and Nazi trading. See also Christopher Simpson, *The Splendid Blond Beast: Money, Law, and Genocide in the Twentieth Century* (Monroe, ME: Common Courage Press, 1995).

53. David Schmitz, *Thank God They're on Our Side*, p. 91. The remark on free trade is Schmitz, summarizing a State Department Report. One official whom Schmitz quotes described the "moderate section of the party, headed by Hitler himself."

54. Long quoted in Schmitz, *Thank God They're on Our Side*, p. 92. Others in U.S. policy circles believed that Germany was a bulwark against communism. Churchill and Roosevelt were certainly more hostile toward Germany. British foreign secretary Lord Halifax described Nazi Germany "as the bulwark of Europe against Bolshevism," quoted in the controversial A.J.P. Taylor, *The Origins of the Second World War* (New York: Touchstone, 1996), p. 137. For the record, Schmitz does not argue that support for Germany at the time was designed to push Berlin toward the Soviets.

55. Linda Lantieri and Janet Patti, *Waging Peace in Our Schools* (Boston: Beacon Press, 1996), pp. xv and 7.

56. Lantieri and Patti, *Waging Peace in Our Schools*, p. 21.

57. Lantieri and Patti, *Waging Peace in Our Schools*, pp. 74–79.

58. Taylor McNeil, "Seduced by War," *Bostonia* (Winter 2004–2005): 21.

59. David Dellinger, "The Future of Nonviolence," reprinted in Staughton Lynd and Alice Lynd, eds., *Nonviolence in America*, p. 403.

Bibliography

Books

Aburish, Said. *Saddam Hussein: The Politics of Revenge.* London: Bloomsbury Publishing, 2000.

Achbar, Mark, ed. *Manufacturing Consent: Noam Chomsky and the Media.* Montreal: Black Rose Books, 1994.

Acheson, Dean. *Present at the Creation: My Years in the State Department.* New York: W.W. Norton, 1969.

Ackerman, Peter, and Jack Duvall. *A Force More Powerful: A Century of Nonviolent Conflict.* New York: St. Martin's Press, 2000.

Aikman, David. *A Man of Faith: The Spiritual Journey of George W. Bush.* Nashville, TN: W Publishing Group, 2004.

Alexandra, John. *Mephistopheles Anvil: Forging a More Human Future.* Spring Valley, NY: Rose Harmony Publishers, 1996.

Ambrose, Stephen. *Ike's Spies: Eisenhower and the Espionage Establishment.* Jackson: University Press of Mississippi, 1999.

American Library Association. *Less Access to Less Information by and about the U.S. Government: A 1981–1987 Chronology.* Washington, DC: ALA, 1988.

Andrepoulous, George J., and Richard Pierre Claude, ed. *Human Rights Education for the Twenty-first Century.* Philadelphia: University of Pennsylvania Press, 1997.

Appy, Christian. *Patriots: The Vietnam War Remembered from All Sides.* New York: Penguin Books, 2003.

Aptheker, Herbert. *The Colonial Era.* New York: International Publishers, 1979.

Bacevich, Andrew. *American Empire: The Realities and Consequences of U.S. Diplomacy.* Cambridge, MA: Harvard University Press, 2002.

_____. *The Imperial Tense: Prospects and Problems of American Empire* Chicago: Ivan R. Dee Publishers, 2003.

_____. *The New American Militarism: How Americans Are Seduced by War* Oxford: Oxford University Press, 2005.

Bailey, Thomas A. *A Diplomatic History of the American People.* 10th ed. Englewood Cliffs, NJ: Prentice Hall, 1980.

Barfield, Owen. *Poetic Diction: A Study in Meaning.* Middletown, CT: Wesleyan, 1973.

_____. *The Rediscovery of Meaning and Other Essays.* Middletown, CT: Wesleyan, 1977.

_____. *Saving the Appearances.* Connecticut: Wesleyan University Press, 1988.

Barnet, Richard. *Roots of War: The Men and Institutions behind U.S. Foreign Policy.* Baltimore: Penguin Books, 1972.

Bartov, Omar, Anita Grossman, and Mary Nolan, eds. *Crimes of War: Guilt and Denial in the Twentieth Century.* New York: The New Press, 2002.

Batatu, Hanna. *The Old Social Classes and the Revolutionary Movements of Iraq: A Study of Iraq's Old Landed and Commercial Classes and of Its Communists, Ba'thists and Free Officers.* Princeton, NJ: Princeton University Press, 1978.

Baumeister, Roy F. *Evil: Inside Human Violence and Cruelty.* New York: W.H. Freeman, 1999.

Beliles, Mark A., and Stephen K. McDowell. *America's Providential History.* Charlottesville, VA: Providence Foundation, 1989.

Bellah, Robert. *The Broken Covenant: American Civil Religion on Trial.* New York: Seabury Press, 1975.

Bennett, William J. *Why We Fight: Moral Clarity and the War on Terrorism.* New York: Doubleday, 2002.

Bercovitch, Sacvan. *The American Jeremaid.* Madison: University of Wisconsin Press, 1978.

Berger, Henry, ed. *A William Appleman Williams Reader.* Chicago: Ivan R. Dee, 1992.

Blum, William. *Killing Hope: U.S. Military and CIA Interventions since World War II* Monroe, ME: Common Courage Press, 1995.

_____. *Rogue State: A Guide to the World's Only Superpower.* Monroe, ME: Common Courage, 2000.

Bodansky, Yossef. *Bin Laden: The Man Who Declared War on America.* New York: Prima Publishing, 2001.

Brzezinski, Zbigniew. *The Grand Chessboard: American Primacy and Its Geostrategic Imperatives.* New York: Basic Books, 1997.

Brisard, Jean-Charles, and Guillaume Dasquie. *Forbidden Truth: U.S.-Taliban Secret Oil Diplomacy and the Failed Hunt for bin Laden.* New York: Thunder's Mouth Press, 2002.

Burns, Robin J., and Robert Aspeslagh, eds. *Three Decades of Peace Education around the World: An Anthology.* New York: Garland Press, 1996.

Bush, George W. *A Charge to Keep: My Journey to the White House.* New York: HarperCollins, 2001.

Butler, Jon. *Awash in a Sea of Faith: Christianizing the American People.* Cambridge, MA: Harvard University Press, 1992.

Butler, Smedley D. *War Is a Racket.* New York: Roundtable Press, 1935.

Cabezudo, Alicia, and Betty Reardon. *Learning to Abolish War: Teaching toward a Culture of Peace.* New York: Hague Appeal for Peace, 2002.

Calvert, Gregory. *Democracy from the Heart: Spiritual Values, Decentralism, and Democratic Idealism in the Movement of the 1960s.* Eugene, OR: Communitas Press, 1991.

Carroll, James. *Crusade: Chronicles of an Unjust War.* New York: Metropolitan Books, 2004.

Central Intelligence Agency. *The Pike Report.* Nottingham, UK: Spokesman Books, 1977.

Cherry, Conrad, ed. *God's New Israel: Religious Interpretations of American Destiny* Englewood Cliffs, NJ: Prentice Hall, 1971.

Chomsky, Noam. *American Power and the New Mandarins.* Harmondsworth, UK: Penguin,1969.

_____. *Chomsky on Anarchism.* Edited by Barry Pateman. Oakland, CA: AK Press, 2005.

_____. *Chomsky on Miseducation.* Edited and introduced by Donaldo Macedo. Lanham, MD: Rowman and Littlefield, 2000.

_____. *Imperial Ambitions: Conversations on the Post–9/11 World.* New York: Metropolitan Books, 2005.

_____. *The Umbrella of U.S. Power: The Universal Declaration of Human Rights and the Contradictions of U.S. Policy.* New York: Seven Stories Press, 1999.

_____. *World Orders: Old and New.* New York: Columbia University Press, 1994.

Chossudovsky, Michel. *War and Globalisation: The Truth behind September 11.* Shanty Bay, Ontario: Global Outlook, 2002.

Clark, Ramsey. *The Fire This Time: U.S. War Crimes in the Gulf.* 2nd ed. New York: International Action Center, 2002.

Clarke, Richard A. *Against All Enemies: Inside America's War on Terror.* New York: The Free Press, 2004.

Cohen, Warren. *The Cambridge History of American Foreign Relations.* Vol. 4, *America in the Age of Soviet Power, 1945–1991.* New York: Cambridge University Press, 1995.

Commission on the Roles and Capabilities of the United States Intelligence Community. *Preparing for the 21st Century.* Washington, DC: U.S. Government Printing Office, 1996.

Cooley, John. *Unholy Wars: Afghanistan, America and International Terrorism.* London: Pluto Press, 1999.

Cone, James H. *Black Theology and Black Power.* New York: Seabury Press, 1969.

Cortright, David. *Soldiers in Revolt: GI Resistance during the Vietnam War.* Chicago: Haymarket Books, 2005.

Crozier, Michel J., Samuel P. Huntington, and Joji Watanuki. *The Crisis of Democracy: Report on the Governability of Democracies to the Trilateral Commission.* New York: New York University Press, 1975.

Daadler, Ivo H., and James M. Lindsay. *America Unbound: The Bush Revolution in Foreign Policy.* Washington, DC: Brookings Institute Press, 2003.

Damico, Alfonso J. *Individuality and Community: The Social and Political Thought of John Dewey.* Gainesville: University Press of Florida, 1979.

DeBenedetti, Charles. *Peace Heroes in Twentieth-Century America.* Bloomington: Indiana University Press, 1988.

Dellinger, David. *More Power Than We Know: The People's Movement toward Democracy.* Garden City, NY: Anchor Press/Doubleday, 1975.

Deloria, Vine Jr. *For This Land: Writings on Religion in America.* New York: Routledge, 1999.

Denner, Mark. *Torture and Truth: America, Abu Ghraib, and the War on Terror.* New York: New York Review of Books, 2004.

Dewey, John. *The Public and Its Problems.* Athens, OH: Swallow Press Books/Ohio University Press, 1954.

Domke, David. *God Willing? Political Fundamentalism in the White House, the "War on Terror," and the Echoing Press.* London: Pluto Press, 2004.

D'Souza, Dinesh. *What's So Great about America.* Washington, DC: Regnery Publishing, 2002.

Dussel, Enrique. *A History of the Church in Latin America: Colonialism to Liberation.* Grand Rapids, MI: Eerdmans Publishing, 1981.

Einhorn, Lois. *Helen Keller, Public Speaker: Sightless but Seen, Deaf but Heard* Westport, CT: Greenwood Press, 1998.

Einstein, Albert. *Ideas and Opinions.* New York: Crown Publishers, 1982.

Eisendrath, Craig. *National Insecurity: U.S. Intelligence after the Cold War.* Philadelphia: Temple University Press, 2000.

Eisenhower, Dwight D. *Mandate for Change: The White House Years, 1953–1956.* Garden City, NY: Doubleday, 1963.

Engelhardt, Tom. *The End of Victory Culture: Cold War America and the Disillusioning of a Generation.* New York: Basic Books, 1995.

Farhang, Mansour. *U.S. Imperialism: From the Spanish-American War to the Iranian Revolution.* Boston: South End Press, 1981.

Ferguson, Niall. *Colossus: The Rise and Fall of the American Empire.* New York: Penguin Books, 2004.

Foner, Eric. *The Story of American Freedom.* New York: W.W. Norton, 1999.

Federer, William J., ed. *America's God and Country: Encyclopedia of Quotations*. Fame Publishing, 1994.
Ford, Franklin. *Political Murder: From Tyrannicide to Genocide*. Cambridge, MA: Harvard University Press, 1985.
Fornari, Franco. *The Psychoanalysis of War*. New York: Anchor Books, 1974.
Franklin, H. Bruce. *M.I.A or Mythmaking in America*. Chicago: Lawrence Hill Books, 1992.
Franklin, Jane. *Cuba and the United States: A Chronological History*. Chicago: Ocean Press, 1997.
The Freedom Fighters Manual. Central Intelligence Agency. New York: Grove Press, 1985.
Freiling, Thomas M., ed. *George W. Bush on God and Country: A President Speaks Out on Faith, Principle and Patriotism*. Washington, DC: Allegiance Press, 2004.
Freire, Paulo. *Pedagogy of the Oppressed*. New York: Continuum, 1998.
_____. *The Politics of Education: Culture, Power and Liberation*. Granby, MA: Bergin and Garvey, 1985.
Fromm, Eric. *The Art of Loving*. New York: Harper and Row, 1956.
Gaddis, John Lewis. *The Cold War: A New History*. London: Penguin Group, 2005.
Galtung, Johan. *Pax Pacifica: Terrorism, the Pacific Hemisphere, Globalisation and Peace Studies*. London: Pluto Press, 2005.
_____. *Peace by Peaceful Means: Peace and Conflict, Development and Civilization*. London: Sage Publications, 1998.
_____. *There Are Alternatives*. Nottingham, UK: Spokesman Books, 1984.
_____. *Transcend and Transform: An Introduction to Conflict Work*. Boulder, CO: Paradigm Publishers, 2004.
_____, and Daisaku Ikeda. *Choose Peace*. London: Pluto Press, 1995.
Galtung, Johan, Carl G. Jacobson, and Kai Frithjof Brand-Jacobson. *Searching for Peace: The Road to Transcend*. London: Pluto Press, 2000.
Gardner, Lloyd. *Imperial America: American Foreign Policy since 1898*. New York: Harcourt Brace Jovanovich, 1976.
Gaylin, Willard. *The Rage Within: Anger in Modern Life*. New York: Simon and Schuster, 1984.
Gilligan, James. *Violence: Reflections on a National Epidemic*. New York: Vintage, 1996.
Gleijeses, Piero. *Shattered Hope: The Guatemalan Revolution and the United States, 1944–1954*. Princeton, NJ: Princeton University Press, 1991.
Goldstein, Warren. *William Sloane Coffin, Jr.: A Holy Impatience*. New Haven, CT: Yale University Press, 2004.
Graham, Billy. *Just as I Am: The Autobiography of Billy Graham*. San Francisco: HarperCollins, 1997.
Griffin, David Ray, ed. *Postmodern Politics for a Planet in Crisis: Policy, Progress, and Presidential Vision*. New York: State University of New York Press, 1993.
Grossman, Dave. *On Killing: The Psychological Cost of Learning to Kill in War and Society*. Boston: Back Bay Books, 1996.
Grossman, Karl. *Nicaragua: America's New Vietnam?* Sag Harbor, NY: The Permanent Press, 1984.
Haavelsrud, Magnus. *Education in Developments*. Tromsø, Norway: Arena, 1996.
Haines, Gerald. *CIA and Guatemala Assassination Proposals 1952–54*. CIA History Staff Analysis, June 1995.
Halpern, James, and Ilsa Halpern. *Projections: Our World of Imaginary Relationships*. New York: Seaview/Putnam, 1983.
Hansen, David T., ed. *John Dewey and Our Educational Prospect: A Critical Engagement with Dewey's Democracy and Education*. Albany: State University Press of New York, 2006.
Harris, Ian M., and Mary Lee Morrison. *Peace Education*, 2d ed. Jefferson, NC: McFarland, 1998.
Hastings, Tom. *Nonviolent Response to Terrorism*. Jefferson, NC: McFarland, 2004.

Hatfield, J. H. *Fortunate Son: George Bush and the Making of an American President.* New York: Soft Skull Press, 2001.
Hedges, Chris. *War Is a Force That Gives Us Meaning.* New York: Public Affairs Books, 2002.
Heffermehl, Fredrik. *Peace Is Possible.* Geneva: International Peace Bureau, 2000.
Hepburn, Mary A., ed. *Democratic Education in Schools and Classrooms.* Washington, DC: National Council for the Social Studies, 1983.
Hersch, Seymour. *Chain of Command: The Road from 9/11 to Abu Ghraib.* New York: Harper Perennial, 2004.
_____. *The Price of Power: Kissinger in the Nixon White House.* New York: Summit, 1983.
Hibbard, Scott, and David Little. *Islamic Activism and U.S. Foreign Policy.* Washington, DC: United States Institute for Peace, 1997.
Hicks, David, ed. *Education for Peace: Issues, Principles, and Practice in the Classroom.* London: Routledge, 1988.
Hiro, Dilip. *Secrets and Lies: Operation "Iraqi Freedom" and After.* New York: Nation Books, 2004.
Hoffer, Eric. *The True Believer.* New York: Perennial Classics, 2002.
Huband, Mark. *Warriors of the Prophet: The Struggle for Islam.* Boulder, CO: Westview Press, 1998.
Human Rights and Security Assistance: An Amnesty International USA Report on Human Rights Violations in Countries Receiving U.S. Security Assistance. Washington, DC: AIUSA, May 1996.
Hunt, Maurice, and Lawrence Metcalf. *Teaching High School Social Studies: Problems in Reflective Thinking and Social Understanding.* New York: Harper and Brothers 1955.
Hunt, Michael. *Ideology and U.S. Foreign Policy.* New Haven, CT: Yale University Press,1987.
Huntington, Samuel. *The Clash of Civilizations and the Remaking of World Order.* New York: Simon and Schuster, 1996.
Hutson, James H., ed. *Religion and the New Republic: Faith in the Founding of America.* Lanham, MD: Rowman and Littlefield, 2000.
Inaugural Addresses of the Presidents of the United States: Grover Cleveland (1885) to George W. Bush (2001). Bedford, MA: Applewood Books, 2001.
Jervis, Robert. *American Foreign Policy in a New Era.* New York: Routledge, 2005.
Johnson, Chalmers. *Blowback: the Cost and Consequences of American Empire.* New York: Owl Books, 2000.
_____. *The Sorrows of Empire: Militarism, Secrecy, and the End of the American Republic.* New York: Metropolitan Books, 2004.
Johnson, Haynes. *Sleepwalking through History: America in the Reagan Years.* New York: Anchor Books, 1992.
Jordon, Winthrop. *White over Black: American Attitudes toward the Negro 1550–1812* Baltimore: Penguin Books, 1969.
Kengor, Paul. *God and George W. Bush: A Spiritual Life.* New York: Regan Books, 2004.
_____. *God and Ronald Reagan: A Spiritual Life.* New York: Regan Books, 2004.
Kennan, George. *American Diplomacy.* Chicago: University Press of Chicago, 1984.
_____. *The Fateful Alliance: France, Russia and the Coming of the First World War.* New York: Pantheon Books, 1984.
Kiesling, John Brady. *Diplomacy Lessons: Realism for an Unloved Superpower.* Washington, DC: Potomac Books, 2006.
Kinzer, Stephen. *Overthrow: America's Century of Regime Change from Hawaii to Iraq.* New York: Times Books, 2006.
Klare, Michael T. *Peace and World Security Studies: A Curriculum Guide.* Boulder, CO: Lynne Rienner, 1994.

Klein, Melanie. *The Writings of Malanie Klein.* Vol. 3, *Envy and Gratitude and Other Works, 1946–1963.* New York: The Free Press, 1975.

Kofsky, Frank. *Harry S. Truman and the War Scare of 1948.* New York: St. Martin's Press, 1993.

Kornbluh, Peter, and Malcolm Byrne, eds. *The Iran-Contra Scandal: The Declassified History.* New York: The New Press, 1993.

LaFeber, Walter. *The American Age: U.S. Foreign Policy at Home and Abroad since 1896.* New York: W.W. Norton, 1994.

_____. *Inevitable Revolutions: The United States in Central America.* New York: W.W. Norton, 1984.

Leary, William. *The Central Intelligence Agency: History and Documents.* Alabama: University of Alabama Press, 1988.

Leshaun, Lawrence. *The Psychology of War: Comprehending Its Mystique and Its Madness.* New York: Helios Press, 2002.

Lewis, Helen Block. *Shame and Guilt in Neurosis.* New York: International Universities Press, 1971.

Lifton, Robert Jay. *Home from the War: Vietnam Veterans — Neither Victims Nor Executioners.* New York: Simon and Shuster, 1973.

_____. *Super Power Syndrome.* New York: Thunder's Mouth Press, 2003.

Lincoln, Bruce. *Holy Terrors: Thinking about Religion after September 11.* Chicago: University of Chicago Press, 2003.

Little, Douglas. *American Orientalism: The United States and the Middle East since 1945.* Chapel Hill: University of North Carolina Press, 2002.

Long, Charles. *Significations: Signs, Significations, and Images in the Interpretation of Religion.* Philadelphia: Fortress Press, 1986.

Lynd, Helen Merrell. *On Shame and the Search for Identity.* New York: John Wiley and Sons, 1967.

Lynd, Staughton. *Intellectual Origins of American Radicalism.* New York: Vintage Books, 1969.

_____. *Living inside Our Hope: A Steadfast Radical's Thoughts on Rebuilding the Movement.* Ithaca, NY: Cornell University Press, 1997.

_____, and Alice Lynd, eds. *Nonviolence in America: A Documentary History.* 5th ed. Maryknoll, NY: Orbis Books, 2002.

Lynd, Staughton, and Thomas Hayden. *The Other Side.* New York: New American Library, 1966.

Macdonald, Douglas. *Adventures in Chaos: American Intervention for Reform in the Third World.* Cambridge, MA: Harvard University Press, 1992.

Magnus, Ralph, and Eden Naby. *Afghanistan: Mullah, Marx and Mujahid.* Boulder, CO: Westview Press, 1998.

Majahan, Rahul. *Full Spectrum Dominance: U.S. Power in Iraq and Beyond.* New York: Seven Stories Press, 2003.

Maley, William, ed. *Fundamentalism Reborn? Afghanistan and the Taliban.* New York: New York University Press, 1998.

Mansfield, Stephen. *The Faith of George W. Bush.* New York: Tarcher/Penguin, 2003.

Marsden, Peter. *Taliban: War, Religion and the New Order in Afghanistan.* London: Oxford University Press, 1998.

Martorella, Peter H. *Teaching Social Studies in Middle and Secondary Schools.* 3rd ed. Upper Saddle River, NJ: Prentice Hall, 2001.

May, Ernest. *American Cold War Strategy: Interpreting NSC 68.* New York: Bedford/St. Martin's Press, 1993.

McDougall, Walter A. *Promised Land, Crusader State: The American Encounter with the World since 1776.* New York: Houghton Mifflin.

McNamara, Robert S. *In Retrospect: The Tragedy and Lessons of Vietnam.* New York: Times Books, 1995.

Mead, Walter Russell. *Special Providence: American Foreign Policy and How It Changed the World.* New York: Routledge, 2002.

Merk, Frederick. *Manifest Destiny and Mission in American History.* Cambridge, MA: Harvard University Press, 1995.

Merryfield, Merry, and Richard C. Remy, eds. *Teaching about International Conflict and Peace.* Albany: State University of New York Press, 1995.

Miller, Ron. *What Are Schools For? Holistic Education in American Culture.* Brandon, VT: Holistic Education Press, 1992.

Mirra, Carl, ed. *Enduring Freedom or Enduring War? Prospects and Costs of the New American 21st Century.* Washington, DC: Maisonneuve Press, 2005.

Moise, Edwin. *Tonkin Gulf and the Escalation of the Vietnam War.* Chapel Hill: University of North Carolina Press, 2004.

Moral, Lucas E. *Lincoln's Sacred Effort: Defining Religion's Role in American Self-Government.* Lanham, MD: Lexington Books, 2000.

Nathanson, Donald L. *Shame and Pride: Affect, Sex and the Birth of the Self.* New York: W.W. Norton and Company, 1992.

Nelson-Pallmeyer, Jack. *School of Assassins.* Maryknoll, NY: Orbis Books, 1999.

Noddings, Nel, ed. *Educating Citizens for Global Awareness.* New York: Teachers College Press, 2005.

Noll, Mark. *America's God: From Jonathan Edwards to Abraham Lincoln.* Oxford: Oxford University Press, 2002.

Parenti, Michael. *Superpatriotism.* San Francisco: City Lights Books, 2004.

Patterson, James T. *Restless Giant: The United States from Watergate to Bush vs. Gore* New York: Oxford University Press, 2005.

Peck, James, ed. *The Chomsky Reader.* New York: Pantheon Books, 1987.

Pelletiere, Stephen. *Iraq and the International Oil System: Why American Went to War in the Persian Gulf.* Washington, DC: Maisonneuve Press, 2004.

Perkins, John. *Confessions of an Economic Hitman.* San Francisco: Barrett-Koehler Publishers, 2004.

Peterson, Owen, ed. *Representative American Speeches, 1988–89.* Number 6. Reference Shelf Series Vol. 61. New York: H.W. Wilson, 1989.

Phythian, Mark, and Nikos Passas. *Arming Iraq: How the U.S. and Britain Secretly Built Saddam's War Machine.* Boston: Northeastern University Press, 1996.

Powers, Thomas. *The Man Who Kept the Secrets: Richard Helms and the CIA.* New York: Knopf, 1979.

Prados, John. *President's Secret Wars: CIA and Pentagon Covert Operations from World War II through the Persian Gulf War.* Chicago: Ivan R. Dee, 1996.

Preble, Christopher. *Exiting Iraq: Why the U.S. Must End the Military Occupation and Renew the War against Al Qaeda.* Washington, DC: Cato Institute, 2004.

Public Papers of the Presidents of the United States of America: John F. Kennedy, 1961. Washington, DC: U.S. Government Printing Office, 1962.

Rashid, Ahmed. *Taliban: Militant Islam, Oil and Fundamentalism in Central Asia.* New Haven, CT: Yale University Press, 2001.

Raviv, Amiram, Louis Oppenheimer, and Daniel Bar-Tal, eds. *How Children Understand War and Peace: A Call for International Peace Education.* San Francisco: Jossey Bass, 1999.

Reardon, Betty. *Comprehensive Peace Education: Educating for Global Responsibility.* New York: Teachers College Press, 1988.

_____. *Educating for Human Dignity.* Philadelphia: University of Pennsylvania Press, 1995.

_____. *Militarization, Security and Peace Education.* Valley Forge, PA: United Ministries in Education, 1982.

Richey, Russell E., and Donald G. Jones, eds. *American Civil Religion.* New York: Harper and Row, 1974.

Ricks, Thomas. *Fiasco: The American Military Adventure in Iraq.* New York: Penguin Books, 2006.

Roland, Alex. *Military-Industrial Complex.* Washington, DC: Society for the History of Technology and the American Historical Association, 2001.

Romero, Oscar. *Voice of the Voiceless.* Maryknoll, NY: Orbis Books, 1985.

Roosevelt, Kermit. *Countercoup: The Struggle for the Control of Iran.* New York: McGraw Hill, 1979.

Russell, Bertrand. *Why Men Fight.* New York: The Century Company, 1916.

Said, Edward. *Culture and Imperialism.* New York: Vintage Books, 1993.

Salisbury, Harrison E., ed. *Vietnam Reconsidered.* New York: Harper and Row, 1984.

Salmon, Gavriel, and Baruch Nevo. *Peace Education: The Concept, Principles and Practices around the World.* Mahwah, NJ: Lawrence Erlbaum Associates, 2002.

Scheff, Thomas. *Bloody Revenge: Emotions, Nationalism and War.* Lincoln, NE: Backin-Print.com, 2000.

Schlesinger, Stephen, and Stephen Kinzer. *Bitter Fruit: The Story of the American Coup in Guatemala.* Cambridge, MA: Harvard University Press, 1999.

Schmidt, Hans. *Maverick Marine: General Smedley D. Butler and the Contradictions of American Military History.* Lexington: University of Kentucky Press.

Schmitz, David F. *Thank God They're on Our Side: The United States and Right-Wing Dictatorships, 1921–1965.* Chapel Hill: University of North Carolina Press, 1999.

Sewell, Sarah, and Karl Kaysen, ed. *The United States and the International Criminal Court.* New York: Rowman and Littlefield, 2000.

Singer, Peter. *The President of Good and Evil: The Ethics of George W. Bush.* New York: Dutton/Penguin, 2004.

Sloan, Douglas. *Faith and Knowledge: Mainline Protestantism and American Higher Education.* Louisville: Westminster John Knox Press, 1994.

_____. *Insight-Imagination: The Emancipation of Thought and the Modern World.* Westport, CT: Greenwood Press, 1983.

_____, ed. *Education for Peace and Disarmament: Toward a Living World.* New York: Teachers College Press, 1983.

Snauwaert, Dale. *Democracy, Education and Governance: A Developmental Conception.* Albany: State University of New York Press, 1993.

Spiritual Perspectives on America's Role as a Superpower. Woodstock, VT: Skylight Paths Publishing, 2003.

Spring, Joel. *The American School, 1642–1992.* New York: McGraw Hill, 1997.

_____. *Education and the Rise of the Corporate State.* Boston: Beacon Press, 1972.

Staub, Ervin. *The Roots of Evil: Origins of Genocide.* New York: Cambridge University Press, 1989.

Steindl-Rast, David. *Gratefulness, the Heart of Prayer.* Ramsey, NJ: Paulist Press, 1984.

Stephanson, Anders. *Manifest Destiny: American Expansion and the Empire of Right.* New York: Hill and Wang, 1995.

Stomfay-Stitz, Aline M. *Peace Education in America, 1828–1990: A Sourcebook for Education and Research.* Metuchen, NJ: Scarecrow Press, 1993.

Tangney, June Price, and Ronda L. Dearing. *Shame and Guilt.* New York: The Guilford Press, 2002.

Taylor, Telford. *Nuremberg and Vietnam: An American Tragedy.* New York: Bantam Books, 1971.

Thornton, Stephen J. *Teaching Social Studies That Matters: Curriculum for Active Learning.* New York: Teachers College Press, 2004.

Tomkins, Silvan. *Affect, Imagery and Consciousness.* New York: Springer, 1963.

Tirman, John. *Spoils of War: The Human Cost of America's Arms Trade.* New York: The Free Press, 1997.

Torricelli, Robert, and Andrew Carroll, ed. *In Our Own Words: Extraordinary Speeches of the American Century.* New York: Kodansha International, 1999.

Trifonas, Peter, ed. *Revolutionary Pedagogies: Cultural Politics, Instituting Education and the Discourse of Theory.* New York: Routledge, 2000.

Trumpbour, John ed. *How Harvard Rules: Reason in the Service of Empire.* Boston: South End Press, 1989.

United Nations and El Salvador, 1990–1995. Vol. 4. New York: The United Nations Blue Book Series, 1995.

United States. Department of State. *Foreign Relations of the United States: 1948.* Vol. 2. *Germany and Austria.* Vol. 3. *Western Europe.* Vol. 4. *Eastern Europe.* Washington, DC: U.S. Government Printing Office, 1973.

_____. _____. *Foreign Relations of the United States: 1950.* Vol. 1. Washington, DC: U.S. Government Printing Office, 1976.

_____. House of Representatives. Permanent Select Committee on Intelligence. *IC 21: The Intelligence Community in the 21st Century.* Washington, DC: U.S. Government Printing Office, April 1996.

_____. Senate. Report to the Committee on Foreign Relations. *Multinational Oil Corporations and U.S. Foreign Policy.* Washington, DC: U.S. Government Printing Office, 1975.

_____. _____. Select Committee to Study Governmental Operations with Respect to Intelligence Activities. *Foreign and Military Service.* 94th Congress, 2nd Session, Report No. 94–755. Washington, DC: Government Printing Office, April 1976.

Van Alstyne, Richard W. *The Rising American Empire.* New York: W.W. Norton & Company, 1974.

Veblen, Thorstein. *The Higher Learning in America: A Memorandum on the Conduct of Universities by Business Men.* New York: Huebsch. Republished by Cosimo in 2005.

Washington, James Melvin, ed. *A Testament of Hope: The Essential Writings and Speeches of Martin Luther king, Jr.* San Francisco: HarperCollins, 1991.

West, Cornel. *Democracy Matters: Winning the Fight against Imperialism.* New York: Penguin Books, 2004.

_____. *Prophecy Deliverance! An Afro-American Revolutionary Christianity.* Philadelphia: Westminster Press, 1982.

Westbrook, Robert J. *John Dewey and American Democracy.* Ithaca, NY: Cornell University Press, 1991.

Williams, William Appleman. *The Tragedy of American Diplomacy.* New York: W.W. Norton, 1972.

Wilson, Joseph. *The Politics of Truth: A Diplomat's Memoir; Inside the Lies That Led to War and Betrayed My Wife's CIA Identity.* New York: Carroll and Graf Publishers, 2004.

Young, Marilyn. *The Vietnam Wars, 1945–1990.* New York: Harper Perennial, 1991.

Yousef, Mohammad, and Mark Adkin. *The Bear Trap: Afghanistan's Untold Story.* London: Leo Cooper, 1992.

Zepezauer, Mark, and Arthur Naiman. *Take the Rich Off Welfare.* Tucson, AZ: Odonian Press, 1996.

Zinn, Howard. *A People's History of the United States.* New York: HarperCollins, 1999.

_____, and Anthony Arnove. *Voices of a People's History of the United States.* New York: Seven Stories Press, 2004.

Articles

"After the Taliban." *The Economist*, 6 October 2001.

Americans for Victory over Terrorism. Advertisement. *New York Times*, 10 March 2002.

Anderson, Guy. "US Defense Budget Will Equal ROW Combined with 12 Months." *Jane's Defense*, 4 May 2005.

Annan, Kofi. "Letter to Colin Powell, July 3, 2002," Press Release NGO Coalition for the ICC, 9 July 2002.

Apple, Michael. "Patriotism, Pedagogy and Freedom: On the Educational Meanings of September 11th." *Teachers College Record* 104, no. 8 (December 2002).

Armstrong, David. "Oil in the Family: George Bush and His Slippery Friends." *Texas Observer*, 12 July 1991.

_____. "Dick Cheney's Song for America." *Harper's Magazine*, October 2002.

Ayub, Gayub. "Psychological War." *The Frontier Post* (Pakistan), 8 November 2001.

Bajaj, Monisha. "Human Rights Education and Student Self-Conception in the Dominican Republic." *Journal of Peace Education* 1, no. 1 (March 2004).

Barber, John. "Wounded and Left on Afghanistan's Plains." *Toronto Globe and Mail*, 29 September 2001.

Barstow, David. "In Haze of Guard Records, a Bit of Clarity." *New York Times*, 15 February 2004.

_____, and Robin Stein. "Under Bush, a New Age of Prepackaged News." *New York Times*, 13 March 2005.

Bazzi, Mohammad. "Alliance Seeks Talks on New Government." *Newsday*, 14 November 2001.

Bellant, Russ. "Secretive Puebla Institute Has Ties to the CIA." *National Catholic Reporter*, 18 November 1988.

Berlowitz, Marvin J., Nathan A. Long, and Eric Jackson. "The Exclusion and Distortion of African American Perspectives in Peace Education." *Educational Studies* 39, no. 2 (2006).

"A Bitter Harvest: The Sufferings of Afghanistan Come to New York." *The Economist*, 15–21 September 2001.

Bloom, Harold. "The Preacher." *Time*, 14 June 1999.

Boot, Max. "Washington Needs a Colonial Office." *Financial Times*, 2 July 2003.

Brock-Utne, Birgit. "The Challenges for Peace Educators at the End of a Millennium." *International Journal of Peace Studies* 1, no. 1 (January 1996).

_____. "Peace Education in an Era of Globalization." *Peace Review* 12, no.1 (March 2000).

Bruni, Frank. "For Bush, a Mission and Defining Moment." *New York Times*, 22 September 2001.

Bumiller, Elisabeth. "America as Reflected in Its Leader." *New York Times*, 6 January 2002.

_____. "The New Slogan in Washington: Start Watching What You Say." *New York Times*, 7 October 2001.

Buncombe, Andrew, and Richard Lloyd Parry. "Bombing Errors Prove Major Test for U.S. Resolve." *Independent* (London), 29 October 2001.

Burkeman, Oliver, and Julian Borger. "The Ex-president's Club." *The Guardian*, 31 October 2001.

Bush, George W. "Address to the Nation." Washington, DC: Office of the Press Secretary. 20 September 2001, http://www.whitehouse.gov.

_____. Human Rights Day press release. Washington, DC, 10 December 2001.

_____. *The National Security Strategy of the United States*, 2002, http://www.whitehouse.gov.

Castro, Fidel. "We Must Defend Our Country." Havana: Havana Domestic Service, 23 April 1961. http://www.marxists.org.

Chomsky, Noam. "After the Cold War: U.S. Foreign Policy in the Middle East." *Cultural Critique*, no. 19 (Autumn 1991).

Christoff Kurop, Marcia. "Al Qaeda's Balkan Links." *Wall Street Journal Europe*, 1 November 2001.

Cockburn, Patrick. "Anti-Taliban Forces Build New Airport to Bring in Supplies," *The Independent* (London), 7 October 2001.

Cohn, Gary, and Ginger Thompson. "Unearthed: Fatal Secrets." *Baltimore Sun*, 11 June 1985.

Commager, Henry Steel. "The Defeat of America." *New York Review of Books*, 12 June 1975.

Csorba, Les T. "President Bush, Part 2." *Newsday*, 21 January 2005.

Cumings, Bruce. "Is America an Imperial Power?" *Current History* (November 2003).

Cummings, Jeanne. "Security Advisers Now Share Blame In Intelligence Row." *Wall Street Journal*, 23 July 2003.

Danner, Mark. "The Secret Way to War." *New York Review of Books*, 9 June 2005.

Editorial, *Jewish Currents* 55, no. 9 (October 2001).

Einstein, Albert, et al. "Letter to the Editor." *New York Times,* 2 October 1948.

Evans, Martin. "Discussing Peace." *Newsday*, 21 October 2001.

Ferguson, Niall. "An Empire in Denial: The Limits of US Imperialism." *Harvard International Review* 25, no. 3 (2003).

Fireman, Ken. "President Plans PR Campaign on War." *Newsday*, 2 November 2001.

Fisk, Robert. "Hypocrisy, Hatred, and the War on Terror." *The Independent* (London), 8 November 2001.

_____. "Osama bin Laden: The Godfather of Terror." *The Independent* (London), 15 September 2001.

_____. "Our Friends Are Killers, Crooks and Torturers." *The Independent* (London), 7 October 2001.

"Gallup International Poll on Terrorism in the U.S. (figures)," n.d., (c. October 2001). http://www.gallup-international.com/terrorismpoll_figures.htm.

Galster, Stephen. "The Afghan Pipeline." *Covert Action Quarterly*, no. 30, (Summer 1998).

Galtung, Johan. "Global Projections of Deep-Rooted U.S. Pathologies." Institute for Conflict Analysis and Resolution: George Mason University. October 1996.

_____. "Moderates All over the World Unite." Speech to the German Peace Movement, Cologne, Germany (14 September 2002), http://www.transcend.org

_____. "September 11, 2001: Diagnosis, Prognosis, Therapy," http://www.transcend. org.

Gargan, Edward. "A Tattered Afghan Alliance a Key for US." *Newsday*, 28 September, 2001.

Gasiorowski, Mark J. "The 1953 Coup d'etat in Iran." *International Journal of Middle Eastern Studies* 19, no. 3 (1987).

Giroux, Henry. "Democracy, Freedom and Justice after September 11: Rethinking the Role of Educators and the Politics of Schooling." *Teachers College Record*, v. 104, n. 6 (September 2002).

_____. "What Might Education Mean after Abu Ghraib: Revisiting Adorno's Politics of Education." *Comparative Studies of South Asia, Africa and the Middle East* 24, no. 1 (2004).

Golden, Daniel, James Bandler, and Marcus Walker. "Bin Laden Family Tied to U.S. Group." *Wall Street Journal*, 27 September 2001.

Goldstein, Amy. "Paige Calls NEA a 'Terrorist' Group." *Washington Post*, 24 February 2004.

Greene, Maxine. "In Search of a Critical Pedagogy." *Harvard Educational Review* 56, no. 4 (November 1986).

Grimmet, Richard F. "Instances of Use of United States Armed Forces Abroad, 1798–1999." Washington DC: Congressional Research Service 96-119F, 19 May 1999.

Grossman, Marc. "American Foreign Policy and the International Criminal Court." Remarks to the Center for Strategic Studies, Washington, DC, May 2002.

Gumbell, Andrew. "Who Is Winning the War of Lies?" *Independent* (London), 4 November 2001.

Haavelsrud, Magnus. "Target: Disarmament Education." *Journal of Peace Education* 1, n.1 (March 2004).

Haines, Gerald. "CIA and Guatemala Assassination Proposals 1952–54." Central Intelligence Agency History Staff Analysis (June 1995).

Hammerich, Else. "Meeting Point Articles." *Transnational Foundation for Peace and Future Research*, n.d.

Harris, Ian. "Peace Education Theory." *Journal of Peace Education* 1, no. 1 (March 2004).

＿＿＿＿＿, Larry J. Fisk, and Carol Rank. "A Portrait of University Peace Studies in North America and Western Europe at the End of the Millennium." *International Journal of Peace Studies* 3, no. 1 (January 1998).

Henderson, Michael. "Acknowledging History as a Prelude to Forgiveness." *Peace Review: Journal of Social Justice* 14, no. 3 (2002).

Hiro, Dilip. "Bush and bin Laden." *The Nation*, 8 October 2001.

Hirshon, Robert. "Letter to the President," May 2002, http://www.fed- soc.org/Publications/barwatchbulletin/barwatchmay2002.htm.

Human Rights Watch. "Afghanistan Crisis of Impunity: The Role of Pakistan, Russia and Iran in Fueling the Civil War." Washington, DC: Human Rights Watch, July 2001).

Jacobs, Andrew. "Peace Signs Amid Calls for War." *New York Times*, 20 September 2001.

Jervis, Robert. "Compulsive Empire." *Foreign Policy* (July–August 2003).

Johnson, Marcia L. "Trends in Peace Education." *Eric Digest* (1998) ED417123.

Khalilzad, Zalmay. "Afghanistan: Time to Reengage." *Washington Post*, 7 October 1996.

King, Neil, and Chip Cummings. "Patience Is a Component of This Military Strategy." *Wall Street Journal*, 28 September 2001.

Kirkpatrick, David D. "In Secretly Taped Conversations, Glimpses of the Future President." *New York Times*, 20 February 2005.

Kirkpatrick, Jeane. "Dictatorship and Double Standards." *Commentary* (November 1979).

Kitzman, Mike. "International Criminal Court." *H-Diplo*, 16 August 2002.

Kissinger, Henry. "The Pitfalls of Universal Jurisdiction." *Foreign Affairs* (July–August 2000.

Klein, Naomi. "Baghdad Year Zero." *Harper's Magazine*, September 2004.

Knecht, Peter, and Peter Freeman, ed. "Background Notes: Afghanistan." U.S. Department of State — Bureau of Public Affairs — Office of Public Communication Department of State Publication 7795-Background Notes Series, Washington, DC: U.S. Government Printing Office, July 1994.

Kraupl Taylor F., and J. H. Rey. "The Scapegoat Motif in Society and its Manifestations in a Therapeutic Group." *International Journal of Psychoanalysis* 34 (1953).

Lincoln, Bruce. "The Theology of George W. Bush." *Christian Century*, 5 October 2004.

Little, Douglas. "Cold War and Covert Action: The United States and Syria, 1945–1958." *Middle East Journal* 44, no. 1 (Winter 1990).

Lynd, Staughton. "Freedom Schools: Concept and Organization." *Freedomways* (April 1965).

＿＿＿＿＿. "Reflections on Class in Early America: Personal Reflections." *Labor: Studies in Working-Class History of the Americas* 1, no. 4 (Winter 2004).

＿＿＿＿＿. "Vietnam and Iraq." *Radical Historians Newsletter*, no. 88 (December 2003).

Mackay, Neil. "John Major Link to Bin Laden Dynasty." *Sunday Herald* (Scotland), 7 October 2001.

Martin, Jerry L., and Anne D. Neal. "Defending Civilization: How Our Universities are Failing America and What Can Be Done about It." A Project of the Defense of Civilization Fund, American Council of Trustees and Alumni (November 2001).

Massing, Michael. "Press Watch." *The Nation*, 22 October 2001.
McCain, John. "2000 Republican National Convention Address." http://www.csmonitor. com.
McCarthy, Sheryl. "U.S. Pays for the Error of Our Ways." *Newsday*, 20 September 2001.
McGrory, Mary. "Contra-Intuitive." *Washington Post*, 8 July 2001.
McLaren, Peter. "George Bush, Apocalypse Sometime Soon, and the American Imperium," *Cultural Studies / Critical Methodologies* 2, no. 3 (2002).
McMichael, William M. "Desert Stronghold." *Airforce Magazine* 82, no. 2 (February 1999).
McNeil, Taylor. "Seduced by War." *Bostonia* (Winter 2004–2005).
Mirra, Carl. *Join Us? Testimonies of Iraq War Veterans and Their Families.* Pamphlet no. 5: Historians against the War, 2006.
Monbiot, George. "America's Pipe Dream: A Pro-Western Regime in Kabul Should Give the US an Afghan Route for Caspian Oil," *The Guardian*, 23 October 2001.
Morse, Jennifer Roback. "Battered America," *Hoover Institute Weekly Essays* (26 November 2001).
"Negroponte Calls Exemption for U.N. Peacekeepers a First Step." U.S. State Department, Washington File, 13 July 2002.
Noonan, Peggy. "Way Too Much God." *Wall Street Journal*, 21 January 2005.
Norris, Pippa, and Ronald Inglehardt. "Islam and the West: Testing the Clash of Civilizations Thesis." John F. Kennedy School of Government, Harvard University, Faculty Research Working Paper Series, #RWP02-015 (April 2002).
Peters, Ralph. "Constant Conflict," *Parameters: U.S. Army War College Quarterly* (Summer 1997).
Powell, Colin. "2000 Republican National Convention Address," http://www.csmonitor. com.
"President Bush Meets with National Security Team." Washington, DC: Office of the Press Secretary, 12 September 2001, available at http://www.whitehouse.gov.
"President George W. Bush, the Bible and Israel." *Yediot Achronot Israeli News*, 11 January 2001.
Priest, Dana. "U.S. Military Trains Foreign Troops." *Washington Post*, 12 July 1998.
Rinaldi, Matthew. "The Olive-Drab Rebels: Military Organizing during the Vietnam War." *Radical America* 8, no. 3 (May–June 1974).
Raphel, Robin. "U.S. Policy toward South Asia," United States Department of State Dispatch 6, no.13 (March 27, 1995).
Rayment, Sean. "Secret MoD Poll: Iraqis Support Attacks on British Troops." *Sunday Telegraph*, 23 October 2005.
Reardon, Betty. "Peace Education: A Review and Projection." Lund University (Sweden), Malmo School of Education, *Peace Education Reports*, no. 17 (August 1999).
"Remarks of European Delegates to the Preparatory Commission," 25 September 2001, compiled by the Washington Working Group on the International Criminal Court.
Richardson, Bill. "Address to the UN Commission on Human Rights." Geneva, Switzerland) 25 March 1998.
Rosenberg, Daniel. "The Holocaust and Business as Usual: Congressional Source Materials," *The Reference Librarian*, no. 61–62 (1998).
Royce, Knut. "A Trail of Distortion against Iraq." *Newsday*, 21 January 1991.
Rubin, James. "Stumbling into War," *Foreign Affairs* 82, no. 5 (2003).
"Rumsfeld Praises Response on Mutual Defense Agreement." Washington, DC: U.S. Department of State Office of International Programs), press release, 21 September 2001.
Scheffer, David J. "Statement before the House International Relations Committee." Washington, DC, 26 July 2000.
Scheidlinger, Saul. "Presidential Address: On Scapegoating in Group Psychotherapy." *International Journal of Group Psychotherapy* 32, no. 2 (April 1982).

Schlesinger, Arthur. "Memorandum for the President, Subject: Cuba: Political, Diplomatic and Economic Problems." NSC-Declassified, 11 April 1972.

Seagupta, Kim, and Andrew Gumbell. "New U.S. Envoy to Kabul Lobbied for Taleban Oil Rights." *New Zealand Herald*, 11 January 2002.

Sheeran, John. "Letter to the Editor." *The Independent* (London), 4 November 2001.

Silverstein, Ken. "Privatizing War: How Affairs of State Are Outsourced to Corporations beyond Public Control." *The Nation*, 28 July 1997.

Snauwaert, Dale T. "Cosmopolitan Democracy and Democratic Education." *Current Issues in Comparative Education* 4, no. 2 (December 2001).

Steele, Jonathan, Ewen MacAskill, Richard Norton-Taylor, and Ed Harriman. "Threat of US Strikes passed to Taliban Weeks before NY Attack," *The Guardian*, 22 September 2001.

Stomfay-Stitz, Aline, and Edyth Wheeler. "Human Rights Education Can Be Integrated throughout the School Day." *Childhood Education* 81, no. 3 (Spring 2005).

Suskind, Ron. "Without a Doubt." *New York Times Magazine*, 17 October 2004.

Synott, John. "Peace Education as an Education Paradigm: Review of a Changing Field using an Old Measure." *Journal of Peace Education* 2, no. 1 (March 2005).

Thompson, James C. "How Could Vietnam Happen? An Autopsy." *The Atlantic Monthly* (April 1968).

United Nations. "Setting the Record Straight: The International Criminal Court (New York: UN Department of Public Information, October 1998.

_____. International Court of Justice. *Case Concerning the Military and Paramilitary Activities in and Against Nicaragua (Nicaragua v. United States of America)*, Judgment 27 June 1986, available at http://www.icjcij.org/icjwww/idecisions/isummaries/isummaries/inussummary860627.htm.

United States. Department of Defense. Joint Chiefs of Staff. Memorandum for the Secretary of Defense. "Justification for US Military Intervention in Cuba" (13 March 1962).

_____. Department of State. "Human Rights Week 2001," http://www.stategov./g/drl/hr/index.cfm?id=5042.

"U.S. Interests in the Central Asian Republics." Hearing before the Subcommittee on Asia and the Pacific of the Committee on International Relations. House of Representatives. 105th Congress, Second Session, February 12, 1998.

"The U.S. Losing Image War." *TheStar.com* (Toronto), 8 November 2001.

"Verbatim," *The Chronicle of Higher Education*, 16 November 2001.

Wahlstrom, Riita. "Peace Education Meets the Challenge of the Cultures of Militarism," *Peace Education Miniprints*, No. 11. Lund University (Sweden), Malmo School of Education (March 1991).

Wayne, Leslie. "America's for Profit Secret Army." *New York Times*, 13 October 2002.

West, Cornel. "Exiles from a City and from a Nation." *The Observer* 11 September 2005.

Wiesel, Elie. "Letter to Honorable Benjamin Gilman," 19 September 2000, http://www.icc.org.

Wilber, Donald. "Overthrow of Premier Mossadeq of Iran." Central Intelligence Agency Clandestine Service Historical Paper No. 208 (October 1969).

Wolin, Sheldon. "The Meaning of Vietnam." *New York Review of Books*, 12 June 1975.

Zakaria, Fareed. "Why Do They Hate Us?" *Newsweek*, 15 October 2001.

Zinn, Howard. "The Power and the Glory: Myths of American Exceptionalism," *The Boston Review: A Political and Literary Forum* (Summer 2005).

Index

221